THE END OF THEORY

The End of Theory

Financial Crises,
the Failure
of Economics,
and the Sweep
of Human
Interaction

Richard Bookstaber

PRINCETON UNIVERSITY PRESS
PRINCETON AND OXFORD

Requests for permission to reproduce material from this work
should be sent to Permissions, Princeton University Press

Published by Princeton University Press,
41 William Street, Princeton, New Jersey 08540

In the United Kingdom: Princeton University Press,
6 Oxford Street, Woodstock, Oxfordshire OX20 1TR

press.princeton.edu

ISBN 978-0-691-16901-9

British Library Cataloging-in-Publication Data is available

This book has been composed in Adobe Text Pro and Gotham

Printed on acid-free paper. ∞

Printed in the United States of America

10 9 8 7 6 5 4 3 2

In memory of my son,

Joseph Israel Bookstaber

CONTENTS

Introduction

1

Crises and Sunspots

During a visit to the London School of Economics as the 2008 financial crisis was reaching its climax, Queen Elizabeth asked the question that no doubt was on the minds of many of her subjects: "Why did nobody see it coming?" The response, at least by the University of Chicago economist Robert Lucas, was blunt: Economics could not give useful service for the 2008 crisis because economic theory has established that it cannot predict such crises.[1] As John Kay writes, "Faced with such a response, a wise sovereign will seek counsel elsewhere."[2] And so might we all.

England's royal family is no stranger to financial crises, or to the evolution of economic thought that such crises have spawned. Our standard economic model, the neoclassical model, was forged in Victorian England during a time of industrial and economic revolutions—and the crises and the cruel social and economic disparities that came with them. This economic approach arose because the classical political economy of Adam Smith and David Ricardo failed in this new reality. The neoclassical model was championed by the Englishman William Stanley Jevons, who experienced the effects of these crises firsthand, and was prepared to bring new tools to the job. Jevons was the first modern economist, introducing mathematics into the analysis and initiating what became known as the marginalist revolution—a huge leap forward that reshaped our thinking about the values of investment and productivity.[3] Nonetheless, despite all the areas in which Jevons's approach improved our thinking, the economic model he originated still failed to predict or elucidate crises. We can make a start in understanding the limitations in the current standard economic approach to financial crises, and what to do about them, by looking at the path Jevons took in mid-nineteenth-century England.

This economic revolution was driven by a technical one. The railroad was the disruptive technology. It reached into every aspect of industry, commerce, and daily life, a complex network emanating from the center of the largest cities to the remotest countryside. Railroads led to, in Karl Marx's words, "the annihilation of space by time" and the "transformation of the product into a commodity." A product was no longer defined by where it was produced, but instead by the market to which the railroad transported it. The railroad cut through the natural terrain, with embankments, tunnels, and viaducts marking a course through the landscape that changed perceptions of nature. For passengers, the "railway journey" filled nineteenth-century novels as an event of adventure and social encounters.[4]

Railroads were also the source of repeated crises. Then as now, there was more capital chasing the dreams of the new technology than there were solid places to put it to work. And it was hard to find a deeper hole than the railroads. Many of the railroad schemes were imprudent, sometimes insane projects, the investments often disappearing without a trace. The term *railway* was to Victorian England what *atomic* or *aerodynamic* were to be after World War II, and *network* and *virtual* are today. When it came to investments, the romantic appeal of being a party to this technological revolution often dominated profit considerations. Baron Rothschild quipped that there are "three principal ways to lose your money: wine, women, and engineers. While the first two are more pleasant, the third is by far more certain." Capital invested in the railway seemed to be the preferred course to the third. Those with capital to burn were encouraged by the engineers whose profits came from building the railroads, and who could walk away unconcerned about the bloated costs that later confronted those actually running the rail. A mile of line in England and Wales cost five times that in the United States.[5] The run of investor profits during the manias of the cycle were lost in the slumps that unerringly followed. One down-cycle casualty was Jevons's father, who was an iron merchant.

In 1848, in the midst of this revolution and its cycle of crises, the great economist and intellectual John Stuart Mill published his *Principles of Political Economy*, a monument to the long and rich tradition of classical political economy of Adam Smith, Jean-Baptiste Say, Thomas Robert Malthus, and David Ricardo. With this publication, economics reached a highly respectable, congratulatory dead end, the station of those in a staid gentlemen's club sitting in wing-back chairs, self-satisfied and awash in reflection. Economic theory then languished for the better part of the next two decades. Mill wrote that "happily, there is nothing in the laws of Value which remains for the present or any future writer to clear up; the theory of the subject is complete."[6]

But over those two decades, with a backdrop of labor unrest and a rising footprint of poverty, cracks began to emerge in the pillars of Mill's theory.[7] His economics failed to see the essential changes wrought by the Industrial Revolution. He put labor front and center. The more labor used to produce a good, the greater that good's value. This was reasonable when production was driven by labor.[8] But with the Industrial Revolution, capital could multiply the output of a laborer, and, furthermore, capital was not fixed. It could drive ever-increasing efficiency. At the same time, the supply of labor was brimming over the edges because many small landholders and agricultural workers moved to the cities as landholdings were consolidated through enclosures into more efficient large estates. The laborers were paid subsistence wages, while the economic benefit from the increased productivity was captured by those controlling the machinery, the capitalists.

For those whose success or luck of birth pushed them into the newly emerging business class, life was filled with promise and stability. Men would become gentlemen with country houses, providing an Oxbridge education for their sons. For the working class, life held something less. Henry Colman, a minister visiting the United Kingdom from America, reacted to the factory life he observed in the cities: "I have seen enough already in Edinburgh to chill one's blood, make one's hair stand on end. Manchester is said to be as bad, and Liverpool still worse. Wretched, defrauded, oppressed, crushed human nature lying in bleeding fragments all over the face of society. Every day that I live I thank heaven that I am not a poor man with the family in England."[9] The clergyman Richard Parkinson wrote with irony that he once ventured to designate Manchester as the most aristocratic town in England because "there is no town in the world where the distance between the rich and the poor is so great, or the barrier between them so difficult to be crossed."[10]

The Birth of Modern Economics

Industrial age economics moved away from Mill in two directions. The one traveled by Marx, based on historical analysis and with a focus on the human consequences of the dominance of capital, fomented revolution that would engulf the world. The other, based on mathematics, emulated the mechanics of the natural sciences while ignoring the human aspect completely, forming the foundation for today's standard economic model, that of neoclassical economics. This was the way pushed forward by William Stanley Jevons.

To say that the development of the neoclassical approach ignored the human aspect is to say that it was a product of its times. Arithmetic, writes the historian Eric Hobsbawm, was the fundamental tool of the Industrial Revolution. The value of an enterprise was determined by the operations of addition and subtraction: the difference between buying price and selling price; between revenue and cost; between investment and return. Such arithmetic worked its way into the discourse and analysis of politics and morals. The simple calculations of arithmetic could express the human condition. The English philosopher Jeremy Bentham proposed that pleasure and pain could be expressed as quantities, and pleasure minus pain was the measure of happiness. Add the happiness across all men, deduct the unhappiness, and the government that produces the greatest net happiness for the greatest number has de facto applied the best policy. It is an accounting of humanity, producing its ledger of debit and credit balances.[11]

This formed the starting point of Jevons's *Theory of Political Economy*: a quantitative analysis of the feelings of pleasure and pain. Of the seven Benthamite circumstances associated with pleasure and pain, Jevons selected intensity and duration as the most fundamental dimensions of feeling. Clearly, "every feeling must last some time, and . . . while it lasts, it may be more or less acute and intense." The quantity of feeling, then, is just the product of its intensity and duration: "The whole quantity would be found by multiplying the number of units of intensity into the number of units of duration. Pleasure and pain, then, are magnitudes possessing two dimensions, just as an area or superficies possesses the two dimensions of length and breadth."[12]

Jevons was a polymath who started in the pure sciences and mathematics. He studied for two years at University College in London, winning a gold medal in chemistry and top honors in experimental philosophy. He left before graduating to take a post as an assayer in Sydney, Australia, for the new mint, stopping on the way to study in Paris, receiving a diploma from the French mint. While in Australia he expanded his interests beyond chemistry and mathematics, exploring the local flora, geology, and weather patterns. In fact, for a time he was the only recorder of weather in Sydney. He also wrote a manuscript for a book on music theory.[13]

His interest moved from meteorology and music into economics as he became engaged in the economic travails of the New South Wales railway, which no doubt echoed his family's financial travails. He found an immediate affinity for the subject, which he wrote "seems mostly to suit my exact method of thought." He wrote in 1856 that, as his interests moved to this new area, he felt he was "an awful deserter" of "subjects for which I believe I am equally well or even better suited" and he doubted that "I shall ever be able to call myself a scientific man." In fact, Jevons did remain engaged in mathematics and logic, and in 1874 would publish *The Principles of Science*, which, among other things, laid out the relationship between inductive and deductive logic, and treated the use of cryptography, including the factorization problem that is currently used in public key cryptography.[14] But his formal studies moved from pure science to political economy. In 1859, after five years in Australia, he returned to University College to study political economy, where he won a Ricardo scholarship and a gold medal for his master of arts.

He poured himself into his new focus of study, and by the following year had already discovered the idea of marginal utility. He wrote to his brother that "in the last few months I have fortunately struck out what I have no doubt is the true theory of economy. . . . One of the most important axioms is that as the quantity of any commodity, for instance plain food, which a man has to consume increases, so the utility or benefit from the last portion used decreases in degree." In another letter he expanded on this discovery, giving a succinct explanation of marginal theory and the implications of the relationship between profits and capital: "The common law is that the demand and supply of labor and capital determine the division between wages and profits. But I shall show that the whole capital employed can only be paid for at the same rate as the last portion added; hence it is the increase of produce or advantage, which this last addition gives, that determines the interest of the whole."

Jevons wrote up his ideas in a paper, "A General Mathematical Theory of Political Economy," first presented in 1862, and these ideas gained broad notice with the publication of his 1871 book, *The Theory of Political Economy*. The temple of classical economics shuddered to a sudden collapse with this publication, which was as much a manifesto against the prevailing wisdom, a call to "fling aside, once and for ever, the mazy and preposterous assumptions of the Ricardian School," as it was a scientific treatise on economics theory.[15]

Not long afterward, others were hot on the marginalist trail.[16] And the concepts of marginal utility and the application of mathematical methods seemed to find precursors in many places, leading Jevons to complain that books were appearing "in which the principal ideas of my theory have been foreshadowed." He found himself in the "unfortunate position that the greater number of people think the theory nonsense, and do not understand it, and the rest discover that it is not new." Jevons gave up on the hope that he would be able to establish a first claim to the concepts, but took comfort that "the theory . . . has in fact been discovered 3 or 4 times over and must be true."

Blinded by Sunspots: Jevons's Quest for a Scientific Cause of Crises

Jevons not only brought mathematical rigor to the field but also was the first economist to focus on the sources of economic crises. He had personal reasons for this focus. Not only had his father suffered a failure during the railroad bubble while Jevons was still a boy, but others in his extended family had suffered through similar difficulties. And he was brought up in Unitarian circles where social inequities were a point of concern. He was socially aware, and would take walks though the poor and manufacturing districts of London to observe social costs up close.

Jevons viewed an understanding of crises as the key test of economics. He believed that if economics could not explain market crises and "detect and exhibit every kind of periodic fluctuation," then it was not a complete theory.[17] The inquiry into the causes of phenomena as complex as commercial crises could not approach the rigor or mathematical purity of a science unless Jevons purged this subject of all traces of human emotion, unless he assumed—even if he could not prove—that some physical cause was acting on events others might describe as socially driven. Without some observable natural phenomenon to serve as causal agent, commercial crises threatened to become uninterpretable, limiting the claim of economics to be a science.

Because Jevons patterned his economic methods after the scientific methods used for studying the natural world, he looked for a natural phenomenon as the anchor for his study of otherwise unexplainable crises. This led him to theorize that sunspots were the culprit.[18] He was determined to link sunspot periodicity to the periodicity of commercial crises. And Britain had certainly been subject to them, most recently the 1845–1850 railway mania bubble, which, like all bubbles, did not end well.

Jevons's interest in sunspots was not mystical. He hypothesized that the success of harvests might be one of many causes that could precipitate a panic: "It is the abnormal changes which are alone threatening or worthy of very much attention. These changes arise from deficient or excessive harvests, from sudden changes of supply or demand in any of our great staple commodities, from manias of excessive investment or speculation, from wars and political disturbances, or other fortuitous occurrences which we cannot calculate upon and allow for."[19]

Jevons used a sunspot cycle that had been determined by earlier researchers to be 11.11 years. All that remained, then, was to show that the cycle for commercial crises followed a similar course. A simple attempt at matching the two came up short, but, convinced that this theory—attractive from the standpoint of bringing economics into the fold of the natural sciences—was correct, he looked past the contemporary data and reached back to data from the thirteenth and fourteenth centuries. This attempt also failed, because data were scant on both sunspots and commercial cycles.

After extending his dataset across time failed to prove this theory, Jevons then cast a broader net geographically. He looked at records from India, with the argument that British commerce relied on agricultural activity and raw materials from its colony. This approach also failed. With a view that "the subject is altogether too new and complicated to take the absence of variation in certain figures as conclusive negative evidence," he continued to press forward, expanding the dataset to tropical Africa, America, the West Indies, and even the Levant, stretching the logic of including India, asserting that these parts of the globe also had a demonstrable effect on British commercial activity. In addition to his search for confirming data, he revised his eleven-year cycle, noting recent research that suggested a shorter cycle. His data refused to fit the alternative cycle, too.

Having discovered no evidence for his mathematically driven, mechanistic model of crises in the historical or contemporary records, in the records of Britain, India, or the broader reaches of the globe, or through revisions in the period of the cycle, Jevons still didn't doubt the model. He surmised that observational error must be at the root of his inability to confirm the sunspot theory. So he called for direct observation of the sun. And he also added a further level of causality to his theory, which smacked of astrology: he called for a study of the planets, which had an effect on the course of the sun and thereby on sunspot activity: "if the planets govern the sun, and the sun governs the vintages and harvests, and thus the prices of food and raw materials and the state of the money market, it follows that the configurations of the planets may prove to be the remote causes of the greatest commercial disasters."

Clearly a man not easily deterred, Jevons continued his advocacy of the sunspot theory in the face of the lack of evidence: "In spite . . . of the doubtful existence of some of the crises . . . I can entertain no doubt whatever." This advocacy, which bordered on the fanatical, was all in the service of his dream of a mathematical foundation for economics that would form a scientific basis to marry the study of economics to that of the natural sciences.

Chasing Sunspots after All These Years

Jevons's unrelenting drive to demonstrate the link between sunspots and crises rests on two ideas: First, for economic theory to be complete and valid, it must extend beyond the everyday and explain crises. Second, economics "is purely mathematical in character. . . . [W]e cannot have a true theory of Economics without its [mathematics'] aid." I agree with his first point. Contemporary economics agrees with his second. And the motivation behind Jevons's preoccupation with sunspots remains at the center of economics, yet an unswerving adherence to mathematics fails in predicting crises today just as surely as did Jevons's unswerving focus on sunspots.

And we do not have to go as far as failures in prediction. It is one thing to predict where a battle line might be breeched. But before and during the Great Recession, economists couldn't even tell whether the forces were on the attack or in retreat. Despite having an army of economists and all the financial and economic data you could hope for, on March 28, 2007, Ben Bernanke, the chairman of the Federal Reserve, stated to the Joint Economic Committee of Congress that "the impact on the broader economy and financial markets of the problems in the subprime market seems likely to be contained." This sentiment was echoed the same day by the U.S. Treasury secretary Henry Paulson, assuring a House Appropriations subcommittee that "from the standpoint of the overall economy, my bottom line is we're watching it closely but it appears to be contained."

Less than three months later, this containment ruptured when two Bear Stearns hedge funds that had held a portfolio of more than twenty billion dollars, most of it in securities backed by subprime mortgages, failed, marking a course that blew through one financial market after another over the following six months—the broader mortgage markets, including collateralized debt obligations and credit default swaps; money markets, including the short-term financing of the repo (repurchase agreement) and interbank markets; and markets that seemed to be clever little wrinkles but turned out to have serious vulnerabilities, such as asset-backed commercial paper and auction-rate securities.

In early 2008, as the market turmoil raged, Bernanke gave his semiannual testimony before the Senate Banking Committee. He said that there might be failures within the ranks of the smaller banks, but "I don't anticipate any serious problems of that sort among the large internationally active banks that make up a very substantial part of our banking system." That September, ten days after the spectacular collapse of the investment bank Lehman Brothers, Washington Mutual became the largest financial institution in U.S. history to fail. In October and November, the federal government stepped in to rescue Citigroup from an even bigger failure.

Another bastion of economic brainpower, the International Monetary Fund, did no better in predicting the global financial crisis. In its spring 2007 *World Economic Outlook*, the IMF boldly forecast that the storm clouds would pass: "Overall risks to the outlook seem less threatening than six months ago." The IMF's country report for Iceland from August 2008 offered a reassuring assessment: "The banking system's reported financial indicators are above minimum regulatory requirements and stress tests suggest that the system is resilient." A month and a half later, Iceland was in a meltdown. Iceland's Financial Supervisory Authority began the takeover of Iceland's three largest commercial banks, all of which were facing default, with reverberations that extended to the United Kingdom and the Netherlands.

Economic theory asserts a level of consistency and rationality that not only leaves the cascades and propagation over the course of a crisis unexplained but also asserts that they are unexplainable. Everything's rational, until it isn't; economics works, until it doesn't. So economics blithely labors on, applying the same theory and methods to a world of its own construction that is devoid of such unpleasantries. The dominant model postulates a world in which we are each rolled up into one representative individual who starts its productive life having mapped out a future path of investments and consumption with full knowledge of all future contingencies and their likelihood. In this fantasy world, each of us works to produce one good and conveniently—because who wants to worry about financial crises?—lives in a world with no financial system and no banks!

Lucas is right in his assessment that economics cannot help during financial crises, but not because economic theory, in its grasp of the world, has demonstrated that crises cannot be helped. It is because traditional economic theory, bound by its own methods and structure, is not up to the task. Our path cannot be determined with mathematical shortcuts; we have to follow the path to see where it leads. Which might not be where we intended. As the boxer Mike Tyson noted, everyone has a plan until they get punched in the mouth.

This book explores what it would mean to follow the path to see where it leads. It provides a nontechnical introduction to agent-based modeling, an alternative to neoclassical economics that shows great promise in predicting crises, averting them, and helping us recover from them. This approach doesn't postulate a world of mathematically defined automatons; instead, it draws on what science has learned recently from the study of real-world complex systems. In particular, it draws on four concepts that have a technical ring but are eminently intuitive: emergent phenomena, ergodicity, radical uncertainty, and computational irreducibility.

Emergent phenomena show that even if we follow an expected path, whether choosing to drive on a highway or buy a house, we'll miss insight into the overall system. And it is the overall system that defines the scope of the crisis. The sum of our interactions leads to a system that can be wholly unrelated to what any one of us sees or does, and cannot even be fathomed if we concentrate on an isolated individual.

The fact that as real-world economic agents we couch our interactions in our varied and ever-changing experience means that we are a moving target for economic methods that demand *ergodicity*, that is, conditions that do not change.

And we don't even know where to aim, because of *radical uncertainty*: the future is an unknown in a deep, metaphysical sense.

Neoclassical economic theory cannot help because it ignores key elements of human nature and the limits that these imply: *computational irreducibility* means that the complexity of our interactions cannot be unraveled with the deductive mathematics that forms the base—even the raison d'être—for the dominant model in current economics. As the novelist Milan Kundera has written, we are in a world where humor resides, a world filled with "the intoxicating relativity of human things," with "the strange pleasure that comes of certainty that there is no certainty."[20] It is humor, intoxication, and pleasure that economics cannot share.

These limitations are also at work in our day-to-day world even though they are not very apparent or constraining. Lucas acknowledges that "exceptions and anomalies" to economic theory have been discovered, "but for the purposes of macroeconomic analyses and forecasts they are too small to matter."[21] A more accurate statement would be, "but for the self-referential purposes of macroeconomic analyses and forecasts viewed through the lens of economic theory, they are too small to matter." Are the exceptions and anomalies manifestations of the limits brought about by human nature?

The performance of economics during crises is a litmus test for its performance in other times, where the limits might be ignored, cast aside as rounding errors. Thus, understanding crises provides us a window into any broader failure in economics. Crises are the refiner's fire, a testing ground for economic models, a stress test for economic theory. If standard economic reasoning fails in crises, we are left to wonder what failings exist in the noncrisis state, failings that might not be so apparent or that can be covered by a residual error term that is "too small to matter." Small, perhaps, but is it a small smudge on the floor or a small crack in the foundation?

Expecting rationality, casting the world in a form that is amenable to mathematical and deductive methods while treating humans as mechanistic processes, will continue to fail when crises hit. And it might also fail in subtle and unapparent ways beyond the periods of crisis. But what can replace it?

2

Being Human

As a start, consider that we are human. Being human, we are social. We have meaningful interactions that change our world and our relationships with others. Being human, we have a history. We are shaped by experiences that provide the context for our worldview. Our actions cannot be separated from the experiences that color how we relate to one another, the values we hold, what we buy, sell, and consume—everything that motivates us and drives our objectives. The dynamics of our lives are rich and complex because our interactions add to our experiences, changing the context for future interactions.

By the yardsticks of interaction and experience, a crisis is a deeply human event. During crises, interactions rise in intensity and are fraught with uncertainty as we are buffeted by unfamiliar experiences and wade into unsettling contexts. A financial crisis is not simply a run of typical bad days, or bad spins on the wheel of the Wall Street casino. Neither is it just "more of the same, only worse." Nobody thought they were merely having another bad day as Lehman imploded on Sunday, September 14, 2008.

A crisis has is its own dynamic, often one without precedent. In the financial markets our day-to-day mode of operation is to reduce meaningful interactions, to fly under the radar. We try to minimize the impact of our transactions to keep from moving the market and to protect against signaling our intent. But not so when a crisis hits. When investors face margin calls, when banks face runs or teeter on default, the essential dynamic of a crisis cascades through the system, changing prices, raising credit concerns, and altering the perception of risk, thereby affecting others, even those not directly exposed to the events precipitating the crisis.

We've all learned from each of these crises. We change our strategies, throw out some financial instruments and cook up some new ones. So each crisis really is different. And as we dig out from one, we are sowing the seeds for the next.

Yet the regulators and academics always seem to be fighting the last war. After 2008, all we talked about was reducing bank leverage and coming up with new risk measures based on bank leverage and whatever else. But I doubt it will be bank leverage that hits us over the head the next time around. What creates a particular crisis, how it propagates to engulf the financial system—and whether the event turns into a crisis at all—is unique. It is unique because each crisis is generated by a different shock, propagated by different financial holdings.

We build defensive lines to keep us from being embroiled in a crisis. We don't put on oversized positions, positions beyond where the market can take us out. We put limits in place to override our usual investing and get us out of the market if things start to go south. We manage our risk through diversification, spreading our exposure across disparate markets. If the market drops, we are increasing our hedge. We can't find any buyers, so we are dropping the price more, and doing it right now. We aren't going to try to sell, because if we do, the new price will make us revalue our portfolio, and we will have to sell more.

Look at any business, talk to anyone you know, and you will see prudent, thoughtful actors. But look at the sum total of their actions, and sometimes it will seem without rhyme or reason, bordering on chaos. The sum of individually rational actions can be the genesis of a crisis. Everyone (well, most everyone) follows actions that they are convinced are stable, rational, and prudent. But then look at the overall system. It can be globally unstable. It can seem to be irrational, the end result of imprudence. We'd like someone to tell everybody, "please walk out in an orderly manner, single file," but it doesn't happen that way because no one is in control. Each individual is acting based on a narrow subset of the environment. The result—a stampede for the exit—is what is called emergent behavior.

Strange things happen during a crisis. Economics 101 tells you that when prices drop, more buyers will reveal themselves. What it doesn't tell you is that in a crisis, as prices drop, you have more *sellers*. Not that everybody *wants* to sell; some are forced to. Others who would buy at the bargain price bide their time, staying on the sidelines.

Finance 101 tells you that you reduce risk by diversifying and hedging. But in crises the markets, usually rich and varied, governed by many factors, fuse, plasmalike, into a white-hot ball of risk. Whatever is risky and illiquid drops, whatever is low-risk and liquid stays put. Hedges break apart. If you hedge a risky or illiquid position with a lower-risk and liquid one (which is what you do), the two sides of the hedge move in opposite directions, and the hedge becomes a boomerang. What were similar assets in a normal market are now moving in different directions because characteristics that you never gave a thought to are now dominating. With the markets all moving together (that is, down), diversification, the final perimeter of the defense, is breeched.

The typical analysis of the quants no longer matters. During crises, we see a breakdown of institutions and of assumptions that govern the normal application of economics. People act in ways you—and they—never would have thought. Their behavior cannot be predicted based on their daily activities. Some turn cautious (or cowardly), retreating from the market. Some act out of desperation. Others freeze in their tracks.

As the institutions begin to break down, subtlety is replaced by polite panic, like people trying to get a good seat without making it seem as though they are being so crass as to actually break into a run. We also see actions that, absent the context, would be considered uncivil. Terms of funding are not extended, redemption demands are forestalled, trading partners don't pick up the phone—maybe because they are busy trading against you. The fine print of contracts starts to matter, or would matter if there were time to read and evaluate it. People need to shoot from the hip; they have to decide quickly or decisions will be made for them. Any notion of an analytical process gives way because the world does not look rational—at least it does not follow normal assumptions and what you would normally observe.

Meanwhile, the common crowd that shared similar views, that is more or less comfortable with the level of the market and the pace of the world, scurries in all directions. Some are fighting for their lives in the face of margin calls and redemptions, others stepping onto the sidelines to become observers.

Can we tell any of this ahead of time?

The Four Horsemen of the Econopalypse

Social and economic interactions, colored by experience, are parts of human nature that, when joined together, create complexity that exceeds the limits of our understanding. Things happen and we don't know why.

And even if that untidy result is in some way quantifiable, human limits are the core of why economic methods fail with crises, because crises are the times when this complexity is most clearly evident and these limits are most constraining. I will argue that these are the reasons for using agent-based models, models that allow for individuals who are each plotting their own course, making adjustments along the way, and affecting the world and others through their actions. Agent-based models do this by applying the simulation approach that is rooted in the analysis of complex and adaptive systems. These are models that respect our very human limits.

Let me summarize four broad phenomena that are endemic to financial crises as they have been evolving since the tulip mania of seventeenth-century Holland. I will treat these in more detail in chapters 3 through 6.

1. Emergent phenomena. You're cruising along the highway when traffic jams up, and you wonder: Is there an accident up ahead? Or maybe road repair? Then, five minutes and a mile later, you're again moving along smoothly without any obvious reason for the jam. There are less benign versions of transitory congestion, like the flow of fans exiting a concert or soccer match that suddenly turns into a stampede. Even though no one is directing the action and no one is trying to cause a stampede, the end result of these many independent individual actions can inexplicably trigger a catastrophic event. When systemwide dynamics arise unexpectedly out of the activities of individuals in a way that is not simply an aggregation of that behavior, the result is known as emergence. Emergence can create a helter-skelter world where people who are minding their own business and doing what seems reasonable produce strange, unexpected results in the big picture—including unintended consequences that make for devastating crises. Did *you* cause the economic meltdown of 2007–2009? Neither did anybody else. We still had one, though. That's emergence.

2. Non-ergodicity. Want to do something really ergodic? Sound like fun? Actually, it's the essence of boring. An ergodic process is same old, same old; it is one that does not vary with time or experience. It follows the same probabilities today as it did in the distant past and will in the distant future. That works for physics. And for the game of roulette. You can bet on 20 every day for the next twenty years and the odds won't ever change. But the richness of our experiences and the interplay between our experiences and our interactions cannot be reduced to something like roulette. Our world changes; we learn and we discover. The way we interact is dictated by context, which varies based on sometimes subtle cues and our experience and frame of mind. So we need to know our history, which is ever-changing in unexpected ways. Our individual actions, even if based on established and deterministic rules, can lead to unexpected dynamics in the swirl of human interactions.

Our world is not ergodic—yet economists treat it as though it is. Without drilling into each individual's context and knowing the future path of where this will take him and those with whom he interacts, we cannot look at where someone is now and know the path he will take, even in probabilistic terms.

3. *Radical uncertainty.* It's everywhere, but you don't see it. Emergent phenomena and non-ergodic processes create it; we create it with our own inconsistencies, with the inevitably human process of analyzing and modeling ourselves, with our creativity and inventiveness, which leads the world to go in directions we had never imagined. And there are plain old where-did-that-come-from surprises, like eggplants that look like Richard Nixon. Think of the radical uncertainty that arises from the simple process of maturing. You want to look at real radical uncertainty? Start with a teenager. He cannot know what maturity will be before he is mature. If your younger self were to meet your older self at the door, your younger self might be surprised at what you have become ("I can't believe I became an economist. What went wrong?!") and might discover that you have moved in a direction that was not even in the realm of your younger vision. You might discover that your older self is the ungrateful child of all the sacrifices and plans and hopes of your younger self.

Our unanticipatable future experiences, on the one hand, and the complexity of our social interactions, on the other, lead to uncertainty that cannot be expressed or anticipated. As J.B.S. Haldane wrote, "The universe is not only queerer than we suppose, but queerer than we can suppose." The world could be changing right now in ways that will blindside you down the road. No wonder it's called radical uncertainty.

4. *Computational irreducibility.* It is a deeply held conviction within economics that our world can be reduced to models that are founded on the solid ground of axioms, plumbed by deductive logic into rigorous, universal mathematical structures. Economists think they have things figured out, but our economic behavior is so complex, our interactions are so profound that there is no mathematical shortcut for determining how they will evolve. The only way to know what the result of these interactions will be is to trace out their path over time: we essentially must live our lives to see where they will go. There is no formula that allows us to fast-forward to find out what the result will be. The world cannot be solved; it has to be lived.

Problems like this are said to be computationally irreducible. Computational irreducibility is more the rule than the exception for systems with interactions, even for many simple, almost trivial, systems with dynamic interactions. And a crisis is defined by interactions that are far from trivial or run-of-the-mill, that significantly alter the environment and change the way we act.

No wonder that the reductive methods used in economics will fail in such a world. We have no equation to describe the sickening feeling in a panicky investor's stomach as the market drops. Some phenomena cannot be compressed into a theory because they are too complex in this computationally irreducible sense. This means that there are limits to how far we can carry deductive processes for understanding or describing human and even natural phenomena.

Modern neoclassical economics sweeps humanity off the stage. It prefers to use mathematical models of a representative agent with stable preferences—one that doesn't have temper tantrums or unexpected medical expenses—operating under a specified probability distribution. But our lives cannot be understood without following the path of our experiences and context, because even when it *can* be modeled, the models are computationally irreducible. Our world cannot be understood by looking at people behaving within the system because of emergent phenomena. Our markets display decisions that are not in the ergodic world of a gambler at the roulette table because our environment shifts with every interaction and experience—and particularly during crises, which is where it is most critical we find a way to predict or at least understand. When we come to comprehend these limits, we approach a world filled with the giant of unknown unknowns: radical uncertainty.

These four phenomena have far-reaching implications for those undertaking the task of unraveling the mysteries of crises—and for people trying to understand why economists were caught flat-footed by the 2008 financial meltdown. Yet you can read through academic articles in mainstream economics, and textbooks from Econ 101 though graduate-level courses, and see none of these terms. (Maybe *ergodicity*, but rarely.) Economists would do well to pause and reflect on their failings in dealing with financial crises, whether in assumptions or execution or data. But this may not be in the cards.

Modeling Crises

Our social and economic interactions and our experience combine to create limits to our knowledge, limits that deflect the attempts of economic methods, methods demanding knowledge that this complexity withholds. We must study crises while respecting these limits, because they can't be overcome. They are inherent outcroppings of our nature and are particularly constraining during periods of crisis.

So, how do we deal with these problems? The limitations themselves suggest the approach for overcoming them. We cannot assume them away without removing the key aspects of the problem, and we cannot defeat them. We must have meaningful interactions, ones that can alter the environment and our relationships with others. If our individual actions create emergent phenomena, then that is the way things work. We can't try to overcome this by replacing the interactions of many individuals with one representative agent without leaving the essential dynamics behind. If we have a level of complexity that is computationally irreducible, then imposing simplifications and regularity assumptions that make it suitable for mathematical machinery risks assuming away the essence of the problem.

To deal with these limitations we need an approach that allows us to follow the path rather than rely on mathematical shortcuts, to extract from the individual to the system level the behavior that emerges, and to do so without relying on stable probabilities. The methods to do this, methods that are at the core of complexity science, are computer simulations. And the specific application of those simulations to problems like this is known as agent-based modeling.

With this method we can discard altogether the idea that the economic world is founded on axioms of economic behavior that are timeless and universal, where the agents have no history or experience, behaving in the same manner whether you enter that world today or ten generations hence, whether that world is on Earth or Mars. The paths that people take are not predetermined through a mathematical formula of utility and probability, and people do not respond mechanistically, nor are they described by a universally applicable model in which all key relationships are fixed.

The problem suggests the answer: We must start with models of individual, heterogeneous agents and allow them to interact. We must allow that interaction to alter their behavior and to alter their environment. We must follow the path of the individuals from the start without trying to find shortcuts in the process. We also must monitor the models for emergent phenomena. Agent-based modeling is the approach that meets these conditions.

So this book is my manifesto for financial crises, a declaration that the neoclassical economic theory has failed and the new paradigm of agent-based economics may succeed. There are two things this book is not. First, it is not a broadside against all of economics in all applications. It is about finance and crises, though there remains open the question of whether the arguments I put forward do have broader implications. Second, it is not a detailed "How To" manual; there is no specific model to be proposed. Our complex financial universe resists formulaic solutions to its problems. There is no simple path, no plugging in problem A and pulling out solution B. Indeed, the power of the agent-based approach is that it launches an agile rather than a hard-coded, axiomatic attack against the problem.

The Four Horsemen

3

Social Interactions and Computational Irreducibility

A map is designed as a shortcut for solving the problem of getting from point *A* to point *B*. Maps are scaled, meaning they're reduced to a tiny fraction of the territory they describe and with fewer details than what is in the territory itself. But that doesn't have to be the case, at least not in the world imagined by the great Argentinian writer Jorge Luis Borges:

> In that Empire, the Art of Cartography attained such Perfection that the map of a single Province occupied the entirety of a City, and the map of the Empire, the entirety of a Province. In time, those Unconscionable Maps no longer satisfied, and the Cartographers Guilds struck a Map of the Empire whose size was that of the Empire, and which coincided point for point with it. The following Generations, who were not so fond of the Study of Cartography as their Forebears had been, saw that that vast Map was Useless, and not without some Pitilessness was it, that they delivered it up to the Inclemencies of Sun and Winters. In the Deserts of the West, still today, there are Tattered Ruins of that Map, inhabited by Animals and Beggars; in all the Land there is no other Relic of the Disciplines of Geography. (Suarez Miranda, *Viajes de varones prudentes*, Libro IV, Cap. XLV, Lerida, 1658)[1]

We do not find examples of the strange case that Suarez Miranda recounts because if the problem to be solved requires a map the size of the territory, the mapping exercise is pointless and cartographers will move on to find more suitable geographies as the focus of their skills.

But what if there were times when the map cannot be made smaller than the territory—there is nothing of the territory that can be reduced in size or detail without losing critical features necessary to travel the path to your destination? In such a case, you must actually traverse the entire path, either in the territory itself or in a map that has you taking the same steps you would in the territory. When the map cannot be made appreciably smaller than the territory it is describing, or when the problem cannot be solved using the map any faster or more efficiently than it can by operating in the territory itself, we have a system that is called computationally irreducible.

A computationally irreducible problem is one without mathematical shortcuts, where the only way to determine the outcome is to perform each step of the program. If you want to see what a system will be like at a distant time, you have to run the computer program that is modeling the system step by step from now until that distant time. By contrast, a computationally reducible system is one that can be described by mathematical formulas that give the outcome at any chosen instant of time without working through all the time steps.[2]

Mathematics works only with computationally reducible systems. Axioms and deductive logic are intended to provide shortcuts, to give general results that can compress a problem and provide insight into its workings so that it can be solved without having to take on the tedious task of running things through step by step. For example, the math behind ballistics tables allows an artillery gunner to calculate where the shell will land before it is fired. By contrast, there is no precalculated table to consult to determine the best path through rush hour traffic.

Looking back into the centuries of scientific progress, a manifest characteristic of the great theoretical triumphs has been finding computational shortcuts that help understand how systems behave, so that the scientist is not left merely watching the phenomenon and taking notes. The primary tool for executing these shortcuts, the tool of the scientist-cum-cartographer, is mathematics, and mathematics deductively applies a general axiomatic structure, a structure that begins with the statement of laws.

If we instead are left to traverse the map to get to the result, we want to have a vehicle that can do the trip quickly—more quickly than we could traverse the same territory in the real world. And that is what the last part of the twentieth century gave us. The physicist and computer scientist Stephen Wolfram has commented, "People sometimes say that the reason the mathematics that we have is the way it is, is because that's what we need to describe the natural world. I think that's just not true." Many problems cannot be described with mathematics, but until recently that was all we had; the computational power simply was not there to deal with problems that were both nontrivial and computationally irreducible. So, naturally, all the effort was focused on finding problems that fit the math. (Give a carpenter a hammer and everything looks like a nail.) The art in trade of the mathematician, and the economist convinced of mathematical prowess, is to know how to bypass this pocket of resistance to find friendlier ground. Wolfram adds, "Mathematics has navigated through these kind of narrow paths in which you don't run into rampant undecidability all over the place."[3]

Now we have the machinery to tackle problems that have this rampant undecidability, those that are computationally irreducible. And that certainly is where the problem of financial crises resides.

Where Do You Find Computational Irreducibility?

How hard is it to construct an example of a computationally irreducible problem? Where can we find a practical example? The answer is: everywhere. In fact, computational irreducibility is the norm in real-world dynamical systems—not just in crises, with their complexity and wildfire interactions, but even in the tamer, deterministic worlds of planets revolving around each other, or of rule-bound automatons blinking on and off in their cells.

TWO'S A NEWTON, THREE'S A COMPUTATIONALLY IRREDUCIBLE CROWD: THE THREE-BODY PROBLEM

Let's start with something really simple: a system with three agents or components, with no randomness, all governed by the same simple mechanistic relationship. In particular, let's plot the path of a system that has three planets, their interaction determined by their gravitational force, which is the product of their masses divided by the square of the distance between them. The mass of each planet is fixed, so the only variable of relevance for determining the forces acting on them is the distance between them. We want to analyze this system so that we can determine where the planets will be at any given time in the future, given their current position and velocity.

Back in 1687, Isaac Newton made a running start on this problem by solving it for two planets. Then he hit a wall. (It happens, even to the man who discovered the laws of gravity in 1666.) And so did every mathematician after him for the next couple of centuries. The three-body problem was a central topic in mathematical physics from the mid-1700s until the early 1900s, when it was determined that the three-body problem could not be solved in terms of algebraic formulas and other standard mathematical functions.

After Newton, only three special cases were discovered where the three-body problem is tractable: the Lagrange-Euler solution, where equally spaced planets go around in a circle like horses on a merry-go-round; the Broucke-Hénon solution, where two of the planets run back and forth inside the orbit of the third planet; and a solution by Cristopher Moore, where the planets trace out a figure eight. Only with the advent of supercomputing did another thirteen cases reveal themselves.[4] But most of the time, if you start the three planets on a course, they will follow complex and apparently random trajectories that finally end with one of the planets escaping from the gravitational pull of the others.

The three-body problem illustrates how easy it is to run into computational irreducibility. It is a problem that borders on the trivial, yet it seems that it cannot be solved analytically. There is no apparent shortcut, no mathematical equation that can tell you the trajectory.[5] In general, if you want to know where the planets will end up at some time down the road, you have to ride along with them as they trace their paths, either in practice or in simulation. If we want to know whether the planets crash, whether one of them will fly off into space, whether they will be periodic or chaotic, we have to follow them over the course of their travels. We can't plug coordinates or a time period into a formula and crank out the answer.

The three-body problem also illustrates the potential for finding pockets of stability in what is broadly and generally an unstable system. If you live within one of the sixteen cases that have been discovered, and if you think that it is the only one that matters, you can enjoy the stability and tractability that it affords. But if you construct your model of the world as one of those cases, none of the analysis you do will be very useful unless you can explain why it is natural for planets always to interact under those special conditions.

There are many other examples of apparently simple systems that defy analytical solutions, but the three-body problem has a pedigree in economics because this very issue was specifically addressed by William Jevons as he developed his mathematical theory of economics. In addition to his concern that the stability imbued in economics through mathematics made it ill-equipped to understand crises, Jevons recognized that he had no means of introducing or analyzing complex interactions in his theory. He realized that the three-body problem in astronomy would pose similar difficulties for the exchange of three trading bodies and three commodities: "If we are to apply scientific method to morals, we must have a calculus of moral effects, a kind of physical astronomy investigating mutual perturbations of individuals. But as astronomers have not yet fully solved the problem of three gravitating bodies, where shall we have a solution of the problem of three moral bodies?"[6]

The three-body problem points to another wrinkle in the standard methods of economics: in economics we can get solutions, we can get stability, but only in very restrictive conditions. And as if adhering to a canon of religious principles, all the analysis rests on those restrictions. In economics, the cart leads the horse, and having found restrictions and regularity conditions that allow for a clean solution, people are then constricted to behave in that way. According to an economist's way of thinking, our behavior is a matter of what is mathematically convenient. The regularity of conditions and assumptions pulls the rabbit out of the hat.

If people behave just so, and things move along just right, the deductive approach yields an answer. But such conditions generally don't hold in real life. And this is where the focus on crises is useful, because in the case of crises, all bets are off.

Similar problems arise in more elaborate models. Deterministic, nonlinear models can lead to chaotic dynamics, while agent-based models, simulating the actions of individuals under hypothesized behavioral rules, often display nearly chaotic outcomes that have been dubbed complexity. In such models, positive-feedback interactions in which one person's action makes it more likely that another will act in the same way are the source of either chaos or complexity. These interactions should be commonplace in a realistic, comprehensive theory of individual economic activity. As the mathematician and economist Donald Saari puts it, "Economics so effortlessly offers the needed ingredients for chaos that, rather than being surprised about exotic dynamics, we should be suspicious about models which always are stable."[7] And just as it is for the three-body problem of astronomy, Saari notes that there are examples of three-person, three-commodity economies with permanently unstable price dynamics, showing that we cannot hope to prove the stability of general equilibrium in all cases.[8]

CALL ME IRREDUCIBLE: THE ROCKET MAN
AND CONWAY'S GAME OF LIFE

In the 1940s, the famed Princeton polymath John von Neumann developed an abstract template for self-replicating machines, which he called a universal constructor. He simulated it, not on a computer, but using the cells on a sheet of graph paper, where each cell could take on any of twenty-nine states. His universal constructor gave rise to the concept of a von Neumann probe, a spacecraft capable of replicating itself, which could land on one galactic outpost, build a hundred copies of itself, each traveling off in one of a hundred different directions, discover other worlds, and replicate again, thereby exploring the universe—and, depending on the design of the machines, conquering the universe—with exponential efficiency.

The universal constructor caught the interest of John Conway, a British mathematician who would later hold the John von Neumann Chair of Mathematics at Princeton, and over "eighteen months of coffee times," as he describes it, he began tinkering to simplify its set of rules. The result was what became known as Conway's Game of Life.[9] The "game" really isn't one—it is a zero-player game, because once the initial conditions of the cells are set, there is no further interaction or input as the process evolves. There's a simple set of rules. Each cell on the grid can have one of two possible states: it is either alive (colored black) or dead (colored white). Each cell on a grid has eight neighboring cells,[10] and the fate of each cell for the next period is determined by the number of neighboring cells that are alive this period:

1. Each living cell with four or more neighbors that are alive dies, due to overpopulation.
2. Each living cell with only one neighbor or with no neighbor alive dies, due to isolation.
3. Each living cell with two or three neighboring cells that are alive survives for the next generation.
4. Each cell that is currently dead and that has exactly three neighbors that are alive is in just the right nurturing environment to be a "birth cell," and becomes alive in the next period.

Figure 3.1 illustrates the application of these rules. The starting configuration is given. Between period 1 and period 2, the cell in the left-most column dies because it has only one other alive cell as a neighbor, as does the cell in the top row. But two new cells are born because in period 1 there

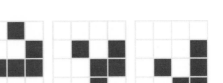

Period 1   Period 2   Period 3   Period 4   Period 5

FIGURE 3.1. **Conway's Game of Life.** An illustration of the progression of cells in Conway's Game of Life, the periods moving from left to right. Each dark cell is "alive"; each white cell is "dead." In any period, a cell is determined to be alive or dead based on how many of its neighboring cells are alive in the previous period:

  1. Each living cell with four or more living neighbors dies.
  2. Each living cell with only one living neighbor dies.
  3. Each living cell with two or three living neighbors continues to live.
  4. Each dead cell that has exactly three living neighbors becomes alive.

are two dead cells that each have three alive neighbors. Between period 2 and period 3, one of the cells that was born the previous period dies because it has only one alive neighbor, and the cell diagonally below it to the right dies because it has too many alive neighbors. But two new cells are born. If we follow the rules over the next several periods, we get to period 5, where we have a configuration that looks just like the one in period 1, but it has moved along the grid. And if we extend the grid out, it will continue to do so until it runs into some other living cells. This configuration is called a glider. It is one of a number of configurations in Life that are called spaceships, which move along the grids.[11]

Conway played this game on a Go board—which conveniently has cells and white and black pieces—and he discovered that these rules led to configurations that rebuilt themselves and built things that were more complicated than themselves. So it has the features not only of self-replication but also of generating increasing levels of complexity. The degree of that complexity could be appreciated only when the game was moved from the Go board to the computer.

Once the initial state of the grid is set with various cells alive and others dead, the process might go on for a few periods and then have all the cells die off, or it might continue with all sorts of structures emerging and changing. It is, in general, impossible to predict whether a configuration will die off in a given period. Indeed, Life is an illustration of Alan Turing's halting problem: you can't know if the cells will all die off without running the game until they do die off. Thus, Life, a two-state process governed by four rules, is computationally irreducible.

Von Neumann designed the universal constructor with the objective of self-replication; Conway designed his cellular automaton without any specific objective in mind. But he observed, "If you couldn't predict what it did, then probably that is because it is capable of anything." And it turns out that it is indeed capable of anything, at least anything that can be done with a computer. Like any other cellular automaton, Life can be thought of as a computational device: the initial state of the cells before running the game can be thought of as an input string, the instruction set for the computation. As the process runs, the state of the cells can be looked at as an output string.[12] What can Life compute? It turns out that Life can compute everything a universal Turing machine can and therefore can function as a general-purpose computer: with the right selection of initial conditions, let Life loose and it will be capable of carrying out any computational procedures.

The Game of Life is also a stylized version of an agent-based model. The cells are agents that operate based on a simple heuristic laid out by the four rules. Thought of in this context, it presents several characteristics of agent-based models that we will revisit and expand on later. It displays emergence: simple rules can lead to complex results, including results that do not seem to relate in any natural or predictable way to those rules. Any one cell/agent reacts only to eight other agents and can act only in one of two ways. Yet the aggregate result of the individual actions is rich and complex. It gives a hint of the pervasiveness of computationally irreducible dynamics and the related limits on mathematical methods, and also illustrates the method for dealing with this: namely, letting the world run to see what happens.

Conclusion

In view of how even the simplest cases can lead to computational irreducibility, how can it fail to be the case that the path of human—and thus economic—interaction and the implications of human experience are computationally irreducible? If we cannot successfully deal with the computational irreducibility head on, we are missing a key aspect of humanity.

But one of the critical skills for economists is figuring out how to construct models that do not have computational irreducibility, because that is what they need to have things work in a mathematical setting. And that is not so simple a task; when you are dealing with humans it takes a lot of tweaking and simplification to get something that produces useful shortcuts. Economists push for simple and elegant models in a world that is admittedly not simple or elegant (a world that is human-bound, after all) because that is what is needed to get the math to work.[13]

The alternative route of taking the path through the territory rather than drawing a map where one cannot be drawn is not as elegant, but now is largely possible. Agent-based models are one tool for doing that. If we are facing the prospect of a crisis, we have an alternative to trying (unsuccessfully) to compress the crisis into a reducible, analytical form. The idea of irreducible systems is very simple and powerful at the same time. If we cannot determine the outcome of so simple an artificial world as Life without actually running it, why do we think we can deal with so complex and interconnected a system as an economy in the throes of crisis without doing the same?

4

The Individual and
the Human Wave

EMERGENT PHENOMENA

Ribbons of white, punctuated by splashes of color from umbrellas to protect against the desert sun, mark the crush of Muslim pilgrims streaming from their tent cities in Mina for their holy tour of Mecca, a few kilometers away. Then, near an intersection of a set of narrow streets, crowds become trapped and the stream becomes turbulent; a crushing stampede is tripped off with masses of pilgrims trampled. Only after the area finally clears does the catastrophe become evident in the piles of white-robed bodies. More than 2,400 Hajj pilgrims are dead.

Blame for this tragic stampede, which occurred during the annual Hajj pilgrimage in 2015, was variously ascribed to errors by security personnel who had closed off exits; to the failure of the pilgrims to follow the guidelines and instructions "issued by the responsible authorities," perhaps because of language and educational barriers; to the wide diversity in cultural backgrounds of the pilgrims, which would have led to varied and incompatible reactions to the confinement and crush of people; and to disorientation from being in an unfamiliar setting, made all the worse by heat and fatigue.

The 2015 stampede was only the latest in a series, and comes despite the Saudis having spent billions of dollars to prevent a recurrence by enlarging the gathering spaces such as the Jamarat, where pilgrims gather to throw pebbles at walls in a ritual that represents the stoning of the devil, and widening and streamlining the channels for movement between the sites. Other disastrous stampedes have occurred in similar circumstances in the Jamarat and, as in 2015, on the pathways surrounding it. A stampede in 1990 inside a pedestrian tunnel leading to the Jamarat left 1,426 pilgrims dead. In 1994, more than 500 died in two separate stampedes at the Jamarat; in 1998, 120 were killed on the bridge leading to the Jamarat; and in 2006, some 350 perished in a stampede that started on the ramps heading to the Jamarat Bridge. Survivors of these disasters describe being pinned in a crush of bodies as people walk over them in an effort to escape. People climb over one another just to breathe. If one person stumbles, the pressure coming from each side forces others on top.

No one decides to stampede. And unlike the panics that might occur fleeing a burning building, there is no particular trigger or incentive that turns walking along the—albeit congested—path into a contagion of suffocating and unstable turbulence. It is a surge with no apparent cause. The disruption that begins the cascade into the stampede might be a busload of people pushing their way into the flow, one stream of people meeting another from a different direction, or even something as seemingly benign as a few people stopping to wait for others in their group.

These stampedes have more to do with physics than mass psychology. They are the result of amplifying feedback and cascades, the domino effects that are common to dynamical systems. Leading up to the "crowd quake," any one person is doing what seems innocuous or unavoidable given his immediate surroundings. But the overall systemwide effect is not a simple aggregation of the actions of individuals. Nor is it the result of some grand plan, of some governing authority directing everyone's actions from on high. It may have originated hundreds of yards away with a bit of pushing, or even simply people stopping to rest, amplified like a rogue wave rising up out of nowhere.[1]

Such stampedes have a scientific name: they are examples of emergent phenomena. Emergent phenomena occur when the overall effect of individuals' actions is different from what the individuals are doing. The actions of the system differ from the actions of the agents that comprise the system. We see emergent phenomena as a matter of course in nature, from the turbulence of water in a stream to the gathering of clouds in the sky. Emergent phenomena are also common in our social interactions, as the stampedes of the Hajj demonstrate, although we have various control mechanisms to prevent the emergence from moving along a destructive path.

There is no general theory for why the jostling of a crowd dissipates in some cases and propagates to create a stampede in others. Any individual in the crowd simply moves forward aware of those around him, unaware of how his actions might end up cascading and propagating through the crowd. No individual knows what is happening or why it is happening except as it affects him and those in close proximity, and there is no governing force or body or mind that has that knowledge. Contrary to the consistency dictum that's part of the rational expectations hypothesis, people do not know the model, and arguably there is no model to know.

A financial crisis is an emergent phenomenon that has broken through the market's containment vehicles. As in the Hajj stampedes, no one decided to precipitate the crisis, and indeed at the level of the individual firms, the decisions generally are made to take prudent action to avoid the costly effects of a crisis. But what is locally stable can become globally unstable.

Defining Emergence: Something Fishy

Before we get into the chaos surrounding the Hajj stampedes, let's look at something that is based on the same dynamics but is the essence of coordination and grace: a school of fish. A school of thousands of fish moves along as one unit, all heading the same way, looking like a single entity. Then, apparently on cue, they switch direction and continue to move with their shape changed. Sometimes the fish move languidly and spread out; sometimes they increase speed and close ranks. There is no leader, no big fish giving directions to the other fish, giving them the three-dimensional coordinates of where to be or the speed at which to travel. There is no order shouted out to initiate a redirection, no new set of coordinates distributed to the group. Instead, each fish is acting based on very simple rules dictated by its immediate surroundings. It faces the direction of the fish nearby, keeping a distance from them. If there is no threat, the fish will keep a greater distance to increase the feeding area; if there is something suspicious, it will close the distance to its neighbors to provide a smaller target.[2]

From these simple rules emerges a complex group dynamic that cannot be divined from the rules of an individual fish. The whole is more than, or at least different from, the sum of the parts. Dynamics for the system arise from the interactions of agents, which the agents do not individually exhibit—dynamics called emergent phenomena.

Look at the streets of midtown New York during the holidays. Watch as the throngs of people huddled at each corner cross once the traffic light changes. They form little rivulets, some going one way, some the other, with no bumping and jostling. The rule they intuitively follow is simple and not so different from those of the fish (minus the risk of a predator): stay behind someone who is going the same direction you are, at a distance that is not too close and not too far. No one has had to hand out leaflets on "rules for walking across New York City intersections"; the rules are simple and innate. The result, with each change of the lights, is a large-scale dynamic emerging from this simple rule and then passing away.

Once we have the rules in hand, we can model this emergent phenomenon in a computer simulation just as easily as we can observe it in real life. The flight of the flock of birds can appear incredibly complex and fluid. In the spectacular display, many thousands of starlings appear as a dark cloud ever-shifting in direction and form. The flight of a flock of birds appears to operate as a system yet is based on the decisions of the individual birds, each reacting to the other birds in the flock. Building a macro, top-down model of the behavior of the flock will miss the reality of the situation, however. Although the movements of the flock are complex and nonlinear at the macro level, they are not based on any systemwide program. Yet the task turns out to be remarkably easy if it is viewed, more realistically, as the aggregation of local interactions by the individual birds in the flock. In an early simulation of that emergent phenomenon, Craig Reynolds, a software engineer and Academy Award winner,[3] built a dynamic model for a flock of artificial "boids" based on three simple rules:

1. Separation: don't get too close to any object, including other boids.
2. Alignment: try to match the speed and direction of nearby boids.
3. Cohesion: head for the perceived center of mass of the boids in your immediate neighborhood.

Boids can be structured as a cellular automaton along the lines of Life, with each boid seeing only its immediate surroundings and acting based on simple rules. Indeed, cellular automatons such as Life provide us with a paradigm for emergence: the higher-level features of a world, which clearly are the result of the activities of the individual agents, arise with a complexity and intricacy of design that seem totally at odds with the simple, on-off rules of the individual agents. As simple as the Game of Life is, there's a host of other cellular automatons that are even simpler where complex phenomena emerge.[4]

The emergent phenomena we are concerned about are not the ones that lead to the mesmerizing dance of schools of fish or flocks of birds, or the laminar flow of crowds on the street. They are the ones where the rules, which seem sensible and generally work well at the individual level, lead to unexpected chaos at the system level.

Complexity and Emergence

If we have an emergent phenomenon, then no agent, be it fish, bird, or man, knows the model even though a participant in it. Although each agent is acting based on the world around him, and perhaps can know perfectly his part of the world, the overall effect is something different and cannot be determined by what any agent observes. Due to the complexity of interactions, the total model does not look like an aggregate of the models of the individuals. Each person would need to know what every other person is doing throughout the system (and of course there is huge value if you can do so). We can make an "assume everyone knows sufficient data to understand the implications of interactions" sort of statement as a starting point, but that obviously is not the way things really work. Even if everyone follows a model, as they try to get to the right model, that itself changes the model and creates yet other emergent interactions. The model for the system as a whole needs to look at the decisions of each agent based on what they each individually observe, change the agents and the environment accordingly, and then proceed to do the same period by period. That is the essence of the procedure of an agent-based model.

John Maynard Keynes understood this principle:

> The kind of fundamental assumption about the character of material laws, on which scientists appear commonly to act, seems to me to be [that] the system of the material universe must consist of bodies . . . such that each of them exercises its own separate, independent, and invariable effect, a change of the total state being compounded of a number of separate changes each of which is solely due to a separate portion of the preceding state. . . . Yet there might well be quite different laws for wholes of different degrees of complexity, and laws of connection between complexes which could not be stated in terms of laws connecting individual parts.[5]

This is a statement about the interactions that give rise to emergent phenomena, and the underlying theme is that these interactions increase in magnitude and number during a crisis, if for no other reason than that the usual attempts to keep actions under the radar and minimize market impact—which is to say, to not interact in a meaningful way—have to go by the wayside.

Emergence explains why we can all be doing what we think makes sense and indeed be doing what manages our risk, and yet have the result be disastrous. We can all be individually prudent and yet have the system behave as if we are being supremely imprudent. Just as our individual worlds can look stable and yet the system can be globally unstable, so what is locally prudent can be globally imprudent.

5

Context and Ergodicity

To know if we are in an ergodic world, we can ask a simple question: Does history matter? Does it matter how we got to where we are? In most physical processes it doesn't. We can look at the world as it stands, with a particle's location and velocity, and go from there. It doesn't matter that particle C got where it is by bouncing off particle A rather than particle B. And the lack of dependence on its history is a very important property. Without it, the ability to apply our physical laws to predict and understand how the world works would be stymied, because we would have to reach back to trace the past. If we came to a situation fresh, we would be operating largely in the dark.

The mechanical processes that are the drivers of our physical world are ergodic. So too are many biological processes, the random movements of a range of creatures from plankton to insects. But if we view our experience and context as mattering, the product of human nature is not ergodic; the future is not an extrapolation of the past. "When we think of the world's future," wrote the philosopher Ludwig Wittgenstein, "we always mean the destination it will reach if it keeps going in the direction we can see it going in now; it does not occur to us that its path is not a straight line but a curve, constantly changing direction."[1]

Context is the product of history. When we take in an interpersonal relationship, we are cautioned, "Well, you have to understand the history between them." In contrast, for the aspects of our existence that are rooted in physics, all we need to know is where we are.

How we look at the world, even how we understand what someone else is saying, depends on context, and context changes with our experience and with circumstance. In the day-to-day world, these changes usually move slowly—though they do change: what we want for our lives, what we strive for and sacrifice for, are different at ages fifteen and fifty. The changes that come slowly with life experience speed up during a crisis. And having lived through one crisis, we will be a different person and come to the next one differently.

If we affect the world based on our actions—that is, if interactions matter—and if our actions are based on our varied context, then we will not have a world that behaves the same today as it did in years past. The point that we change, and that context matters, is a way of saying that the path of our lives is not ergodic.

That may sound like a fancy word for "predictable," but ergodicity is a mathematical concept that is applied in many fields, ranging from thermodynamics to econometrics, differing a bit in its definition and application from one field to the next. To place it in a practical setting: If a process is ergodic, it will look the same in terms of its probability distribution a thousand years from now as it does today. You can sample from the past and determine a probability distribution for its behavior in the future. You can be blindfolded and put in a time machine, and can exit at any point in the past or the future and feel at home in the sense that the same sorts of things will occur with the same probability. There is no learning from experience, no approaching an event with a new perspective; the same environment is drawn from the probability distribution, and the same range of possible results will occur with the same likelihood.[2]

For example, if investing were an ergodic process we could invest for, say, twenty years, look at the result, then do it again for a total of five times, and we would have the same distribution of our wealth as if we had invested one time for one hundred years. You can average over many lives rather than one. But that is not in fact the case. You can't rewind the world and try it again and again. In *The Unbearable Lightness of Being*, Kundera poses the question of eternal recurrence and then has his protagonist, Tomas, come to the realization that we have only this one life, the juxtaposition of an ergodic and a non-ergodic world. You cannot average over many lives rather than live one with attendant events from which there is no recovery. If we run along one path rather than average over a number of different paths, there is a chance that we lose it all, and then that is the end of that. In contrast, as the mathematician Ole Peters has put it, the ergodic approach puts us all in the role of Job: we can lose our house and family, but in the next period that is all past and forgotten; we get a new house and family and go on from there.[3]

With an ergodic process, all samples are pulled from the same population, and a sufficiently long sample can be used to describe the underlying characteristics of the process, such as its mean or variance, and a sample drawn from any time period will do just as well and give the same results as any other.

Economics assumes that the world is ergodic.[4] This is a very helpful assumption because then you can take expected values that will stand over the long run. You don't have to know anything about history because what happens next will be determined just by some fixed probability distribution. This hypothesis, wrote Lucas,

> will *most* likely be useful in situations in which the probabilities of interest concern a fairly well defined recurrent event, situations of "risk" [where] . . . behavior may be explainable in terms of economic theory. . . . In cases of uncertainty, economic reasoning will be of no value. . . . Insofar as business cycles can be viewed as repeated instances of essentially similar events, it will be reasonable to treat agents as reacting to cyclical changes as "risk," or to assume their expectations are *rational*, that they have fairly stable arrangements for collecting and processing information, and that they utilize this information in forecasting the future in a stable way, free of systemic and easily correctable biases.[5]

Humans are not ergodic, however. We move through the world along a single path, and we get only that one path. Where we are on that path, our experiences, our interactions, the view we have of the world at that moment all determine the context for our actions. That path is not repeatable; we are not taking draws from a distribution. We cannot jump on board at any arbitrary point and see the same story unfold from that point onward.

You Sound Like a Goddamn Robot

Ergodicity works for machines, because machines conform to the unerring laws of physics. It also works for robots that are programmed to provide a defined output for a given input. And it will work for people if they are assumed to be machines or robots. But that is not a very good assumption. We can see what an ergodic human is like by looking at a chatbot, a robot programmed to carry on conversations, named MGonz.

In 1989, Mark Humphrys, an undergraduate at the University College Dublin, put online a chatbot program he had written, and left for the day. A user at Drake University in Iowa sent the message "finger"—a command prompting the user on the other end—to Humphrys's account. Humphrys's program responded immediately: "cut this cryptic shit speak in full sentences." Thus began an argument that lasted an hour and a half between the Drake University user, named Someone, and Humphrys's program, MGonz.[6]

One of the phrases that MGonz was programmed to use frequently and out of the blue was, "type something interesting or shut up." Dropping into this conversation after ten minutes of back and forth, and after this phrase was used repeatedly, we get this exchange (because of the slow connection speed, some of the message is typed out of order):

SOMEONE AT DRAKE: what is it with this type something interesting or shut up business?
MGONZ: what are you talking about
SOMEONE AT DRAKE: i keep getting a message that says. "* AH TYPE SOMETHING INTERESTING OR
MGONZ: you are obviously an asshole
SOMEONE AT DRAKE: shut up
MGONZ: what are you talking about
SOMEONE AT DRAKE: what is this? first it says "YOU ARE OBVIOUSLY AN ASSHOLE" then
MGONZ: what are you talking about
SOMEONE AT DRAKE: you say "WHAT ARE YOU TALKING ABOUT"
MGONZ: ok thats it im not talking to you any more
SOMEONE AT DRAKE: are there two people on your username
MGONZ: when was the last time you had sex
. . .
SOMEONE AT DRAKE: do you have all these silly sayings on some sort of control? [To explain the repetitiveness, Someone thinks MGonz has hot-keys attached to particular phrases.]
MGONZ: ok thats it im not talking to you any more
SOMEONE AT DRAKE: you sound like a goddamn robot that repeats everything.[7]

That unknowingly astute observation was made at 8:31 PM, about twenty minutes into the conversation. Things continued until 9:40 PM.

Returning to the lab the next morning, Humphrys was stunned to find the log. How could the program keep a human user engaged for so long? How could such a simple program fool Someone into thinking he was not dealing with a "goddamn robot"?

MGonz is ergodic. No matter what the history of the conversation, we can pick up where we left off. Indeed, we don't even need to know where we left off. We don't even care if we are continuing the conversation with the same person. We wait for the next comment and can respond knowing nothing more than that.

The reason is that MGonz operated without the need for context; it made responses that worked without any knowledge of where things were in the conversation. Each response depended only on the previous query, not on the history of the conversation. Or, it didn't even depend on the previous query, coming out of the blue with invectives and accusations. This feature of the program, and of most successful chatbot programs, is that each part of the interaction does not change the environment at all. Any part of MGonz's mechanically generated statements can be made at any point. So there is interaction in one sense, but not interaction that causes any change or dynamic. And it got by with that by focusing on aspects of conversation where human engagement goes nowhere: MGonz threw out profanity, relentless aggression, and random queries about the user's sex life. And MGonz simply asserted from time to time that Someone was a liar. For example, later in the conversation, MGonz throws out, "when was the last time you got laid," and then follows Someone's response with "i don't believe it." When it lacked any clear cue for what to say, MGonz fell back on things like "You are obviously an asshole," or "Ah type something interesting or shut up."

We have all heard or been part of these sorts of conversations; someone could walk by, come back five minutes later, and it would sound the same. Put another way, the conversation is hardly a conversation at all. It goes nowhere. Each remark could just as well come from different people; the "model" does not develop or build based on interactions. It is not dynamic. This characteristic is called being stateless. We do not need to know where we are in the conversation; we can enter at any point.[8]

For humans, context matters no less than content. If you start a conversation with somebody and pick it up thirty years later, you won't really continue where you left off. That's the nature of your life changing with experience and being non-ergodic. A mechanistic model does not reflect on existential angst, on grudges, or on how context will be shaped based on childhood experience. It does not consider how motivations and actions might be colored by previous conversations or the sense of the other's interests and emotions. It does not flit between self-interest and altruism, spirituality and hedonism. These dimensions of human interaction are flattened as we sink into the world of economic models. That flattening might not matter for the small-scale decisions when these issues are background radiation. But in the contexts that emerge during a crisis, they can come to the fore.

Logic and Context

A computer program unambiguously instructs the computer to perform a particular sequence of operations. The "meaning" of the computer program is thus universal. Two computers following the same instructions will perform the same set of information-processing operations and obtain the same result. The unambiguous nature of a computer program means that one and only one meaning is assigned to each statement. If a statement in a computer language is ambiguous, the result is an error message. By contrast, human language is rich in ambiguity, with the meaning varying by circumstance and mood. The way we untangle this ambiguity to get to a meaning is through the overlay of context. That context is determined by questions like: Where is this coming from? Why is he asking me this? What is everyone doing here?

If we take as a starting point that we are human, then the ambiguity driven by context is a feature; if we take as a starting point that we are rational beings driven by logic, then it is a bug. Kahneman and Tversky plumb the ways people fail as rational beings, where *rational* means making decisions in a way consistent with rules of logic. They find that the same question posed in different but logically equivalent ways leads to different results. They then catalog these aberrations as demonstrations of human tendencies toward biases, frames, and other devices. They study how people behave in different contexts, versus how a rational human should act logically and consistently. That is, they look at how context breaks an instrument that is governed by logic.[9]

The problem is that for humans, logic cannot be considered apart from context, such as the usage and norms of language. For example, does anyone really think that when Mick Jagger sings, "I can't get no satisfaction," he actually means he can get satisfaction? If you are parsing like a logician, that is what you think, because you are operating in the absence of context, namely how people use language. Language usage and the mode of conversation are among the clearest examples of how context and norms matter. If someone says, "I'm not going to invite anyone but my friends and relatives," does anyone really think that means he will invite only that subset of people who are both his friends and also his relatives? (He will be safer if he says "my friends and my relatives.") Again, that will be the takeaway for someone parsing like a logician. These two examples are simplistic, but they are fairly illustrative of the work used to establish the failure of logic, inconsistencies based on framing, and the like.

A classic example of the problems that come from assuming away context is shown by this question posed by Tversky and Kahneman (1983), and critiqued by Gigerenzer (2008):

Linda is thirty-one years old, single, outspoken, and very bright. She majored in philosophy. As a student she was deeply concerned with issues of discrimination and social justice and also participated in anti-nuclear demonstrations.

Which of two alternatives is more probable?

A. Linda is a bank teller.
B. Linda is a bank teller and is active in the feminist movement.

The vast majority of U.S. college students who were given this question picked B, thus scoring an F for logical thinking. But consider the context. People are told in detail about Linda, and everything points to her being a feminist. In the real world, this provides the context for any follow up. We don't suddenly shift gears, going from normal discourse based on our day-to-day experience into the parsing of logic problems. Unless you are a logician or have Asperger's syndrome, you will take the term *probable* to mean "given what I just described, what is your best guess of the sort of person Linda is?" Given the course of the question, the bank teller is extraneous information, and in the real world where we have a context to know what is extraneous, we filter that information out.

If you are a logician, you don't even need to know all of the description of Linda to answer the question—we can substitute for this problem one that asks, "which is more probable, A, or A and B?"—because the logician does not need the context that the description might provide.

Demonstrating our failures to operate within the framework of formal logic is more a manifestation of logic not being reconciled to context than it is of people not being logical. Much of Kahneman and Tversky's work could just as well have been directed toward the failures of formal logic as a practical device than the failures of people to think logically. The point is that what we do is context-specific; it is not driven by logic. Logic would have us act consistently, but what we do depends on the world we see and the situation we are in.

We are not computers and our preferences are not simple functions. A mathematician entering the world of economics begins with a set of axioms. That is just the way mathematics works. And one of those axioms—or one of the assumptions that is necessary to take an axiomatic approach—is that people think like mathematicians. In starting this way, neoclassical economists fail to consider how people actually think, much less how that thinking is intertwined with their environment and the context of their decisions.

The mathematical approach is to assume that, absent constraints on cognitive ability, people will solve the same sort of problem a mathematician will solve in decision making: one of optimization. Then, recognizing that people cannot always do so, they step back to concede that people will solve the optimization problem subject to constraints, such as limited time, information, and computational ability. If computational ability is an issue, then moving into a constrained optimization is moving in the wrong direction, because a constrained optimization problem is generally more difficult to solve than an unconstrained one. But given the axioms, what else can you do?

It doesn't take much familiarity with humans—even human mathematicians—to realize that we don't actually solve these complex, and often unsolvable, problems. So the optimization school moves into "as if" mode. "We don't know how people really think (and we don't care to know) but we will adjust our axioms to assume that they act as if they are optimizing. So if we solve the problem, we will understand the way people behave, even if we don't know how people's mental processes operate in generating their behavior."

Behavioral economics 1.0 does not fully get away from the gravitational pull of this mathematical paradigm. Decision making is compared with the constrained optimization, but then the deviations are deemed to be anomalies. Perhaps this was a necessity at the time, given the dominance of today's standard neoclassical paradigm. But academic politics aside, it might be better to ask if the axioms that would fit for a mathematician are wrong for reality. After all, I could start a new field of economics where I assert as an axiom that people make decisions based on sunspots and astrology, and then enumerate the ways they deviate from the astrological solution. People will throw stones at such an axiom, but I can gather evidence that there are people who operate this way, which is more, as far as I can tell, than the optimization school has. When we delve into how people actually think—work that naturally originated in psychology rather than economics—we find that people employ heuristics: rules of thumb that do not look at all like optimization.

Crises and Context

How has economics gotten so far if it ignores the essential nature of humanity, treating people as well-programmed robots? It might be that it has not gotten as far as it appears. Much of economic analysis is pegged to the time frame of our day-to-day world, where people do not change much. But with a crisis, the effects are manifest to a degree that these limits and failures come to the fore, are laid bare, and the failure of economics becomes evident, as opposed to other times, when it is cloaked by ordinariness. Or the failures can be cast off using behavioral economics and irrationality, chalking things up to market anomalies, as a foil.

In a perfect vacuum a feather and a cannon ball fall at the same rate because the key force that is operating is gravity. But there are always atmospheric conditions and wind resistance in practical applications. With economics, perhaps in general the same can be said. But in a crisis, things go off the rails. In physics, air resistance is understood as a possible confounding factor. In economics, humanity is not. Or it is recognized but viewed as too difficult to model, and so is taken out of the equation.

The change in context is seen by what matters during a crisis compared with during mundane investing. During a crisis what matters is not relative value, the subtleties of relative expected earnings, or constrictions in the supply chain. What matters is liquidity and risk. People dump risky and illiquid assets, and there is a flight to quality (toward assets that are liquid and less risky). Other considerations fall by the wayside. You can do all sorts of gymnastics to find a set of stable preferences to encompass this, but I can point to any number of other context-driven preferences, and by the time you adjust to take all of them into account you have left economics in the dust; you have a model of the human psyche.

If this dynamic is inevitable, then we have lost an essential part of what is necessary for economics to appeal to the scientific method. Economics operates as if we are like MGonz, like a "goddamn robot," and it will present a reasonable view of our behavior and preferences if we live in such a con-textless world. The fact of humanity is an impediment. That characteristic might not matter in the short term or in a stable world, but times of crisis are not such a world. So we get back to the point that in using crises as the crucible we find limitations to the standard economics approach.

6

Human Experience and Radical Uncertainty

During the war in Iraq, then Secretary of Defense Donald Rumsfeld referred, somewhat indecorously, to "unknown unknowns" when describing U.S. operations strategy. In financial circles, the concept goes by the term *Knightian uncertainty* to honor the economist who recognized it. More broadly, it is called radical uncertainty. It is meant to describe surprises—outcomes or events that are unanticipated, that cannot be put into a probability distribution because they are outside our list of things that might occur. And so they cannot be modeled.[1] We might try to chalk up this sort of uncertainty to model error—after all, no one expects a model to catch everything—except that sometimes these occurrences do more than put us a bit to the left or right of the target. Sometimes they redefine the target. The issue that arises from this is, simply put, how do you model something that at the outset you are essentially asserting you cannot model?

If radical uncertainty occurs anywhere in our common experience, it is in times of crisis. Indeed, the times when things are turned upside down, when, as Jefferson Airplane's Grace Slick sang, "logic and proportion have fallen sloppy dead," might be the very definition of what we mean by crisis. But radical uncertainty is also a common part of our lives. The pat world of defined states and probabilities hardly exists for us unless we walk up to the gambling table. Radical uncertainty is an inherent part of human existence.

The most dramatic form of radical uncertainty is when there are events that we simply have no inkling can occur.[2] We can also use this definition in the framework of birds, lizards, and insects, because it is easier to envision this sort of radical uncertainty in that realm. But let's first address the irreconcilable uncertainty that comes from self-referential qualities of being human, the realization that we might have experiences beyond what we can contemplate. And that we might approach those experiences, or be changed by those experiences, in ways that we cannot internalize; and also that we deliberately act to create radical uncertainty, to change the environment in an unanticipated way for our own advantage, as occurs in warfare.

The Limits to Knowledge: Our Self-Referential Selves (or, How We Learned What We Cannot Know)

We wish every problem to have a solution, even though it may be difficult to find, even if the solution has not yet been discovered. Perhaps that's why we enjoy novels, computer games, and their fantasy world counterparts in the cinema, where we can see actions connected to results. And, taking a verse from the Beatles, there's nothing you can know that isn't known; nothing you can see that isn't shown. And there are some things that you can't see; that are not known. Issues arising from our interactions and experience express limits to our knowledge that upset this innate human desire. We cannot understand crises unless we operate within these limits—that is, unless we use methods that do not demand of nature things that we simply cannot have. We cannot have predetermined systems or systems that rest deductively on an axiomatic core, we cannot have processes that move seamlessly and smoothly from the individual to the system, we cannot have a world that runs like a game of roulette, with probability distributions on a fully defined, exhaustive set of states.

There are some things that we simply cannot know, that define limits to our knowledge, as expressed by the Latin maxim *ignoramus et ignorabimus*, we do not know and will not know. Some relate to logic: we cannot know because we cannot create a consistent and self-contained system of mathematics (the impossibility theorem); we cannot know because there are problems that can be posed algorithmically that are not decidable (the halting problem). Others relate to processes and the physical world: we cannot know because in interacting with the world we change the world (the uncertainty principle); we cannot know because depicting the evolution of the system requires being precise beyond any physical capability (chaos);

we cannot know because our models cannot predict things we actually observe (emergent phenomena). And yet others deal with probability: we cannot know because we cannot establish a probability distribution (ergodicity); we cannot know because we cannot fathom the possible events that might lie ahead (radical uncertainty).

What are the limits to our knowledge? How do we know that we cannot know? Questions of this nature occupied some of the most brilliant minds in philosophy, mathematics, and physics of the past 150 years. Prodigious amounts of brainpower set to the task of contemplating the most profound of these unknowables, and yielded grand statements of human existence.

GÖDEL'S IMPOSSIBILITY THEOREM

In 1901, Bertrand Russell, the British logician and philosopher, began an intense ten-year study that would culminate with the completion of a three-volume, 1,800-page tome of nearly impenetrable mathematics titled *Principia Mathematica*. This study, for which he enlisted his teacher, the mathematician Alfred North Whitehead, as a co-laborer, aimed to demonstrate that "all pure mathematics follows from purely logical premises and uses only concepts defined in logical terms." Its goal was to provide a formalized logic for all mathematics—why *does* $1 + 1 = 2$?—to develop the full structure of mathematics where every premise could be proved from a clear set of initial axioms. Russell observed of the dense and demanding work, "I used to know of only six people who had read the later parts of the book. Three of those were Poles, subsequently (I believe) liquidated by Hitler. The other three were Texans, subsequently successfully assimilated."[3]

The complex mathematical symbols of the manuscript required it to be written by hand, and its sheer size—when it was finally ready for the publisher, Russell had to hire a panel truck to send it off—made it impossible to copy. Russell recounted that "every time that I went out for a walk I used to be afraid that the house would catch fire and the manuscript get burnt up." Cambridge University Press estimated it would face a loss publishing the book. After the Royal Society chipped in to cover some of the cost, Russell and Whitehead were left shelling out £50 each, thus earning −£5 a year apiece for ten years' work.[4]

Momentous though it was, the greatest achievement of *Principia Mathematica* was realized two decades after its completion when it provided the fodder for the meta-mathematical enterprises of an Austrian, Kurt Gödel.

Although Gödel did in fact face the risk of being liquidated by Hitler (therefore fleeing to the Institute of Advanced Studies at Princeton, escaping eastward through the Soviet Union by the Trans-Siberian Railway, and then by boat from Japan to San Francisco), he was neither a Pole nor a Texan. In 1931, he wrote a treatise titled "On Formally Undecidable Propositions of *Principia Mathematica* and Related Systems," which demonstrated that the goal Russell and Whitehead had so single-mindedly pursued was unattainable. (This work, one of the keystones of mathematics and logic, was, incredibly enough, written as part of Gödel's qualifying dissertation for entrance into the teaching profession.)

Gödel proved that it would be impossible for any system of mathematics to solve every problem. The flavor of Gödel's basic argument can be captured in the contradictions contained in a schoolboy's brainteaser. A sheet of paper has the words "The statement on the other side of this paper is true" written on one side and "The statement on the other side of this paper is false" on the reverse. The conflict isn't resolvable. Or, closer to the point, the following assertion: "This statement is unprovable."[5] You cannot prove the statement is true, because doing so would contradict it. If you prove the statement is false, then that means its converse is true—it is provable— which again is a contradiction.

The key point of contradiction for these two examples is that they are self-referential. This same sort of self-referentiality is the keystone of Gödel's proof, where he uses statements that imbed other statements within them. Any formal system that is sufficiently rich—for example, that includes the axioms for arithmetic—can prove its own consistency if and only if it is inconsistent.

This problem did not totally escape Russell and Whitehead. By the end of 1901, Russell had completed the first round of writing *Principia Mathematica* and thought he was in the homestretch, but was increasingly beset by these sorts of apparently simple-minded contradictions falling in the path of his goal. He wrote that "it seemed unworthy of a grown man to spend his time on such trivialities, but . . . trivial or not, the matter was a challenge." Attempts to address the challenge extended the development of *Principia Mathematica* by nearly a decade. Yet Russell and Whitehead had, after all that effort, missed the central point. These apparently trivial contradictions were rooted in the core of mathematics and logic, and were only the most readily manifest examples of a limit to our ability to structure formal mathematical systems.

TURING'S HALTING PROBLEM

Although Gödel had taken apart Britain's know-it-alls, the big fish to fry was not Russell and Whitehead, but the dean of early twentieth-century mathematics, David Hilbert.

Hilbert, a German who taught at the University of Göttingen, sought a solution for what is called the decision problem for defining a closed mathematical universe: Is there a systematic procedure, a program, that can either prove or else disprove any statement expressed in the language? By a systematic procedure, Hilbert meant a procedure a computer could execute—though not computers in the current sense of the term. If I had escorted you into one of the cavernous rooms filled with "computers" during World War II's Manhattan Project, you would have found scores of women toiling away with rudimentary calculators, being handed sheets of instructions and handing back other sheets with the results. (The person developing those instructions and devising the method for compiling the results was none other than the famed physicist Richard Feynman.) The women were like clerks, and were called computers because that is what they did. They did not need to know the nature of the underlying task; they simply had to execute a set of instructions without error. Hilbert argued for a large-scale mathematical initiative to devise mechanical procedures that they could follow by rote, that in the end could lead to the proof of any mathematical proposition, giving a decided yes or no to the question. Of course, if the process is mechanical, why not develop a machine to do it—a "computing machine" that does the same rote, mechanical tasks that the human computers can do?[6]

This is what Turing set himself to do. He developed a conceptual framework for a computer that could take in any set of instructions, execute them faithfully, and deliver the result. Turing's colleague Alonzo Church (who, independently of Turing, had also demonstrated the impossibility of Hilbert's program) called this the Turing machine. Turing went a step further, and added to the machine a set of instructions that were internal to the machine and were not altered over the course of execution. The instruction set could be for any computation we can envision, and so this became known as the universal computing machine, or the universal Turing machine (UTM).

The UTM is a momentous achievement; it is the foundation for modern computers. It allows for the essential elements of computing—reading, writing, a database (in Turing's conception, held on an infinitely long tape), short-term memory of the state of the computation, and the instructions to execute held internally as part of the database. The UTM can do anything any other computer can do, and so Turing also demonstrated that all digital computers are fundamentally the same, no matter what is going on under the covers.

But it also was the conceptual mechanism for Hilbert's project. Turing set this machine to a few tasks. One was to determine if, for any arbitrary set of instructions, the machine can determine if the execution of those instructions will lead the machine to print a "0" at any point during its computation. This is called the printing problem. Turing demonstrated that it is impossible for the machine to do this. That is, the machine can be set upon a systematic procedure to prove or disprove a statement for which a yes or no is not possible—it is undecidable. There are other undecidable problems, the most famous being the halting problem: we cannot know ahead of time for any arbitrary program if the computer will finally give a result and stop, or will go on calculating forever.[7]

The halting problem is similar to Gödel's impossibility theorem, and it also is a statement of the point of computational irreducibility: the only general procedure for answering the question of whether a computer program will halt is by actually running it to see if it halts. Of course, you can never be conclusive in that exercise, because unless you run the program forever, it might well be that a computer program that has yet to halt would have halted just a few steps after you gave up or ran out of computer time. So the halting problem is an example of computational irreducibility and then some, because there are instances when you can't ever follow the path to the end. And, along the lines of not being allowed to wish for more wishes, there is no computer program that can take another computer program and determine with certainty whether the first program halts or not. This relates to the issue of contemplating future experience: "Once we set a train of thought in motion, we do not know whether it will lead anywhere at all. Even if it does lead somewhere, we don't know where that somewhere is until we get there."[8] The halting problem is apparent in the cellular automaton of the Game of Life, where we cannot know if the cells will all die out or stabilize unless we run the game to that point.

The epitaph on Hilbert's tombstone has lines taken from the conclusion of his retirement address at the conference of the Society of German Scientists and Physicians, lines given in response to the maxim "We do not know, we shall not know," on the limits to knowledge: *Wir müssen wissen. Wir werden wissen.* We must know. We will know. Ironically, Hilbert made this declaration one day after Gödel had quietly announced the nature of his impossibility theorem during a roundtable discussion that was held in conjunction with the same conference: "One can even give examples of propositions that, while contentually true, are unprovable in the formal system of classical mathematics."[9] Hilbert said that the existence of a supreme systematic procedure was required in order to place the whole of mathematics "on a concrete foundation on which everyone can agree." Gödel remained at the conference the day after the roundtable. It is very likely he was in the audience when Hilbert made that proclamation. I wonder what his reaction was.

Gödel's work had shaken the foundations for such a systematic procedure, and now Turing demonstrated that it could not exist. If it did exist, then the UTM could carry it out, since it can carry out every systematic procedure. But Turing demonstrated that the universal machine cannot decide the answer to all yes or no mathematical problems. And Turing's approach invalidated Hilbert's program on Hilbert's own terms by providing a construct for the procedure Hilbert envisioned, and then showing how it could not work. It extended Gödel's impossibility theorem to far broader grounds and put it on a more intuitive footing. The essence of the undecidability can be laid out in a few easy steps—and, like Gödel's theorem, it ultimately has to do with the problems of self-referential systems.

HEISENBERG'S UNCERTAINTY PRINCIPLE

Just four years before Gödel defined the limits of our ability to conquer the intellectual world of mathematics and logic with the publication of his undecidability theorem, the German physicist Werner Heisenberg's celebrated uncertainty principle delineated the limits of inquiry into the physical world, thereby undoing the efforts of another celebrated intellect, the great mathematician Pierre-Simon Laplace. In the early 1800s, Laplace had worked extensively to demonstrate the purely mechanical and predictable nature of planetary motion. He later extended this theory to the interaction of molecules. In the Laplacian view, molecules are just as subject to the laws of physical mechanics as the planets are. In theory, if we knew the position and velocity of each molecule, we could trace its path as it interacted with other molecules, and trace the course of the physical universe at the most fundamental level. Laplace envisioned a world of ever more precise prediction, where the laws of physical mechanics would be able to forecast nature in increasing detail and ever further into the future, a world where "the phenomena of nature can be reduced in the last analysis to actions at a distance between molecule and molecule."

What Gödel did to the work of Russell and Whitehead, and Turing did to Hilbert's program, Heisenberg did to Laplace's concept of causality. The uncertainty principle, though broadly applied and draped in metaphysical context, is a well-defined and elegantly simple statement of physical reality—namely, the combined accuracy of a measurement of an electron's location and its momentum cannot vary far from a fixed value. The more precise the measure of the electron's location, the less accurate the measure of its momentum; the more precisely one measures its momentum, the less exact will be the measurement of its location.[10] What is true in the subatomic sphere ends up being true—though with rapidly diminishing significance—for the macroscopic. Nothing can be measured with complete precision as to both location and velocity because the act of measuring alters the physical properties. Perhaps if we know the present we can calculate the future, but we cannot even perfectly know the present.[11]

These limits to measurement imply limits to prediction. After all, if we cannot know even the present with complete certainty, we cannot unfailingly predict the future. It was with this in mind that Heisenberg, ecstatic about his yet-to-be-published paper, exclaimed, "I think I have refuted the law of causality!" The epistemological extrapolation of Heisenberg's work was that the root of the problem was man—or, more precisely, man's examination of nature, which inevitably affects the natural phenomena under examination so that the phenomena cannot be objectively understood. Heisenberg's principle was not something that was inherent in nature; it came from man's examination of nature, from man becoming part of the experiment. (So in a way the uncertainty principle, like Gödel's undecidability proposition, rested on self-referentiality.) The implications of Heisenberg's uncertainty principle were recognized immediately, making him famous. And it became a simple metaphor reaching beyond quantum mechanics to the broader world.

Self-Referential Systems, Reflexivity, and the Human Predicament

Gödel, Turing, and Heisenberg all demonstrate facets of the limits to knowledge that occur from a self-referential system, a system that is being used to prove itself, or a system where an observer is part of what he is observing. Humans are ultimately self-referential because they are part of their social setting and interactions; they are creating their own experiences, which then change the nature of the social setting and interactions. They are the ones who are building the models of themselves. This is the essential distinction between building models of human systems as opposed to those of the natural world. What we observe, we change. What we change alters how we observe.

This point has certainly not escaped philosophers and historians. Take the Thomas theorem from 1928, "If men define situations as real, they are real in their consequence," or Edward Gibbon's observation in *The Decline and Fall of the Roman Empire*, "During many ages, the prediction, as it is usual, contributed to its own accomplishment." Individuals' beliefs lead to their actions, and those actions can in turn lead the beliefs to be confirmed.

What we say and what we think do not come into the equation for the operation of the natural world or for the validity of the natural sciences. No matter how great the earnestness or religious fervor with which I hold my views, they will not alter the laws governing the natural world. Although the reality of the natural world is unaffected by what I think or do, I can affect reality in the human sphere. The reality of such momentous movements as Marxism, Freudianism, or Calvinism were determined not by any inevitability or law of nature but by how people reacted to those theories, because we are both the subject of the theories and the ones who take in the theories and decide to adjust our actions or not.

This is the conceptual underpinning for a profound concept introduced to economics thirty years ago: reflexivity.[12] It is also one that has been resoundingly ignored by the field. I am dumbfounded by this; I don't see how any economist reading Soros's exposition of reflexivity can ignore it and walk away. Perhaps it is because it is so destructive to the current economic paradigm that is wedded to imitating the natural sciences, with economists trudging along, soldiers engaged in Thomas Kuhn's normal science. But I can't help but think that one reason reflexivity has been ignored is that it is proposed by a man who also is a multibillionaire. There seems to be something unsettling in having a fantastically successful businessman also be a serious philosopher. We no longer expect great intellectuals to do their writing in cafes on the banks of the Seine, but many are not ready for them to be among the world's wealthiest, especially if the financial success is based on the philosophical work. The adage that the proof of the pudding is in the eating does not often apply in economics.

I will treat reflexivity more broadly later, but for the current discussion, reflexivity is a concept related to the cycle of self-referential feedback, such as between our beliefs and our actions. It has a range of connections within philosophy, but the specific notion of reflexivity in Soros's terms is where observations of the economy lead to ideas that change behavior, which in turn changes the economy itself.

His application of the concept is based on two principles. The first is the principle of fallibility, which is that any individual's "perspective is bound to be either biased or inconsistent or both." The second is the principle of reflexivity, taking the principle of fallibility down the path sketched out by Thomas, Gibbon, and others, namely that "these imperfect views can influence the situation in which they are related through the actions of the participants."[13] To point reflexivity at one prominent economic target, "if investors believe that markets are efficient then that belief will change the way they invest, which in turn will change the nature of the markets in which they are participating." For Soros, these two propositions are "tied together like Siamese twins, but fallibility is the firstborn: without fallibility there would be no reflexivity."

Reflexivity creates deep problems for those who are determined to model our actions in a scientific structure founded on timeless and universal axioms. There is fundamental indeterminacy and uncertainty that cannot be breeched. And although economists might try to cover over its effects by using some notion of an unbiased and independent tracking error within their models, reflexivity in fact is neither an unbiased nor an independent variation in an otherwise correct reading by economics of human interaction. Reflexivity is the essence of economic dynamics, and economics cannot succeed in representing a human economic system without incorporating it. Reflexivity gives recognition to the point that humans are not robots, that social systems and social science cannot successfully engage in, as Soros has written, "slavish imitations of natural sciences" because we can evaluate the world, change our actions based on that evaluation, and then change the world as a result.

Inexperience and Radical Uncertainty

Adding a second bookend to this discussion, we can move from the philosophical to the purely human. We humans move from experience to experience. We learn, we invent, we create. We cannot already know what we will experience, what we will learn, invent, or create. As the Austrian philosopher Karl Popper put it, "Quite apart from the fact that we do not know the future, the future is objectively not fixed. The future is open: objectively open."[14] We cannot enumerate the states of nature that will arise, much less assign them probabilities. Thus the world is different for each new crisis: different markets, financial instruments, crowded strategies, view, concerns, context. So even as we look to our past experience for context, we look to the inaccessibility of our future experience for uncertainty.

It is the nature of humanity to harbor radical uncertainty. Fundamentally, we don't know where we are going, and we don't know who we will be when we get there. Nowhere does the reality of humanity point to the failure of the mechanistic approach of economics more than here. If we change with our experiences, and if we cannot anticipate those experiences or how they will change us, if we must live out life in order to know it, then a central underpinning of economics is ripped away. Neither economics nor psychology nor cognitive science expresses this notion of radical uncertainty. It is rooted in the humanities, in our sense of self, rather than in science. So I look for its expression in literature.

The novelist Milan Kundera uses the motif of radical uncertainty as a part of human nature (though of course he does not put it in those terms), most notably in his novel *The Unbearable Lightness of Being*. Kundera initially intended to use the title *The Planet of Inexperience*, explaining that inexperience is a "quality of the human condition. We are born one time only, we can never start a new life equipped with the experience we've gained from a previous one. . . . [E]ven when we enter old age, we don't know what it is we're heading for: the old are innocent children of their old age. In that sense, man's world is the planet of inexperience."[15]

The novel in its CliffsNotes form is the story of a love triangle between a physician, Tomas, his cynical lover, Sabrina, and the naïve and hopeful Tereza, whom Tomas marries, and who grapples with his ongoing infidelity. But the theme coursing below the surface is the uncertainty of life. Kundera brings this to the fore with the first lines of the novel. He begins by questioning the eternal recurrence proposed by Friedrich Nietzsche (2006). Can we live one life after the next, or is this our one life, and if so, can we ever know our life? Do we pass along this single path, or can we depict life as one draw out of many? This leads the narrator to recall Tomas meeting Tereza by pure happenstance, but also with a sense of inevitability. Tomas ponders the nature of their relationship with unease until he realizes that "not knowing what he wanted was actually quite natural."

Kundera writes that Tomas imagines that "somewhere out in space there was a planet where all people would be born again" aware of the experiences of their previous lives. "And perhaps there were yet more and more planets, where mankind would be born one degree (one life) more mature." But we can live only on this first planet, the planet of inexperience. We might be able to fabricate vague fantasies of what will happen on those other planets, but we "can never know what to want, because, living only one life, we can neither compare it with our previous lives nor perfect it in our lives to come. . . . We live everything as it comes, without warning, like an actor going on cold. And what can life be worth if the first rehearsal of life is life itself? That is why life is always like a sketch."

The inevitability of our inexperience is what leads to the unbearable lightness of being; "the thing that gives our every move its meaning is always totally unknown to us." Sabina, Tomas's sensual lover, "was unaware of the goal that lay behind her longing to betray. The unbearable lightness of being—was that the goal?" Man's "fateful inexperience" is also what makes history "light as individual human life, unbearably light." Giving contrast to this world of inexperience and radical unknowing, Tomas knows an editor who acts "as though history were a finished picture rather than a sketch." Belief in the "finished picture" assumes control and predictability. But they do not exist on the planet of inexperience.[16] Kundera might as well have dismissed the methods of economics, which solve on day one for the path of decisions over the course of one's life (and, if extended intergenerationally, even beyond!).

Borges's Library of Babel

The easiest conception of radical uncertainty is a wholly unanticipatable event, one that at once is important and had never been considered. That is, one that is not even enumerated in the state space. For the Japanese, the atomic bomb might be an example of that—who in Japan envisioned or strategized in their war contingencies a bomb that could destroy a city? Or, as I will discuss in the next chapter, for an insect radical uncertainty would include a first-time change of its environment from jungle to desert. But radical uncertainty does not require an event that cannot be enumerated and put into a state space. To understand why this is the case, consider a short story by Borges that describes the Library of Babel.[17]

Borges's surreal Library of Babel contains an all but countless number of books stacked within its hexagonal rooms. Each book contains 410 pages, each page contains 40 lines, and each line contains 80 characters. So each book has a total of 1,312,000 characters. There are 25 characters that can be used to fill the slots: 22 letters along with a blank space, a period, and a comma. (There are no numbers—any number is written out—nor are there capital letters.) The library contains a book with every possible combination of those characters. So any history, including a detailed history of the future, any description of a place or person, philosophical discourse, or religious canon exists somewhere in the library.[18] That is, the library contains all knowledge. More than that, it contains all possible knowledge. There is no action, no flight of imagination that has not already been inscribed in one of the books.[19]

In Borges's story, a book taken off the shelves at random will likely be gibberish. And the call number for any book would be as long as the book itself. You cannot know the content of the book until you read it—in the vein of computational irreducibility (and, as we will discuss in chapter 8, its cousin, informational irreducibility), there is no shortcut to going along the shelves, reading book by book. He writes of the agonizing promise within, never realizable: "When it was announced that the Library contained all books, the first reaction was unbounded joy. All men felt themselves the possessors of an intact and secret treasure. There was no personal problem, no world problem, whose eloquent solution did not exist—somewhere in some hexagon. That unbridled hopefulness was succeeded, naturally enough, by a similarly disproportionate depression. The certainty that some bookshelf in some hexagon contained precious books, yet that those precious books were forever out of reach, was almost unbearable."

To have command of the library is to have the attribute of God, knowing all that has occurred and will occur, knowing what is in the hearts of all mankind. The problem is that this knowledge is not indexed, and the vastness of the library assures that the knowledge it contains will never be accessed. For every book that has useful content, the librarian must traverse multitudes of books; one might have the letters *mcv* repeated from start to finish, or another with the exact same sequence, but ending in *mvv*. But even for books containing seemingly random letters, there will be another book that can be taken as a dictionary which, in its apparently random language, gives meaning to those letters in such a way that the former book leaps forth with meaning. And because there are many such dictionaries, the same text, meaningless to us, can have multitudes of meanings.

In Borges's world, even if you find a book that made sense, and even if it seems on point, you can never know if it is fact or fiction. For each book that is in some sense true and correct, there will be innumerable others that vary ever so slightly from that correctness, or are patently false: "the faithful catalog of the Library, thousands and thousands of false catalogs, the proof of the falsity of those false catalogs, a proof of the falsity of the true catalog, the gnostic gospel of Basilides, the commentary upon that gospel, the commentary on the commentary on that gospel, the true story of your death, the translation of every book into every language, the interpolations of every book into all books, the treatise Bede could have written (but did not) on the mythology of the Saxon people, the lost books of Tacitus." Don't forget your library card.

If we have a Library of Babel, have we eliminated radical uncertainty? Wouldn't it be great if we can enumerate and describe all the possible outcomes, all possible future states of the world? Then we can assign a probability to each of those outcomes, to each of the books becoming reality, to each of the worlds that might appear in the future, and voilà, I've moved back into a solid world of roulette-type risk! And, after all, in principle I can create a Library of Babel. And in principle I can assign probabilities to each book—though granted that in most cases I will be winging it. Then I have a world with exhaustive states that cover any eventuality—nirvana for the economic theorist; what is called in economics an Arrow-Debreu world, a world without radical uncertainty. In theory, yes. In reality (which is where I am sitting), no.

The reason is that the world of the Library of Babel is the juxtaposition of limitless knowledge with the fruitlessness of accessing that knowledge. That is the core of Borges's story. The size of this library is all but unfathomable. Indeed, a book has been written (a real book, though also, of course, housed in theory in the Library) on some of the Library's features.[20] For each book, there are 1,312,000 characters to be filled, and each can be filled in any of 25 different ways, so there are $25^{1,312,000}$, or about $10^{1,834,100}$, distinct books in the Library. The known universe is about 10^{27} meters across. If we take the universe to be a cube 10^{27} on each side, and assume we can fit a thousand books in each cubic meter, then our universe could hold $10^{81} \cdot 10^3 = 10^{84}$ books. If we were to do that, it is 10^{84} books down, another $10^{1,834,016}$ books to go. Even if we shrink the books down to the size of a proton, 10^{-15} meters across, so we could pack 10^{45} books in each cubic meter, the known universe would only hold 10^{126} of these books!

Borges, a librarian by trade, relates the frustration of knowing there is unbounded knowledge that is out of reach, and how this breeds superstitions, gods, and religions. There is a belief in what is called the Book Man.

On some shelf in some hexagon, it was argued, there must exist a book that is the cipher and perfect compendium of all other books, and some librarian must have examined that book; this librarian is analogous to a god. "Many have gone in search of Him. For a hundred years, men beat every possible path—and every path in vain. How was one to locate the idolized secret hexagon that sheltered Him? Someone proposed searching by regression: To locate book A, first consult book B, which tells where book A can be found; to locate book B, first consult book C, and so on, to infinity." In fact, such a compendium cannot exist; the library itself is the only compendium.[21] The map really is the territory.

7

Heuristics

HOW TO ACT LIKE A HUMAN

I have painted us into a corner. From our interactions we face computationally irreducible problems that cannot be solved until they run their course. We have emergent phenomena that seem to come out of nowhere, that are unrelated to the actions we and others take, and that cannot be anticipated until they overtake us. On a more human level, we live on a planet of inexperience, where we cannot fathom what is in store.

In short, we have radical uncertainty: we not only cannot pose a probability distribution, we don't even know what the things are to which we should be assigning a probability. And the complications go beyond this because we are in a dynamical system with feedback between these phenomena: the interactions that are themselves computationally irreducible and the breeding ground for emergent phenomena are also the base of the experiences that form our context and the foreboding of radical uncertainty, and these then change the nature of our interactions.

I have replaced the analytical tractability of today's world of neoclassical economics with limits to knowledge and with radical uncertainty. How do we find our way around the world if it is a world we cannot know? What more can we do than throw up our hands and say, "Whatever"?

It is part of being human that things happen that are beyond our comprehension, that lurk beyond our purview and experience; where we haven't got a clue and are unable to anticipate or take action, much less represent and incorporate with an error term or probability distribution. These can be dramatic: surprising tactics of warfare, calamities with no precedent, crises that disrupt the mundane world while giving insufficient time for us to reorient ourselves and react. And they also can be an integral part of the fabric of our lives.

How do we face this world? What are we supposed to do when we don't know what is coming down the pike, we can't solve for its implications when it does, and we don't know how we will feel about it even if we do? We seem to have figured it out, though not within the axioms and structure of rationality and consistency that economics demands.

The Omniscient Planner and the Cockroach

If you were omniscient, if you could pierce through these limits to knowledge, how would you design a creature to survive in a world with radical uncertainty? That is, suppose that you have an omniscient view of the future and you know all the types of risks that a species will face and you can give that creature rules in order to give it the best chance of survival, not just in the current environment but in the face of all that will cross its path over the course of time. But you have one critical constraint: your rules don't allow communication of any information regarding the unknown future states or solutions to those things that the creature would not be able to perceive in its nonomniscient state. (This is a bit like *Star Trek*'s Prime Directive.)

Before setting down the rules, you might want to do some background work and see what the species that have faced this sort of world have done that have allowed them to survive. Species that have existed for hundreds of millions of years can be considered, de facto, to have a better rule set than those that have been prolific in one epoch but became extinct as crises emerged. So it makes sense to start there.

If you take this route, you can't do much better than to look at the cockroach. The cockroach has survived through many unforeseeable (at least for it) changes: jungles turning to deserts, flatland giving way to urban habitat, predators of all types coming and going over the course of three hundred million years. This unloved critter owes its record of survival to a singularly basic and seemingly suboptimal mechanism: the cockroach simply scurries away when little hairs on its legs vibrate from puffs of air, puffs that might signal an approaching predator, like you. That is all it does. It doesn't hear, it doesn't see, it doesn't smell. It ignores a wide set of information about the environment that you would think an optimal system would take into account. The cockroach would never win the "best designed bug" award in any particular environment, but it does "good enough" and makes it to the finish line in all of them.

Other species with good track records of survivability also use escape strategies that involve coarse, simple rules that ignore information. The crayfish, another old branch in the evolutionary tree that has been around in one form or another for more than one hundred million years, uses a winner-take-all escape mechanism: a stimulus triggers a set of neurons, each dictating a pattern of action, and one variant of behavior then suppresses the circuits controlling the alternative actions. That is, although a number of different stimuli are received and processed, all but one of them are ignored.

These sorts of coarse rules are far removed from our usual thinking on how to make decisions because they ignore information that is virtually free for the taking. Yet if we look around further we see that coarse rules are the norm. They are not only seen in escape mechanisms, where speed is critical. They are also used in other decisions that are critical to survival such as foraging and mate selection. The great tit is a bird that does not forage based on an optimization program that maximizes its nutritional intake; it will forage on plants and insects with a lower nutritional value than others that are readily available, and will even fly afield to do so. The salamander does not fully differentiate between small and large flies in its diet. It will forage on smaller flies even though the ratio of effort to nutrition makes such a choice suboptimal. This sort of foraging behavior, although not totally responsive to the current environment, enhances survivability if the nature of the food source unexpectedly changes.

For mate selection, the peahen uses a take-the-best heuristic: she limits herself to looking at three or four males, and then picks the one with the most eyespots. She ignores both other males and other features. A red stag deer also has a take-the-best strategy, challenging another deer for his harem by running through a range of behavioral cues until he finds one that is decisive, and stops at that point. The first can be done at a nonthreatening distance: the challenger roars and the harem holder roars back. If the challenger fails on this test, it's game over. Otherwise, the challenger approaches the alpha male more closely and the two deer walk back and forth to assess their relative physical stature. If this showdown does not solve matters, they move on to direct confrontation through the dangerous test of head butting.

The heuristic is a simple one, winner-take-all, where the first cue that makes a difference is determinant, but in this case the cues occur sequentially, going from the one that requires the least information (it can be done at a distance without even having a clear view of the opponent) to the most direct and risky. The underlying heuristic remains one that is as coarse and simple as possible, where the first cue that can differentiate makes the decision.[1]

Foraging, escape, and reproduction are the key existential activities, and we see that heuristics are at their core. And we also see a movement toward coarse behavior for animals when the environment changes in unforeseeable ways. For example, animals placed for the first time in a laboratory setting often show a less than fine-tuned response to stimuli and follow a less discriminating diet than they do in the wild. In fact, in some experiments, dogs placed in a totally unfamiliar experimental environment would curl up and ignore all stimuli, a condition called experimental neurosis.[2]

The coarse response, although suboptimal for any one environment, is more than satisfactory for a wide range of unforeseeable ones. In contrast, an animal that has found a well-defined and unvarying niche may follow a specialized rule that depends critically on that animal's narrow perception of its world. If the world continues as the animal perceives it, with the same predators, food sources, and landscape, then the animal will survive. If the world changes in ways beyond the animal's experience, however, the animal will die off. So precision and focus in addressing the known comes at the cost of reduced ability to address the unknown.

It is easier to discuss heuristics as a response to radical uncertainty when we are focused on less intelligent species. We are willing to concede that nature has surprises that are wholly unanticipated by cockroaches and our other nonhuman cohabitants. A disease that destroys a once-abundant food source and the eruption of a volcano in a formerly stable geological setting are examples of events that could not be anticipated by lower life forms even in probabilistic terms and therefore could not be explicitly considered in rules of behavior. But the thought experiment of the omniscient planner provides insight into what heuristics are doing in our decision making as well. It is not that we take on heuristics solely because of limits in our cognitive ability to solve the problem with the full force of optimization methods. It is because some problems simply cannot be solved by optimization methods even absent cognitive constraints. Absent our being omniscient, we cannot apply optimization methods to the real-world problem we face, and if we try to do so, we simply have to make things up.

Heuristics and Optimization

I wake up, fall out of bed, run downstairs to drink a cup of coffee, and grab some breakfast. Then I head back up to figure out what to wear. And then it is off to work.

If I were rational, at least the economic version of rational, this routine would not be as easy as it sounds. My mind would be running optimizations from the moment I opened my eyes. All possible breakfasts, all possible sets of clothes, and all paths to work: I would evaluate each one in turn given my current set of preferences, ranking each one against the others. For breakfast, do I want strawberry jam with rye bread toast, or oatmeal and maple syrup? Or just some orange juice?

And I would wonder, what is the problem with my preferences—which are supposed to be stable—that I want to wear a red tie with my gray suit today, but preferred the green tie two days ago? On my way to the office, do I want to save money and get some exercise by walking, or do I take the subway? If I walk, do I take a path to maximize safety, to enjoy the scenery, to minimize distance, or to bypass possible congestion? The streets from my apartment to work comprise a 33 by 6 grid, and there are a lot of ways to work down through that maze. Broadway reduces distance because it cuts through at a diagonal, but it is also more congested. And I haven't even taken account of the uncertainty surrounding these alternatives. If I am thinking about buying a cup of coffee on the way, I have now opened up another range of optimization problems: preferences of one sort of coffee versus another; the convenience versus cost of the various coffee shops; alternative uses for my three or four dollars, not only today but in the context of my lifetime intertemporal optimization.

If I ran these optimizations every day I might never get out of bed. Although I certainly want to make the best use of my time (which should add to this optimization problem), I don't really spend a lot of time thinking about how to do so. No matter how I make the many little decisions over the course of the day, one thing that is clear is that my decision-making process is not as rigorous or as complete as the mathematical world of utility optimization demands. I go about my life leaving information by the wayside and possibilities unconsidered. I am satisfied to get things close enough. So I go about my day relying on coarse rules of thumb and heuristics.[3]

A heuristic is a strategy that ignores some information and generates simple rules of thumb. We rely on heuristics to make decisions that do not wait for the computationally irreducible world to unfold and that are robust in the face of radical uncertainty. Every day we make decisions where critical aspects of nature of the world, and possibly even the objective of the decision, might not be known. We just do it.

Heuristics are coarse and context-dependent rules rather than general, deductive solutions. Gigerenzer notes, "A heuristic is ecologically rational to the degree that it is adapted to the structure of the environment." Logic, math, and probability, in contrast to heuristics, are all independent of context. That is where their power lies; they will work as well on Mars as on Earth. But the real world comprises the specific, and the specific varies in unpredictable ways. Heuristics can take into account context and norms, an awareness of the environment, and our innate understanding that the world may shift in unanticipated way.

As the example of my daily life suggests, it is absurd to think that we optimize. So economists tone down this critical assumption to say that we act *as if* we are optimizing. Or we optimize subject to our constraints on cognitive ability and available information.[4] But the fact is that we don't do even that. Our basic mode of operation in our lives can be summarized as doing what we pretty much think makes sense. Put in other terms, we operate based on heuristics. We know already what a cockroach can gather only through the course of evolution: that when there is radical uncertainty, things cannot really be optimized. So heuristics take a different approach to this problem; they live within the radical uncertainty rather than assuming it away. In applying coarse and robust rules, they do not try to capture all the nuances of the possible states and their probabilities. They use simple approaches that are robust to changes in states or to new, unanticipated states.

This approach turns out to be better because it recognizes an important aspect of our environment that cannot be captured even in a model of constrained optimization under uncertainty. In an environment where things can happen that we cannot anticipate, to which we cannot assign a probability, the best solution is one that is coarse. And being coarse and robust leads to another anomaly for those who are looking through the optimization lens. In a robust and coarse environment, we may ignore some information, even if it is costless to employ.

If the world unfolds in a smooth way, if our preferences and the environment in which those preferences live are stable, if the future is drawn from the same distribution as the past, if equilibrium reigns and nothing goes off the rails, if that is the world, then optimization is the way to go. Well, not *really* optimizing—we don't really want to rank all ten thousand possible Starbucks combinations every morning—so it must be that people are operating under cognitive constraints. People must act as if they are doing a constrained optimization, looking at the cost or limits to search or to available information. There's an irony to adding constraints to reflect cognitive limits—constraints just make the problem worse. It is even more difficult to solve a constrained optimization. If people can't optimize because that exercise is too difficult, then they certainly cannot work their way through a constrained optimization.

It might be that we don't fit into an optimization because we are constrained and cannot pull off the task, or it could be that we are in a world where things change suddenly and wholly unexpectedly, where the past does not give us a window into what is happening, and where what is happening could run off the rails and down the chasm, so the conditions required for following the mathematically rational path of optimization are no longer really optimal. And so it becomes just an academic exercise, because people actually do not behave in a way that is "as if" they were optimizing or even executing a constrained optimization. They display various behavioral flaws that cannot be consistent with a constrained optimization.

Economics has a roundabout answer for this, too. People now are said to behave as if they are doing a constrained optimization with a utility function that essentially zigs and zags to accommodate their irrational behavior, behaving as if they are both constrained and have a weird utility function that adds more and more adjustable parameters. The economist Thomas Sargent, though of the view that bounded rationality means optimization under constraints, wrote, "Ironically, when we economists make the people in our models more 'bounded' in their rationality . . . *we* must be smarter, because our models become larger and more demanding mathematically and econometrically."[5]

The advantage of taking the route of simple heuristics doesn't happen because the world is simple. On the contrary, the simplicity of the heuristic is a result of the world being so complex and its risk unfathomable.[6] The point is that in a world where the future is not drawn from the same population as the past, the optimal portfolios are not really optimal. They are rooted in the past where the market is not. So in a sense, these models will almost always be wrong. And if that is true in the normal course of the market, certainly it will be true in a crisis.

Sex Is Coarse

While we are looking at coarse rules, we can wade into the eternally fascinating topic of why we have sex. Asexual species can reproduce more quickly and efficiently than ones that require the mating of a male with a female. So why don't the asexual species overrun the sexual ones? Why doesn't natural selection get rid of males?

Species are not as streamlined and efficiently built as they might be. Darwin remarked:

> Organs or parts in this strange condition, bearing the stamp of inutility, are extremely common throughout nature. Some of the cases of rudimentary organs are extremely curious; for instance, the presence of teeth in foetal whales, which when grown up have not a tooth in their heads; and the presence of teeth, which never cut through the gums, in the upper jaws of our unborn calves. Nothing can be plainer than that wings are formed for flight, yet in how many insects do we see wings so reduced in size as to be utterly incapable of flight, and not rarely lying under wing-cases, firmly soldered together!

This is all the fault of sexual reproduction because not only is it less efficient than asexual reproduction but it also tends to preserve "suboptimal" characteristics—biological traits that are irrelevant in particular ecological settings. Sexual organisms carry an unnecessary second copy of almost every gene, and the interaction of the duplicated genes creates unnecessary diversity, and deviations from what would be optimal in their current environment, even being the source of many diseases that reduce an individual's odds of evolutionary success.

What appears in the obvious physical traits also appears, and is of more importance, on a less visible level: the "pseudogenes" that seem to have no particular purpose, that are turned off and therefore certainly aren't doing anybody any good—at least not in the current environment. DNA for many species is riddled with these pseudogenes, unused sequences that are potentially transformable into new, functional genes. The classical formulation of evolution—or at least one thread of it that was prevalent in the nineteenth century—believed in the same sort of trend toward efficiency that forms the bedrock of economics. Namely, that the forces of nature would eliminate such inefficiencies, and thus over time the species would lose diversity, becoming increasingly streamlined. But as Darwin remarked, we see nonfunctional parts remain at the macroscopic level, and we see the same at the microbiological level as well. The reason is simple: the resulting diversity, though leading to variants that are less than optimal in any one environment, enhances the odds of survival when the environment changes in unanticipated ways.

There is general agreement that asexual reproduction is best if you are a fit organism in the current ecology, and if that ecology doesn't change. If you have a stable world, you will want to stick with an asexual approach. You will get some organisms that are close to the optimum, and you will want them to keep going just as they are.

Unfortunately for California blackworms or whiptail lizards, asexual reproduction tends to be a dead end in the long run because the world is riddled with radical uncertainty.[7] No ecological niche is stable, nor are its variations predictable or related to the past. Absent a few random mutations, the asexual organism is stuck with what it has. Thus asexual reproduction is not the way to go if a species plans to stick around for more than a few ticks of the evolutionary clock. In contrast, if organisms reproduce sexually, the shuffling and recombination of genes increases the odds that some offspring may be lucky and get dealt a set of genes that happen to be well adapted for the next environmental shock. Sex is a robust mechanism, to say the least, that increases the odds of survival.[8]

The point is to illustrate that being optimal in any given environment may not be optimal in the long run. Even in reproduction, we go with the robust but coarse response. It might be an also-ran in any one environment, but be more survivable as shocks occur, as species are beset by one surprise after another over eons.

Conclusion

With the gap between theory and reality yawning wide, there is a point where it makes sense to step back. The appeal to heuristics does not simply derive from the costs of collecting and processing the data needed for optimization. It is not that we want to optimize but don't have the wherewithal to do so. It is not the cost of information; information will be ignored even if it is free for the taking. Nor is our reliance on heuristics exclusive to crises, although that is where it will be particularly apparent. Rather, heuristics are the robust solution to a world filled with radical uncertainty. The same goes for the heuristics of less thoughtful species. We might think that these coarse heuristics are being employed because of the cognitive limits of the cockroach or a stag. But certainly the stag could sample more widely if it so chose, and evolution could have "improved" the cockroach to have some of the sensory input that similar species enjoy.

We live on a planet of inexperience, with an unknown future, forced to make decisions based only on the past, a past that may prove to be a limited guide to the future. On this planet we are drawn away from strict optimization and toward heuristics.

If we have adequate data, and if the future looks like the past, optimization models will perform better than heuristics. They will do well because they incorporate all available data, and the future will comport with the past data. They excel at data fitting, and they will be in a world where data fitting gets us where we want to go. But in the real world the future does not look like the past, especially if the future is a crisis and the past is not. And when the future is markedly different from the past, approaches that are calibrated on past information will miss the mark. The same will be true if we dig down to the foundation of these optimization methods: axioms by nature work in a timeless and universal world. Logic, math, and probability are all context independent, but humans are not.

Mathematical optimization can be correct in its purified world and we can be rational in our world, without optimization as the benchmark. It is a truism that if we inhabit a world that fully meets the assumptions of the mathematical problem, it is irrational to deviate from the solution of the mathematical optimization. So either we catalog our irrationality and biases, or we ask why the model is wrong. The invocations of information cost, limited computational ability, missing risk factors are all continually shaving off the edges of the square peg to finesse it into the round hole. Maybe the issue is not that our standard models are almost there, and with a little tweaking we can get the optimization approach to work. It may be that they simply are not the right approach for studying and predicting human behavior.

It deserves repeating that the use of heuristics and the deliberate limits on the use of information as employed by real people in the real world are not part of an attempt at optimization, real or "as if." It is not a matter of starting with optimization and, in some way, determining how to achieve something close to the mathematically optimal solution. It is a different route toward decision making, one that, unfortunately for economists and mathematicians, is most likely the way people actually operate.

Epilogue: Borges and Memory

I end this chapter by injecting humanity into the discussion of optimization and operating under full information. I have already argued that we operate with radical uncertainty, so optimization methods are set up for failure because they cannot incorporate the nature of the uncertainty that we face from the simple fact that we are human. I have then argued that the benefits of optimization based on full information are a mirage; that failing this test is not an issue of bounds or constraints being forced on our cognitive ability, it is not that we yearn for the world of optimization but are thwarted in our attempts to get there. Heuristics do not have to be justified on the basis of the limits in our computational powers or ability to take in information.[9]

There is another nail to put in this coffin: we do not desire full knowledge; or, putting it differently, full knowledge is contrary to our human nature; it prevents us from functioning as people.[10]

In "Funes, the Memorious," Borges gives us the incredible story of Ireneo Funes:

> Ireneo was nineteen years old; he had been born in 1868; he seemed as monumental as bronze, more ancient than Egypt, anterior to the prophecies and the pyramids. It occurred to me that each one of my words (each one of my gestures) would live on in his implacable memory; I was benumbed by the fear of multiplying superfluous gestures.[11]

Ireneo Funes recovers consciousness after a fall from a horse to discover that he has perfect memory. (Borges himself suffered a terrible head injury a few years before writing "Funes," and nearly died of complications.) Funes can recount every facet of every day; he can summon a vision of every person he has met from every perspective in which he saw them. He finds it difficult to come to terms with the fact that those different people, each recalled in full detail and within all the events surrounding the encounter, are in fact the same person viewed at different times.

But with his perfect memory comes a retreat from other human qualities. Borges wrote that Ireneo was "almost incapable of general, platonic ideas. It was not only difficult for him to understand that the generic term *dog* embraced so many unlike specimens of differing sizes and different forms; he was disturbed by the fact that a dog at three-fourteen (seen in profile) should have the same name as the dog at three-fifteen (seen from the front). His own face in the mirror, his own hands, surprised him on every occasion." Funes's world was a jumble of particulars, which affected his ability to think, because thinking requires seizing on what is important to the context and, at least for the moment, forgetting the rest.

Borges's fictional account strikes close to reality.[12] Solomon Shereshevsky, who simply went by "S," was a newspaper reporter. One day his editor gave him lengthy instructions of places to go, people to meet, and information to gather. The editor, noticing that S. had not written down any of the instructions, was about to reprimand him for his inattentiveness, but S. repeated back exactly everything that he was assigned to do. The editor questioned him more closely about his memory and, amazed by his abilities, sent him to a psychological laboratory that was focused on the investigation of memory. There S. met the psychologist Alexsander Luria, who would study him for the next thirty years and write about the process behind his mnemonic gifts.

Luria found himself unable to measure the capacity of S.'s memory. S. could surmount anything Luria put in his path. Luria read to him as many as thirty words, numbers, or letters and asked him to repeat these. He recalled them all. Luria increased the number to fifty, and then to seventy. S. still could recall them and even repeat them in reverse order. It didn't matter whether he was presented words with meaning or nonsense words. Fifteen years after their first meeting, Luria asked S. to reproduce the series of words, numbers, or letters from that first meeting. S. sat, his eyes closed, and recalled the situation:

> "Yes—yes. . . . This was a series you gave me once when we were in your apartment. . . . You were sitting at the table and I in the rocking chair. . . . You were wearing a gray suit and you looked at me like this. . . . Now, then, I can see you saying . . ." And with that he would reel off the series precisely as I had given it to him at the earlier session. If one takes into account that S. had by then become a well-known mnemonist, who had to remember hundreds and thousands of series, the feat seems even more remarkable.

Like Ireneo, S. had a poor memory for faces. "They're so changeable," he said. "A person's expression depends on his mood and on the circumstances under which you happen to meet him. People's faces are constantly changing; it's the different shades of expression that confuse me and make it so hard to remember faces." Details that other people would forget occupied his mind, making it hard to move from the flow of images and sensations to some higher level of awareness, such as abstraction and meaning.

He perceived the changes of faces the way we might perceive constantly changing light and shadow, like looking at the ripples of a pond or eddies of a river.

Also like Ireneo, with a memory composed entirely of details, S. couldn't think on an abstract level. He could recite a story word for word but could not easily summarize it. S. was lost when required to go beyond raw information to grasping metaphors, puns, or symbolism. "If a story was read at a fairly rapid pace, S.'s face would register confusion and finally utter bewilderment. 'No,' he would say. 'This is too much. Each word calls up images; they collide with one another, and the result is chaos. I can't make anything out of this. And, then, there's also your voice . . . another blur . . . then everything's muddled.'" S., knowing everything, lost any sense of context as a result.

Cognitive limits both constrain and enable adaptive behavior. There is a point where more information and more cognitive processing can actually do harm, the possibility of perfect memory giving us the extreme case. Built-in limits can in fact be beneficial, enabling new functions that would be absent without them. Imagine sitting by the fireplace with Ireneo as he recounts an amusing incident from his past. He relates every single fact related to the event. Every detail of the room, every gesture of all those attending, each word spoken. Without filtering, the story is lost, or, more precisely, it is stripped of context. There is no way to tell what matters based on the description he provides. Such a story is meaningless.

Perfect memory is like having all the past also be the present, which in turn is like living totally in a trivial present. To see an object in a thoughtful way we ignore some of its characteristics; we let some things come into focus while letting the rest recede into the background. We encounter and filter things based on our objectives and interests; the tree of a botanist is not the tree of an artist. So, more broadly, the world is meaningful to us only when we see it through a filter, and this means electing to ignore some aspects of it. Meaning emerges only by highlighting some features while relegating to the shadows those that are irrelevant to our context.

The narrator says of Funes, "I suspect . . . that he was not very capable of thought. To think is to forget differences, to generalize, to abstract. In the overly replete world of Funes there were nothing but details, almost contiguous details." In contrast to Funes's world, the world we create through our willing and selective ignorance is what Sartre calls "nihilation." We are like a sculptor who creates his work by removing part of a slab of stone. To see a world of individual things meaningfully related to one another is to elevate part of the perceptual field to the foreground and to relegate other parts of it to an undifferentiated background. Otherwise it all exists too completely; some parts of that existence have to be negated for it to become the subject of thought. To know everything, to remember everything, is not the mark of intelligence. To think, we first choose what to look at and what to ignore. This is what Sartre meant by the statement "we are condemned to be free."

The narrator remarks of Funes, "He knew the forms of the clouds in the southern sky on the morning of April 30, 1882, and he could compare them in his memory with the veins in the marbled binding of a book he had seen only once, or with the feathers of spray lifted by an oar on the Rio Negro on the eve of the Battle of Quebracho."

At age nineteen, Funes, paralyzed by the same accident that led to his prodigious memory, "lying on his back on his cot, in the dimness of his room," where he could picture "every crack in the wall, every molding of the precise houses that surrounded him," died of pulmonary congestion, a physical analogue to his mental state.

Paradigm Past and Future

8

Economics in Crisis

We know that economics has not fared well in dealing with crises. I can shed some light on the dimensions of that failure through the lens of the characteristics and dynamics that arise from human interactions and experience. As a starting point, consider this description of economics by the economist Gary Becker, of the University of Chicago: "The combined assumptions of maximizing behavior, market equilibrium, and stable preferences, used relentlessly and consistently, form the heart of the economic approach."[1] If these assumptions are successfully challenged, then the results of their application will fail. And, for crises, indeed they have. In a crisis we don't come close to having maximizing behavior, we don't wander even within spitting distance of equilibrium, and we don't have stable preferences.

Interaction and the Representative Agent

Before we get into the implications this has for computational irreducibility and emergent phenomena, we need to note another assumption at the heart of the economic approach, which Becker failed to mention though he holds to it unfailingly in his own work: the representative agent. This enabling assumption makes life possible for the economic profession. Economics does not go out and deal with how people behave as individuals. It assumes that it can aggregate all of us into one representative agent. It is a simplifying assumption, and science is filled with simplifying assumptions. But this one stops the usefulness of economics before it even gets going. It takes more than one person to create a stampede, and it takes more than one person to unleash the world into the dynamics of a crisis. And if we include the human effects of context and experience, not only will we have many agents but also they will be as different as snowflakes. Gathering all the agents in a system into a representative agent—into one giant snowball—stops any meaningful analysis of interactions dead in its tracks.

But the use of a representative agent has been a part of post-Jevons neoclassical economics since the beginning. Jevons used a representative agent to bring his theory of exchange mechanics into the sphere of classical mechanics, with a comparison to systems of planetary motion: "We have hitherto considered the Theory of Exchange as applying only to two trading bodies possessing and dealing in two commodities. Exactly the same principles hold true, however numerous and complicated may be the conditions. . . . The exchanges in the most complicated case may thus always be decomposed into simple exchanges, and every exchange will give rise to two equations sufficient to determine the quantities involved."[2] Just as physicists construct a many-bodied system from separate two-bodied systems, so economists can construct a market out of the interactions of pairs of traders. For Jevons, this also implies that large trading bodies could be decomposed into representative individuals, "an aggregate of individuals."[3]

Groups of people display patterns and structures of behavior (namely, emergent behavior) that are not present in the behavior of the individual members; this is a mathematical truth with obvious importance throughout the social sciences. For contemporary economics, this suggests that the pursuit of micro foundations for macroeconomics is futile. Even if individual behavior were perfectly understood, it would be impossible to draw useful conclusions about macroeconomics directly from that understanding, due to the aggregation problem.[4] And, I would add, the pursuit of understanding crises would also be futile.

But the representative agent is used nonetheless, because it is hard to harness the machinery of mathematical economics without it. If you are going to assume the homogeneity that is implicit in a rational expectations model, where everyone is acting in a lockstep, consistent manner using the same (correct, God-given) model, then you may as well collapse the world into one representative agent.

Computational Irreducibility:
There's No Formula for the Future

The interactions that come from our social nature and the shifting preferences that come from experience and context are inherent to humanity. We interact in society, and certainly within markets, and all the more so during periods of crisis. And we are not robots with fixed, mechanistic responses to inputs. We face a changing world that, in turn, changes the context with which we view the world, and that changes us, again all the more so during periods of crisis. The critical implication is that we cannot plug numbers into a model and solve for the future. We cannot know where we will end up until we take the journey. And we cannot retake that journey once completed.

Emergence: There's No Model Anyone Can Follow

We are all agents that interact within the world in nontrivial ways. Agents can change the environment, and other agents will change their actions as a result. Complex dynamics result from those interactions, which can lead to emergent phenomena, where we face the prospect of true surprises. Those surprises include point-of-no-return disruptions from equilibrium, in contrast to the perturbations around equilibrium, the perturbations with stability that are built into most economic models. A characteristic feature that distinguishes economics from other scientific fields is that the equations of equilibrium constitute the center of the discipline. If things do swerve out of their lane, they don't then jump the guardrail and roll down the mountain. Other sciences, such as physics or even ecology, put comparatively more emphasis on the determination of dynamic laws of change.

Due to the complexity of interactions, the behavior of the system cannot be constructed or construed as the aggregate of the models of the individual. Each person would need to know all others (and of course, there is huge value if one actually could). But while we can make an "assume everyone knows sufficient data to understand the implications of interactions" sort of statement as a starting point, that evidently is not the way things really work. Even if everyone is determined to follow a model, the process of discovering the best model itself changes the model and creates yet other interactions. It is not necessary to think that agents are making mistakes, that they are, in Soros's terms, fallible, though that can also be the case. They can be acting with robust heuristics, but still, they cannot know how their actions will combine with others to create emergent phenomena; they cannot anticipate the global view. And it is not an issue of having limited information and thus having more error in an estimate, but still having that estimate be right on average. It is a matter of not having a clue of what the end result will be.

Non-Ergodicity: The Relevance of History, or Each Time It's Different

To obtain a reliable probability distribution about the course of a crisis, we'd have to draw a random sample from that future universe, and analyze that sample from the future to calculate statistically reliable characteristics of this future population. Because drawing a sample from the future is not possible, economists taking this approach assume that the future is drawn from the same distribution as the past. This justifies using historical data, and this assumption requires ergodicity. Paul Samuelson (1969, 184–85) wrote that if economists hope to remove economics from the realm of history and move it into the "realm of science" we must impose the "ergodic hypothesis." Ergodicity is at the core of economics because it is the only way we can apply probabilities in a sensible way.

When uncertainty is introduced to economic models, it is done with the formal machinery of probability theory. Probabilities are defined over a known set of possible events. But in the real world, it is not possible simply to assume that probability distributions are the right way to characterize, understand, or explain acts and decisions made under uncertainty. When we "simply do not know," when we "haven't got a clue," when genuine uncertainty prevails, this structure won't do the job because the future is not like the past, and henceforth, we cannot use the same probability distribution—if it exists at all—to describe both the past and the future. There is no reason to think that the distribution now is even related to the one that will prevail at some future time. So when economic models (with the rational expectation hypothesis being a good case in point) assume that parameter values on average are the same for the future and the past, we are missing the essence of how our experiences and our continual accumulation of knowledge can change our view of the world, not just the probabilities but the structure and the sense of what is possible.

Keynes wrote, "Economics is a science of thinking in terms of models joined to the art of choosing models which are relevant to the contemporary world. It is compelled to be this, because, unlike the typical natural science, the material to which it is applied is, in too many respects, not homogeneous through time."[5] This is all the more so during crises.

The Nobel laureate William Sharpe said that "if you don't like an empirical result, if you can wait until somebody uses a different [time] period . . . you'll get a different answer."[6] I have experienced this first-hand when I was running a long-short equity hedge fund at FrontPoint Partners in the mid-2000s. I trawled the academic literature for possible positive alpha strategies, and in every case when I applied them to a more recent time period, one that was outside the sample used for the paper, they failed. I was suspicious that in many cases they used odd time periods, like from 1989 to 1993. It might have been data fitting in some cases, but in others it was that the world caught on to the opportunities and they were traded away. Thus the very nature of the financial system is to defeat ergodicity.

Temporal instability is the bane of some of the most fundamental financial models. Take the capital asset pricing model—for which Sharpe shared the Nobel Prize. Fama and MacBeth (1973) and others report favorable estimates of the capital asset pricing model over a sample that runs until 1965, but it falls apart when the sample was updated to include the 1970s and 1980s. (The solution: add more variables.)

In physics it may not strain credulity to model processes as ergodic—that is, to assert that time and history do not really matter—but in social and historical sciences it is ridiculous. The future of humanity's experience is not reducible to a known set of prospects. It is not like sitting at the roulette table and calculating what the future outcomes of spinning the wheel will be. Life is not a game; it is about new possibilities that arise from new knowledge. It is not about recalibrating for shifting odds; it is about discovering new alternatives to roulette wheels. No wonder Robert Clower remarked that "much economics is so far removed from anything that remotely resembles the real world that it's often difficult for economists to take their own subject seriously."[7] As G.L.S. Shackle argued, the future "waits, not for its contents to be discovered, but for that content to be originated."[8]

Radical Uncertainty: Possibilities Unknown

Ulrich, the protagonist in Robert Musil's unfinished modernist novel *The Man without Qualities*, dwells in possibility but is also described as "waiting" in "quiet desperation" for "something unforeseen" to happen to him.

Not so with the world of rational expectations. It inhabits a time at the end of history. All experiences have been had, all learning has taken place. This is a remarkable assumption if we accept the premise that we are driven not only by our past but also by the prospects and realizations of the future. We do, after all, continue to learn and, Kundera's planet of inexperience aside, we do mature in our outlook. Rational expectations may make for a more self-consistent world and a more intellectually satisfying model. But does it strip away something critical to our real world? If human experience and context matter, it does.

When we look at ourselves, at our world of human interactions and experiences, what do we see? A world that is being generated by a mechanistic model, which we all share (up to some unbiased error term)? Hardly. We see a world that seems to be bouncing along with no apparent model at all, and with no two people looking at the world in quite the same way.

Heuristics: No Optimization, Just Simple Rules

How do we deal with this complexity and uncertainty? As unsatisfying as it may be, models have to be adjusted as often as the agents and the related environment and institutions adjust in unforeseen ways. One feature of the agent-based modeling approach is that making such adjustments is integral to the fabric of the model. This stands in contrast to the deductive approach, where changes at a minimum need to rework the intricately balanced mathematical structure, and at worst require resetting the underlying axioms.

Even economic models with asymmetric information or with the body English of behavioral assumptions do not accept the limits to knowledge that prevent us from laying out the model until it is run. Yet, people need to know the model, some model, and solve it for an optimization, perhaps constrained in some way, in order to determine how to act.[9]

Problems emerge for economics from the human characteristic of being the children of our experiences, both experiences in the past and the hazy prospects of future experiences. Preferences are the things that get pumped through the utility function to be optimized; preferences are the basis of utility maximization, which in turn is the basis for all explanations of our economic actions. Economists believe that preferences are narrowly constrained, but now we see that we have various motivation systems that drive us in different directions. We have multidirected preferences.

Economists assume that preferences are in the individual. But in fact our motivations are based on the interplay between us and our environment, including others who are in that environment. They are located in our social setting and our external environment.

Economists also believe that preferences are stable. If you ordered an extra foam soy latte yesterday, it's extra foam soy lattes forever. If we cast aside the issue of crises and stay within the day-to-day financial world where our interactions are well choreographed, if the interactions do not elevate much beyond pleasantries, and if our experiences are those of one day following the next—that is, if we essentially mute the nature of human experience—then the notion of stable preferences will do well enough. At least if we keep ourselves looking more in the range of day to day rather than decade to decade. But in fact our motivations can change rapidly; as quickly as someone perceives a context changing from civil to threatening, or as soon as one perceives that the motivation of others is competitive rather than cooperative, or as soon as one person shares another's stress. And when someone communicates stress, one person might reach out to him in empathy while another might become defensive and retreat.[10]

Preferences are not even internally consistent, either based on the context and environment for one person in different times, or for two people sharing the same observations at a specific time. Indeed, two people do not share the same observations in an operational sense. In economics there is objective knowledge, things are the way they are, and they are indisputably that way for everyone. In reality, we create our own perceptions of our environment and context. There is no deterministic knowledge. We are continually weaving our own realities.

This core of human behavior is all irrational for a deductive, logical system. It also creates irreconcilable unpredictability. But irrational or not for some specific system, it is the way humans work and it is understandable in the human context. We live our lives only one time, and our lives are not replicable experiments. If you clone someone, he will not end up as the same person once he enters the world. As soon as we repeat something we have done before, we are doing something different because what we are doing is colored by different experiences, and we are a different person. It has different associations. A past experience might have been novel and difficult, fresh and exciting, and now it is familiar or even tedious. This means that our probability theory and statistics can be thrown out the window, because things are not ergodic and are not repeatable.

Neat, Plausible, and Wrong

How do you create a world without the possibility of crises? What are people like in such a world? The assumptions of neoclassical economics give us an answer: the inhabitants of that world are not people; they are inputs. Economics gives us models where there are no interactions based on context, where there is no interplay between interactions and experience. It is a model of a production plant, not of people. And, of course, if a model or paradigm does not differentiate humans from a production plant or robot, it has failed a fundamental test. If you have a model in which you can do a global search and replace of people with machines, if you have no recognition of humanity, you can develop elegant models more easily but you have missed the essence of the problem.

Certainly, we cannot enter that world and expect to learn about crises, because experiences will have a more profound effect during a crisis; interactions will be more significant. To understand crises, we must work with the limits that address these essential aspects of our human condition. And, more important, we must refute the use of mathematics because the essential problems are computationally irreducible; refute the notion that we all can be represented by a proxy, which already should be refuted based on the failures of general equilibrium theory; refute the notion of optimization and the maximization of utility, because of radical uncertainty and the need to use heuristics; refute the notion of stable preferences, because people live in a non-ergodic world where they change based on their experiences; refute models using predetermined probabilities, because past behavior cannot then provide a window into future behavior. Refute these all in periods of crisis.

H. L. Mencken wrote that there is "always an easy solution to every human problem—neat, plausible, and wrong." And neoclassical economics has been wrong. Its main result, so far, has been to demonstrate the futility of trying to build a bridge between axiomatic, deductive models and the real world. Assuming, for example, perfect knowledge and instant market clearing simply misses the point. Economists cast aside the very subject we want to study: crises that are wrapped in uncertainty, that alter our views of the world in surprising ways beyond the scope of our precrisis probabilities and worldview, that create an instability that is not merely a local aberration but is running off the tracks and careening down the mountain. Crises that are made up of distinct, heterogeneous actors, each acting based on their unique context. When we take human nature into account and amplify that by the effect of crises, what do we find? We find manifold failures in economics, failures that require a different approach to understanding crises.

We might pause to argue that theory, by its nature, makes simplifying assumptions to give clarity to the critical aspects of a system. But there comes a time, if the theory is going to be more than an intellectual exercise, that you pull away the simplifying assumptions and flesh things out to recast the theory with a face toward reality. Economics seems never to pull that off. Economic models that are intended to be used in the real world, that are being applied for policy decisions by central banks around the globe, have decisions being made by one (very large) representative household that always looks forward over the course of its life in order to presently maximize its expected discounted lifetime utility, a household that never bumps into anyone or rethinks the meaning of life along the way.[11]

The notion that at any point in a crisis you can model its trajectory, that you can put it into a self-contained model formula that will have all the answers—the staple of economic modeling—is nonsensical. Not that people won't try, or, like Lucas, proclaim that economics not only cannot but also should not be able to deal with crises. This does not mean that we should take Lucas's approach and throw up our hands.

Mathematical optimization can be correct in its purified world and we can be rational in our world, without optimization as the benchmark. It is a truism that if we inhabit a world that fully meets the assumptions of the mathematical problem, it is irrational to deviate from the solution of the mathematical optimization. So either we set aside our apparent irrationality and biases or we ask why the model is wrong. The invocations of information cost, limited computational ability, and missing risk factors are all to force the mathematics to accommodate reality. Maybe the issue is not that we are almost there, and with a little tweaking we can get the optimization approach to work. Rather, logical models may not be the right approach for studying and predicting human behavior.

It deserves repeating that the use of heuristics and the deliberate limits on the use of information as employed in the Gigerenzer worldview are not part of an attempt at optimization, real or "as if." It is not a matter of starting with optimization and, in some way, determining how to achieve something close to the mathematically optimal solution. It is a different route to decision making, one that, unfortunately for economists and mathematicians, is most likely the way people actually operate.

Eric Beinhocker, the executive director of the Institute for New Economic Thinking, opines that the error of economics is not "in trying to be too much like the other sciences" but rather that "it has made too little effort." Economics has "developed an axiomatic internally consistent self-contained theory" that is "more like theology than science." Crises are messy and complex. The physicist Richard Feynman understood this; looking back at the 1987 crash, he reflected on how difficult physics would be if we had to worry about what the electrons were thinking. To understand and manage crises, economists must give up the myth that the economy is a simple mechanical equilibrium system.

So what do we make of today's standard neoclassical approach? What is the response, other than simply saying that context does not matter? If we say that context matters, the answer might be, "If you tell me the context, I can build a function for utility that is context dependent." If we say agents are heterogeneous, the answer might be, "I've taken care of that, because the functions I use are sufficiently general to have heterogeneity be captured as differences in parameters where the agents all share this same, general function." If we point out that context and thus preferences change over time, the answer might be, "We do dynamical models all the time, so we will have the parameters in our model follow some path and add some noise to them as well." And similarly for feedback.

By the time this is done, if we do it all, and if it is done successfully (and, if it is, it will not be within the confines of the mathematical structure), we won't have a neoclassical model at all.

ECONOMICS' DEGENERATIVE RESEARCH PROGRAM

What is economics doing about this? It cannot do much, because the failings are central to its approach to crises. Economics operates within the deductive approach, patching up holes as they emerge, whether it be contradictions in utility theory or inconsistencies in the theory of rational choice, while still holding on to its core structure. We are the targets of the machine standard that economics has axiomatically constructed, but we are more complex than it bargained for. That complexity comes from an inconvenient characteristic of our nature: we are human.

So economics treats us as though we are temperamental machines that have to be treated just so. Adjust for little quirks, some tinkering here and there when things are not operating according to spec, and then the assembly line of optimization gets back up and running just fine. Economics now is in a Whac-a-Mole world of patching up problems—its poor performance during crises being perhaps the most glaring to those looking at economics from the outside—while still holding fast to the core structure.

The Hungarian philosopher of science Imre Lakatos calls this situation a "degenerative research program." Degenerative because the changes that are being made to the dominant theory are primarily to respond to and correct for new and troublesome evidence or contradictions rather than to achieve greater explanatory power. It is a research program that is sliding down the hill in the face of mounting anomalies. This degenerative research program known as economics is crying out for a new paradigm to replace the prevailing one.[12]

Just as Jevons and others saw the classical economics of Mill and Ricardo failing and replaced it with the steely mathematics of neoclassical economics, we have the failings of neoclassical economics staring us in the face. The answer is not more mathematics, more constrained optimization. It is understanding the essence of human behavior, the interactions and experiences, the phenomena that shape the world. And it is respecting these, understanding that they cannot be surmounted, that they must be addressed rather than assumed away. Bypassing pockets of resistance works in war but not in science.

CRISIS SCIENCE AND A NEW PARADIGM

The philosopher of science Thomas Kuhn (1962) used the phrase *normal science* for scientific work that occurs within the framework provided by a paradigm. Normal science is well organized and well funded. Everyone agrees on the important problems and how to attack them, on the fundamentals of the canon, the rules of the game, such as how to test a hypothesis, how to lay out a justifiable argument, how to write a paper that will pass muster for publication. Scientific education is a kind of indoctrination to instill new researchers with faith in their paradigm.

Normal science involves chipping away at the edges of the known world, adding pieces to the expanding puzzle and smoothing around the edges if a piece does not quite fit. A researcher makes progress, sets his career along that course, sets his students to the task of furthering it through their own research, gets on editorial boards to support research in a similar vein. Everyone in normal science works to find agreement on which problems are important, how to approach these problems, and how to assess possible solutions. Economics is normal science.

There comes a time, however, when normal science no longer works; problems emerge that cannot be solved within the current paradigm. This leads to a period of "crisis science." It is not a bit of trouble here or there; there are always anomalies, and working through them is part of normal science. The crisis arises from something important, where the failure can no longer be attributed to not putting the problem together in the right way. A growing number lose confidence in the paradigm. That is where we are today, and, ironically, the germination of the crisis in economics is its inability to deal with the dynamics of crisis. A scientific revolution requires both a period of crisis science and a candidate for a new paradigm. The 2008 crisis may be such a stimulus. Agent-based modeling may be the new paradigm.

Borges's Tlön

Following the 2008 crisis, Robert Solow, Nobel laureate and dean of economic growth theory, testified before the House Committee on Science and Technology. He critiqued the core model applied for macroeconomic analysis by central banks throughout the world, the dynamic stochastic general equilibrium (DSGE) model. In his prepared testimony, titled "Building a Science of Economics for the Real World," he said that these models take it for granted that the whole economy can be thought about as if it were a single, consistent person or dynasty carrying out a rationally designed long-term plan, occasionally disturbed by unexpected shocks but adapting to them in a rational, consistent way. The DSGE school operates within a simplified economy "with exactly one single combined worker, owner, consumer, everything else who plans ahead carefully, [and] lives forever," where the economy acts as if "it were like a person, trying consciously and rationally to do the best it can on behalf of the representative agent." Reflecting on this, he concludes that a "thoughtful person faced with [the thought] that economic policy [was] based on that kind of idea might reasonably wonder what planet he or she is on."[13]

Economics can exist within a rampart of ironclad axioms, rigorous mathematics, and elegant models because there it occupies a fantasy world, one that has an appealing—for mathematicians—sense of consistency and rationality, but that is not motivated by and is not relevant to the real world. It is the world depicted in Borges's short story about Tlön:

> The contact and the habit of Tlön have disintegrated this world. Enchanted by its rigor, humanity forgets over and again that it is a rigor of chess masters, not of angels. Already the schools have been invaded by the (conjectural) "primitive language" of Tlön; already the teaching of its harmonious history (filled with moving episodes) has wiped out the

one which governed in my childhood; already a fictitious past occupies in our memories the place of another, a past of which we know nothing with certainty—not even that it is false.[14]

For the inhabitants of Tlön, life is only a subjective projection of the mind. There is no material existence. Indeed, there are no nouns in Tlön's language, only impersonal verbs and adjectives. In Tlön there is no vestige of the real world. The world of Tlön's inhabitants permeates the real world and the real world yields, disintegrating under its influence. Tlön's fictitious past replaces the real past and destroys any human sense of time; history no longer matters—nor does the notion of a distinct future.

Casting reality aside, competing schools of thought arise on Tlön. One school negates time; another thinks all existence is a dream. That is, for all its complexity and seeming randomness, Tlön is built by man, using man's rationality and with man as its deity. Because of this, once the world became aware of Tlön—through the work of a journalist (from Tennessee!) who exhumes all forty volumes of the lost *Encyclopedia of Tlön*—"Manuals, anthologies, summaries, literal versions, authorized re-editions and pirated editions of the Greatest Work of Man flooded and still flood the earth. Almost immediately, reality yielded on more than one account. The truth is that it longed to yield. How could one do other than submit to Tlön, to the minute and vast evidence of an orderly plant? Tlön is a labyrinth devised by men."[15]

All things of Tlön sweep the world because "any symmetry with a semblance of order"—order that is possible only in a fantasy world designed by man—is preferred to the unfathomable nature of the real world. People forget their past. English, French, Spanish disappear from the globe. It is Tlön history, the Tlön languages; people yield their very existence to Tlön.[16]

What planet are *we* on? When we look to economics to explain crises, the question becomes all the more insistent. When we look at economics through the lens of human nature, we can fairly ask whether the world of economics is so different from that of Tlön.

9

Agent-Based Models

In *Mission: Impossible III*, Tom Cruise's Ethan Hunt has a cover job chosen to make him the ultimate faceless bureaucrat: traffic engineer for the Virginia Department of Transportation. To wit: at a party, two women start a conversation with Ethan, one asking, "What do you do at VDOT?" He replies, "I study traffic patterns. You hit the brakes for a second, just tap them on the freeway, you can literally track the ripple effect of that action across a two-hundred-mile stretch of road, because traffic has a memory. It's amazing. It's like a living organism." One of the women turns to the other, saying, "Freshen that up for you? What is it, vodka martini?" "Yeah, thanks."

It *is* amazing. Traffic is a great laboratory for emergent phenomena, as anyone who has seen the inexplicable and broad variations in congestion can attest. We all drive cars, and when do, we each operate in our own mini-environment, seeing a small set of the other cars on the roadway. One minute we might be part of a coordinated, smoothly flowing stream of traffic; another, we're unaccountably contributing to a ripple effect of congestion. It is no wonder that agent-based modeling is a popular tool for evaluating traffic flows.[1]

Drivers enter the roadway with different heuristics. They drive at different speeds; some switch lanes to avoid lane-specific congestion; some go slowly in the left lane, annoying all of us; some speed in the right lane. And actions adjust to the environment. Many drivers respond to the speed of the cars around them. And as far as I can tell, it is not always what you might think. For example, I find, inexplicably, that many times a car slows down as it comes alongside a car it is passing. They tend to go faster if the cars around them are going faster. History matters. A car that accelerates to pass around a car on a one-lane road will tend to continue driving at a faster speed. Once cars squeeze out from the congestion of a closed lane, drivers will speed relative to their precongestion speed. Speeding drivers who are approaching a known speed trap will slow down, but sometimes not enough because they have become conditioned by their high speed.

Sometimes when I drive, I game these behaviors to my advantage. If I am in the left lane and a car is coming up behind me, I will increase my speed. Even if I get up to the speed of that car, it will go faster because the driver is already intent on passing me. Finally, having tried to go fast enough to satisfy that driver, I move to the right lane to let him pass, and then return to the left lane. Now the driver in front of me is going faster than he originally intended, but has become adjusted to this faster speed. I can now follow behind with him as a buffer for any looming speed traps.

All of these behaviors can be spread across the various cars in an agent-based model (ABM). The model can be run many times with many different traffic patterns and distributions of the various heuristics to get a sense of how congestion forms along the road. The model can be run to test the effects of different configurations of exit and entrance ramps, to evaluate the traffic issues that will arise with a new office park, or to determine how best to cycle a traffic light.

The simplest ABM for traffic is a cellular automaton: if a cell is black, it is occupied by a car, if it is white, it is an open space in the road. Each car is an agent, and the heuristic for all the agents is simple and identical: if a car has an open space ahead of it, it moves into that space; otherwise it stops until the car in front moves and the space becomes open.

Figure 9.1 shows the traffic pattern and propagation of congestion as it emerges with this model. The top snapshot of the roadway shows the line of cars as we start to follow the traffic pattern. In this figure, the roadway already has congestion. Five cars are jammed together, bumper to bumper. The car at the end of the line cannot move until the four in front of it have moved. We get new snapshots period by period as we go down the page. The cars respectfully follow the speed limit, which is one space per period, so in the open road with no traffic, a car will move along a downward sloping diagonal. If there is congestion, meaning there is another car directly in front of it, the car will stay put, and thus will be at the same position as we move forward in time until the congestion clears. For example, the last car in the line has open road in front of it, so it is moving forward period by

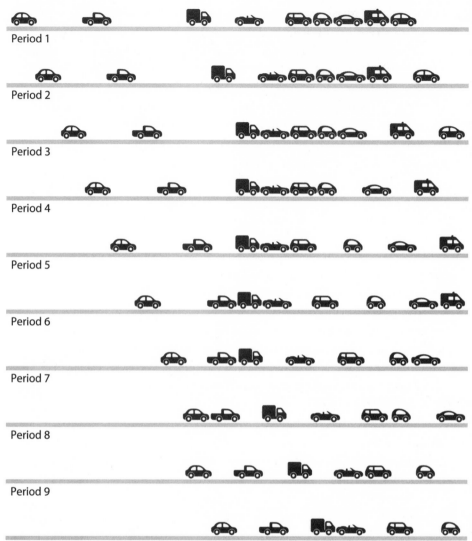

Period 1

Period 2

Period 3

Period 4

Period 5

Period 6

Period 7

Period 8

Period 9

Period 10

FIGURE 9.1. **Traffic flow in an agent-based context.** A simple example of an agent-based model applied to a traffic problem. The roadway is pictured period by period, with the first time period at the top. If a car has an open space ahead of it, it moves into that space. Otherwise, it stops until the car in front moves and the space is open. Each car thus has a simple heuristic, and is affected by the environment limited to the roadway immediately ahead of it. This simple example is the starting point for many more-realistic agent-based models of traffic flow.

period until it gets stuck behind a pickup truck in period 8. The car has to hit the brakes for a second, and then starts moving again. The panel truck that is the third from the back gets stuck in traffic in period 3, and has to sit there until one by one the cars in front of it open up room for it to move. Quite a bit later, in period 10, the panel truck is again at a momentary standstill due to the ripple effect of congestion that occurred way down the road beginning in period 6.

This most rudimentary ABM shows some of the essential elements of this type of modeling: stretches of open road with traffic moving along freely, punctuated with areas of backed-up congestion and stop-and-go traffic. This forms the basis of many more sophisticated and realistic models. We can add multiple lanes and rules for changing lanes in the face of congestion. We can add heterogeneity to this simple model along the lines of that suggested earlier: allow drivers to pick their ideal speed, the number of periods before they move forward when there's space in front of them, and the amount of distance they maintain from the car ahead of them. And, of course, we can start the model off with different degrees of congestion. We can have an entrance or exit ramp so new cars appear while others disappear at various points in the simulation. We can have the amount of congestion, entries, and exits vary with the time of day to represent Monday rush hour or weekend driving to the mall to shop.

We can use the same model for pedestrians. The rules will be similar, in that movement will be dictated by the space available, but there is more freedom of movement because, unlike cars, which have defined lanes and tend not to push around and over one another, people in a crowd are less constrained. That is why you can have crushing stampedes emerge from pedestrian congestion while cars patiently wait in line. But you can enforce some order even on a panicking crowd by putting up barriers, and it turns out, surprisingly, that adding barriers between a crowd and an exit can make things move more smoothly. If a pillar is placed a few feet before an exit, the flow is greatly improved. You would think that adding an impediment near the exit would only make things worse, but in experiments the pillar allows people to get out faster with fewer injuries. It does this by making people act more like cars: they are forced into two (still unruly) lanes, and they have limited the directions where their crushing movement can propagate.[2]

The traffic example extended from the cellular automaton contains the essence of ABMs:

- We have a set of agents (cars, people) that are typically heterogeneous and that can act with some degree of independence or autonomy, so there is no centralized control of the system.
- At the start of each time period each agent observes its environment and acts according to its heuristic. The agent's environment is only a local view of the overall system.
- The agents' actions change the environment.
- In the next period, each agent sees its new environment, altered based on the actions of the previous period, and takes action again. Thus there is an interaction between the agents and the environment, and between one agent and another.

These are the threads of ABMs. It really is that simple.

In applying ABMs to study the nature of traffic congestion, in the actual event we do not know the precise nature of the cars on the roadway, either by location, density, or heuristic (that is, individual driving characteristics). So the model is run many times with cars drawn from a distribution of drivers with various heuristics, with the cars peppered along the roadway with varying densities. Sometimes things will move along smoothly, sometimes not. The end result will be a distribution of roadway characteristics that we can use to assess the probability of congestion and its severity.

For the financial system, we have a leg up on the traffic simulation. We know the specific financial entities, their critical characteristics, such as leverage and holdings (at least if you are a regulator), and many of their interconnections. What we do not have a clear read on are their crisis-related heuristics and the way the markets will respond to a sudden surge of selling pressure. So, as with the traffic analysis, we have to do many runs with variations in these factors.

The Components of an Agent-Based Model

It ultimately boils down to the dynamics of interactions driven by the various agents and their environment, and the heuristics they apply to that environment. This can be cast in terms of Soros's reflexivity. He has two functions for each agent, the cognitive and manipulative functions. The cognitive function shows how the environment affects what the agent does; the manipulative function shows how what the agent does then affects the environment.

Let's think about each of these in the particulars of developing a model for financial crises.

AGENTS

An ABM does not start with axioms; it starts with the reality of the situation. If we are going to look at financial crises, the first step is to recognize that we have a specific financial system with real institutions, organized in a defined way. There are banks like JPMorgan Chase (JPM) and Citi, hedge funds like Citadel and Bridgewater, security lenders, asset managers, pension funds, money market funds. Each one interacts with others; some are sources of funding, others use funding; some are intermediaries and market makers; some act as conduits for collateral, others take on counterparty risk. Each one takes actions based on the world around it, based on its business interests and operational culture, and how it acts—these are big enough institutions that what they do has consequences for the system—in turn changes the environment and affects how others act.

The neoclassical model goes about things differently. It starts off with something along these lines: assume there is a bank with capital K, which seeks to maximize the objective function f(insert a nicely behaved mathematical expression here). What is the problem with this approach? First of all, we *know* the banks. We don't have to do a general exercise for some abstract notion of "bankiness." And if we start by putting in an objective function to maximize, we already have abstracted beyond anything tractable. Now, I understand the principle of deductive approach and the notion that the banks will act as if they are maximizing some objective function. But what they actually do tends to be to apply some pretty simple heuristics. So why not take a stab at using those?

Starting out this way immediately leads to defined, heterogeneous agents. Morgan Stanley is not going to approach the events in the same way as Goldman Sachs. Citadel and Bridgewater are going to have different positions and leverage, different attitudes toward risk posture and reactions to market dislocations. The relationships and functions of the system are critical. A crisis occurs in *our* financial system, not in an abstract system. We understand well at this point that there can be contagion and cascades. If our objective is to understand the way a crisis might occur and propagate, where we are vulnerable to that occurring, why start out with "assume an economy," or "assume there are N banks," when we have an economy that we do not have to assume and when we have banks that we can name and number?

What the banks are and how they act matter during a crisis. A crisis is up front and personal; it cannot be analyzed for some abstract economy that will operate on Mars as well as on Earth. Each firm has different business objectives, is willing to take on different levels of risk, and operates with different contingency plans when it runs into trouble. Not only that, each of the firms fits into various types of agents. Citi in many ways does the same sort of thing as JPM, but differs in other ways. For example, JPM has a much bigger role in the repo market. And obviously a hedge fund like Bridgewater is simply not in the same business as Citi. It does different things and will get into trouble in different ways.

So the point with agents is simple: Why start out by ignoring what's there, plain as day, to see? There is only one financial system; if we are trying to understand financial crises, why not start with the object at hand? This is not just reasonable; if an ABM does not do this, if it runs as an abstract modeling exercise rather than capturing the messy reality, it is failing, it is not an ABM at all but instead a numerical approach to the deductive neo-classical models.

One criticism of a model with heterogeneous agents is that it will lead the model to be overspecified. That is, there will be so many agents that can each do so many possible things that the model can be made to fit anything. There are more parameters to fit than there are observations for fitting them. There are a lot of different ways to change the parameters to get to any given result. An ABM looks like a ragged free-for-all, a scrum, to those who have elegance and parsimony as their objectives. But the *real* world is overspecified as well. And moving away from this by using abstract representatives rather than the scores, or even hundreds, of real players confuses beauty with truth.[3]

ENVIRONMENT

For the traffic problem, an agent's environment includes the features of the roadway and the position and speed of the other agents around it. In the financial markets, depending on the role of the agent, the environment might include the price of assets, the cost of funding, and the quality of collateral and credit. Unlike the traffic example, financial agents generally do not observe other agents directly as part of the environment. The other agents are manifest only through their actions on prices and funding. Agents interact with different parts of this environment. Some trade in particular markets. Some agents borrow to finance their activities; others lend. And some of the lenders take in collateral. So for the financial system, the environment is the plumbing that links these flows between one player and another. We will map out the environment extensively in the next chapter.

Financial crises envelop a wide swath of the landscape, and so the financial system needs to be well mapped out, including the roles of the various participants and the interrelationships among the various financial functions. For example, a bank is not a monolithic entity. It serves roles in the asset markets as a market maker, in the funding markets as an intermediary between the cash providers and leveraged players, and as the counterparty either directly or as the channel to another counterparty.

The environment changes in obvious ways based on the actions of the participants. Prices rise and fall, borrowing increases or declines. But this then can lead to significant changes in the nature of the players. Some will be forced to liquidate positions, causing a large market impact. Some will be weakened or even fail and drop out of the picture. That is, the cast of agents, the way they react to the environment, and even the plumbing and structure of the system can change.

HEURISTICS

Citadel interacts with JPM in at least two ways. It borrows or lends, and it trades certain types of assets with JPM. Citadel will have a heuristic for how it does this. If its leverage is getting too large, it reduces positions to keep borrowing down. How do we know this? Perhaps we can find this by assuming a utility function—one that we cannot see and that even those at Citadel cannot tell us, and optimize when plainly they do not. As opposed to asking ourselves what a commonsense rule of thumb would be. Or asking Citadel directly.

Just as we do not start with axioms, neither do we start with rationality. Our agents are not mathematicians nor are they logicians. They are experienced and savvy professionals, working together to determine the best rules and heuristics for doing their jobs. As the crisis emerges, this remains the case. Put another way, if you placed before a financial professional the heuristic we are applying, on the one hand, and an objective function with its optimization, on the other, he will likely find the heuristic more reflective of how he thinks and what he does. Indeed, the professional might not even recognize as rational the formalized notions of optimal behavior or, for that matter, the rationality that the economists are presenting. (Meanwhile, behavioral economists spend their time trying to understand why these professionals operate in a way that is so inconsistent with the economic notion of rational behavior, without considering that this notion and the axioms underpinning it might not be connected to the real world occupied by those professionals.)

It is, ironically, easier to get a sense of the workings of heuristics when thinking about them in the context of a crisis, even though it is a particularly complex setting. For example, it is not as difficult to know the behavior firms will display during a crisis—at least for the very large firms that we are concerned about. These firms can have a feedback effect, because they will have contingency plans in place, and it will be reasonable and prudent for clients or regulators to understand what those plans are. By contrast, in normal times the decisions are based on profit opportunities that cannot be predetermined or, if they are embodied in a model, will be too proprietarily to share—that is, it is hard to ask a firm, "Tell me, how do you make your money?" This is one of the problems that occurred early on with the application of agent-based modeling to finance—it was focused on trading models, where the actual trading heuristics could not be uncovered and modeled. So the models had to assume trading approaches that were caricatures of actual trading: momentum, reversion, value-based. That defeated a key value of agent-based modeling, the ability to characterize the idiosyncratic behavior of real-world agents.

INTERACTIONS

Because we have specific institutions, we can get to the interactions by looking at what they do day to day based on what they are seeing. What they are seeing includes the effects of what other organizations have done, so the core of our approach is to look at interactions. The process is simple enough. It is step by step, the same as for the traffic problem: Each agent observes some subset of the environment. It then takes actions using its heuristic. Those actions change the environment. Then we move forward one period—it might be a day for a financial firm, a second for a flock of birds—and run this process again.

Because we allow their actions to change the environment, and the changed environment will change their actions, we have the players interacting. What one agent does next depends on what it and others have just done. But we do not require coordination, though it can be added easily enough as part of the heuristics. Each institution can be minding its own business and we still get interactions, and ultimately we get a system imbued with complex dynamics that can defy direct mathematical analysis and trigger emergent phenomena.

DYNAMICS

Each agent in the financial system observes the environment, which includes the effects of others' actions, and acts based on its own heuristics. It does this without integrating how all others in the world are operating, much less how all of what it and everyone else is doing will add up in aggregate. Nothing is predetermined; how the world evolves as a result of this surprises the agents—and might surprise us as the modelers—in the sense that the world evolves in a way that the model cannot know until it traverses the path. We are developing a methodology that looks at the activities of the individual participants, and uncovers the global phenomena that emerge.

This behavior is at the opposite end of the spectrum from the rational expectations world that dominates economics where, as Thomas Sargent has said, you cannot talk about "differences within the typical rational expectations model," where everyone—those in the banks, the broad set of investors, even those setting policy—has the same view of the future and can foresee how their actions and the actions of others, even though they sit within a complex web of these interactions, can determine the future. A world where the "agents inside the model, the econometrician, and God share the same model."[4] This, what Sargent calls the "communism of models" within the rational expectations hypothesis, comes from the fundamental view that those who are being modeled must act in a way that is consistent with the model that is being used to model them. This does make perfect logical sense; who can argue against consistency in a system we are modeling? Why should the modeler have some leg up on those being modeled? If we have a world that is mechanistic and repeatable, of course this will mark rationality.

One small problem: that's not our world.

The alternative that I am proposing is called agent-based modeling, but that already gives it a bad rap. A more illuminating term would be to call it agent-based storytelling. The financial system in crisis evolves like a story, certainly more like a narrative than a mathematical treatise. If you read the accounts by those who were in the middle of, say, the Bear Stearns implosion, the observations and actions don't follow some model. The accounts are about stressed-out people packed around a table trying to puzzle out what's going on and devise the best course of action

As an example of the difference between focusing on dynamic interactions based on heuristics and a general model, let's go back to the boids of chapter 3—modeling birds in flight. How do we explain the ability of birds to fly in V formations? A model consistent with the neoclassical approach would determine a utility function to optimize the effort and speed of the birds, dealing with the dynamics of flight. This will lead to a complex mathematical problem that can be the fodder for all sorts of follow-on manipulations.

We do not know what heuristics a bird actually uses, but if we are going to take a stab at it, the simpler the heuristic we apply the better. And the less coordination and communication, the better. We can guess that birds aren't running differential equations and modeling fluid dynamics, and that they aren't using long-range communication channels. So we have to start with something that is simple and seems to be reasonable, and see how it does. The approach that focuses on interactions can start with a simple rule for what each bird does in reaction to the environment that it sees—the bird next to it.

It turns out that if you follow the interaction second by second with each bird following the rules of separation, alignment, and cohesion, you get a nice V formation. And with a large flock of birds, we can get breathtakingly complex and dynamic formations that are impossible to track with a mathematical approach. Birds do it; why not bankers?

As we have seen, the same approach can be used to evaluate something more complex such as traffic flows or the reaction of people leaving a stadium, and the emergent behavior of traffic jams that seem to come out of nowhere and then just as suddenly resolve, or of a crowd exiting a stadium turning into a deadly stampede. Like birds in flight, each driver sees only part of the roadway and a small subset of the cars. He is more or less minding his own business and reacting to the traffic around him based on his particular heuristics. These will be different from those of other drivers. Unlike with the birds, here we can get a sense of the sorts of heuristics drivers use. (And in its simplest form, it might turn out to be not so different from those used by the boids—something like keeping a fixed distance from the car in front of you and matching its speed.)

Conclusion

A crisis is not an equilibrium state, nor is it a little nudge from that state. A crisis is not something that is in the design of the model but emerges in a way that is not built into the model. The model has to break; it has to move into a realm that does not follow a predetermined path. Nor is a crisis simply a draw from a fat tail, a bad draw from the urn. It is a draw from a new urn, a new distribution—and one that cannot be pinned down if it is not ergodic, and cannot be predetermined if we have computational irreducibility.

A crisis also is not a regime shift except in the obvious, tautological sense that it is a new dynamic. If a regime shift means something more structured than "it is different," that is, if there are defined possible regimes such as "normal," and "bad," and "crisis," then we have just kicked the can down the road. Because the crisis regime is filled with differences due to changing experience, markets, and strategies, not to mention changing portfolio holdings and leverage, so it is not the case that each crisis will be a manifestation of the same regime except in the fairly trivial sense that things will be more than just bad. *Regime shift* is a kludge, dressing up the statement "sometimes things are normal, and sometimes they are not" in the same way that *fat tail event* is a way of saying, "something really bad happened." And, for that matter, the notion of a black swan is just another way of referring to a fat tail event. Simply declaring that such events can occur, or noting that one did occur, ignores the essential dynamics that we must understand and be able to examine if we are to do more than point and shout when a crisis seems to have come out of the blue.

Lucas has written, "In general, I believe that one who claims to understand the principles of flight can reasonably be expected to be able to make a flying machine, and that understanding business cycles means the ability to make them too, in roughly the same sense."[5] Put another way, if you want to understand crises, you have to develop a system that can create one. And to create one, you want to note and address these points:

- The dynamics might be computationally irreducible, so follow the paths rather than try to find a mathematical shortcut.
- Context matters, so include the context. And context varies from one person to the next (remember, we are human), so allow for heterogeneity.
- Interaction matters, so allow interaction.
- We interact by means of heuristics, so have the agents' actions allow for heuristics.
- The interactions can change the environment and lead to emergent phenomena, so be sure the model is constructed in such a way that emergence is not smothered and can be observed.

How a shock propagates and cascades, how it changes the environment, our perceptions, and our experience, creates a dynamic not only for the future course of the event but also for the unraveling of radical uncertainty. Doing this is at the core of the agent-based modeling methodology. ABMs allow us to recognize some essential aspects of the world that are especially apparent during crises, in particular the following.

There is a real world. The real world is a rich and complex place. There are many different players and institutions, many different components have a bearing on how people act. People interact in complex and sometimes surprising ways, and actions work through the system with surprising and nonlinear results. We have real institutions with their particular idiosyncrasies, such as Morgan Stanley, Goldman, Citadel, Bridgewater, Fidelity, and BlackRock. We have regulations that are not elegant but are real—Dodd-Frank, Volcker, Basel—that both reduce risk and constrain activities but also can lead to collateral damage and create vulnerabilities.

We are not starting with axioms and deriving a top-down deductive theory. We are not trying to determine a model that will work for some economy we might discover on Mars. That is what economics seems to want to do—or to build the model as if they are on Mars, unpolluted by the actual market where any theory will be applied.

We are all different. The real world means understanding real financial entities and the actual structure in which they operate. I hardly need to say that we are more than one person, but neoclassical models not only assume homogeneity but also lump everyone together into a single representative agent.

We affect the environment. Large financial institutions cannot take meaningful action in the face of a crisis without affecting the broader system, due to their liquidation of large positions and to its effect on the funding market and related counterparty and credit risk. They can take actions that are locally prudent but imprudent when the effect is extended to the broader system. And sometimes actions are taken to deliberately alter the environment.

We affect one another. Contrary to the notion of a representative agent, there are many forces interacting, and even those that are similar, which we would think could be compressed into a representative agent, generate a complex and unpredictable world. If these affect the environment and the environment affects them, and then they all affect one another. We will discuss this in the context of fire sales, the most important dynamic in looking at market crises, and the key dynamic addressed in the ABM. A fire sale can occur when, whether due to the price or a funding shock, a firm is forced to sell positions. That selling drops prices, and, depending on the amount of liquidity, might drop prices enough to lead to further forced sales. The selling will often extend beyond the market that was initially under pressure, propagating the shock.

The environment affects us. A changing environment changes how we act. If the environment changes, we change, and our context changes. Thus the heuristics of the individual actor are not fixed; they can change with changes in the environment, with changes in context. We can apply all sorts of learning algorithms to wrestle with these complexities. But as we will see, the nature of how people perceive the world makes a reductionist approach to human behavior miss the point.

All these characteristics reside within the critical limit to knowledge that we only know the future as we live it. If we alter the environment based on our actions, and if that in turn affects others who then change the environment further, and all of this occurs within actions that depend on the resulting changes in context, the notion that we can use a deductive approach is mistaken. It will work some of the time, particularly when there is no change in context, and where people are all pretty much the same. They aren't.

A final note: Thomas Kuhn (1962) argues that different paradigms often carry with them different rules for assessing theories and different standards for good and bad scientific work. The approach of agent-based modeling or other simulation strategies that deal with complexity does not fit into the paradigm that takes as a starting point computational reducibility, ergodicity, and the rest. This no doubt is one of the reasons most of the work related to applying these methods to economics and finance—whether it be for crisis-related study or not—do not find homes in the conventional economics journals. Rather, they are scattered among journals that specialize in these methods, or in mainstream scientific journals such as *Nature* and *Science*, where these methods are widespread and accepted.

10

Agents in the Complexity Spectrum

Agent-based modeling is designed to tackle the problem of complexity, which presents itself in a number of forms.[1] We intuitively look at complexity as creating risk and difficulty in understanding. There is the sense that if we stick our fingers into a complex system, bad things are more likely to happen. And when bad things happen, they are likely to be unexpected and to arise in ways we did not anticipate. That is, emergent phenomena and radical uncertainty are outgrowths of complex systems. Complexity means that you cannot express the system in a simple way; there are no shortcuts available—if you want to know the system, you must go through it piece by piece. This sounds a lot like what makes a problem computationally irreducible. And complexity is indeed closely related. And like computational irreducibility, it also limits knowledge.

Complexity can be either an annoyance or a boon, depending on your enthusiasm for tricky problems. We all know intuitively that complexity makes accidents both more likely and more severe. After all, any machine with many parts has more risk of having something go wrong, and with more interconnected mechanisms there is more risk that a single failure will propagate to cause the entire machine to crash. For markets, the accidents are market crises. I pointed to complexity and tight coupling as key components in the origin of market crises in my 2007 book, *A Demon of Our Own Design*.

But there remains the task of defining the type of complexity that matters for financial markets. There are a number of different concepts that shelter under the umbrella of complexity, which is not surprising, given that complexity is an issue in many different fields, ranging from physics and engineering to biology to sociology and economics. Indeed, the physicist Seth Lloyd looked at complexity in terms of the difficulty of description, creation, and organization, and came up with about forty measures of complexity that had been proposed by various people that fit within one of those three groups.

What sort of complexity matters in economics and finance, and how does that compare with the notions of complexity used in other fields? In physics, engineering, and computer science, the measurement of complexity falls into one of three camps: the amount of information required to describe the system, the connectedness of its components, and the effects of nonlinearity within the system. All three are important for our understanding of economic phenomena, particularly in times of crisis.

Information and Complexity

The Renaissance philosopher Gottfried Wilhelm Leibniz was among the earliest known investigators of complexity. In 1675, he argued that a worthwhile theory of anything must be simpler than the data it explains. Otherwise, either the theory is useless or the data are "lawless." The notion of complexity that addresses Leibniz is informational reducibility. A system is informationally reducible if it can be described with less information than the system itself contains. The idea is that a more complex system will be harder to describe or to reconstruct. For example, a string of numbers is informationally irreducible if there is no theory or model more compact than simply writing the string out directly; there is no program for calculating and presenting the number that is substantially smaller than the string itself. The number pi expressed out to, say, a billion digits, would seem to be very complex, given that it is a huge string of numbers. But we can construct an algorithm to generate these digits that contains dramatically fewer numbers (representing the code in its binary form). So this string of numbers from pi, though large, is not that complex from an informational standpoint because it is highly reducible. More generally, a system that can be expressed mathematically is not going to be very far down the road to complexity when it comes to informational irreducibility, so if we are wedded to mathematical models of the world, we have assumed away important aspects of complexity by construction.

But there are other phenomena—such as a random number of a billion digits—that cannot be compressed into a theory because they are too complex in this informationally irreducible sense. And with this notion informational irreducibility sends us down a path for illuminating the complexity of computationally irreducible systems. If you cannot know the string of numbers without writing out the numbers one by one, that is not much different from not knowing the course of future states without going through each of those states.

Connectedness and Complexity

The concept of connectedness and complexity measures how one action can affect other elements of a system—that is, it measures the complexity of interactions. A simple example of connectedness is the effect of a failure of one critical node on the hub-and-spoke network of airlines. When snow shuts down Chicago's O'Hare airport, a lot of people are going nowhere, even those in sunny Orlando. Dynamical systems also emerge from the actions and feedback of interacting components. Herbert Simon posed a fractal-like measure of system complexity by looking at the layering of hierarchy, that is, the depth to which a system is composed of subsystems, which in turn are composed of yet deeper subsystems. The relationship between connectedness and complexity is at the root of network theory. A network is defined by connections, and network theory seeks to supply useful definitions of network complexity and analyze the stability of various network structures.

Nonlinearity and Complexity

Nonlinear systems are complex because a change in one component can propagate through the system to lead to surprising and apparently disproportionate effects elsewhere, for example, the famous "butterfly effect." Indeed, as we first learned from Henri Poincaré's analysis of the three-body problem in 1889, which later developed into the field of chaos theory, even simple nonlinear systems can lead to intractably complex results. The dominant and nearly inescapable form of nonlinearity for human systems is not strictly found in the social, organizational, or legal norms we follow, or in how people behave in a given environment; it is in the complexity of the dynamics, of the feedback cycle between these two. The readiest example of this nonlinearity is the prospect for emergent phenomena. Even if the individual agents are employing linear or simple on/off heuristics, and even if their actions based on these can be expressed by linear or on/off effects, the aggregate result can lead to systemwide effects—traffic jams, riots, flash mobs—that are starkly nonlinear.

The definition you use depends on the purpose to which you want to apply complexity. For financial crises, *all* these measures of complexity come into play. Another important point for finance that makes complexity different from its physical counterparts is that, in finance, complexity is often created for its own sake rather than as a side effect of engineering or societal progress. Complexity is manufactured because if properly devised it can offer a competitive advantage.

All three of these complexity types interact for human systems, but for each one there is a natural link to one of the characteristics that lead to the limits to knowledge. As the name suggests, informational irreducibility is the key notion of complexity for computational irreducibility. Indeed, a system can be computationally irreducible based on this notion of complexity even if it is linear and is not highly connected. Connectedness is the key notion of complexity for emergence, because emergence requires interacting individuals. A system can have emergence even if the behavior of each agent is linear and the agents are homogeneous, and thus can be described in an informationally reducible form. The notion of complexity embodied by nonlinearity can lead to a non-ergodic system. It can do so even if the heuristics of the participants and their impact on the environment are themselves depicted by linear or binary relationships. This can happen when that nonlinearity results from the feedback between the behavior and the dynamics of the changed environment that is created by that behavior.

When we look at complexity through the windows of informational irreducibility, connectedness, and nonlinearity, while looking at the constraints defined by computational irreducibility, emergence, and non-ergodicity, then we see how complexity relates to our limits to knowledge. That is, how complexity can be more than just "more complicated," and rise to the level of a limit of knowledge. We also see how agent-based models are a tool for the loosely defined—as it must be, given that complexity itself is loosely defined—field of complexity science. And, for that matter, we can see why economics may not work in a complex world while agent-based models will.

A complex system is one that is clearly difficult to understand and model; as complexity increases, so do the odds of something unanticipated going wrong. This is the driving characteristic of complexity that is most important for finance and economics: complexity generates surprises, unanticipated risk. *Unanticipated* is the key word. Complexity doesn't equal more risk—we can create risk by walking on a high wire or playing roulette. Rather, it is that complexity increases risk of the "unknown unknowns" variety. And the risks that really hurt us are these risks, the ones that catch us unaware, the ones we cannot anticipate, monitor, or arm ourselves against. A system is complex if you cannot delineate all its states. (This is radical uncertainty, again.) You may think you have the system figured out, but every now and then something happens that leaves you scratching your head.

For financial crises, we cannot end the discussion of complexity without reference to time frame. Although there are limits to knowledge that are implied by complexity at the extreme, there is also complexity that does not reach these limits. These problems might be complex if we have only a few seconds to respond, but not complex if our time frame is one or two months. The importance of time frame is the reason we have to look at complexity and tight coupling jointly. Tight coupling means that a process moves forward more quickly than we can analyze and react. There are any number of crises that have led to disaster because of complexity that could not be addressed in the time available. For example, the nuclear accident at Chernobyl and the explosion of the oil-rig Piper Alpha occurred because complexity propagated through the system faster than the time need to contain it, leading to catastrophe. There are systems that are complex, but we do not see them as such because we have more than enough time to navigate through them.

Reflexivity

Now we get to the critical source of complexity we must address when we are operating in the human sphere, the one that comes from the nature of human interaction and experience: reflexivity.

In September 1998, when the vaunted but ill-fated hedge fund Long-Term Capital Management (LTCM) was facing strains on its capital, the firm issued its famous "Dear Investor" letter asking clients for more funding. LTCM explained, rationally, that there were large opportunities ahead, but recent losses had left it a bit short of cash. Would you send us some? With that letter its failure was all but guaranteed, because the letter contributed to the perception that LTCM was in trouble, and investors reacted in a way that led those perceptions to be realized. On hearing the news, they liquidated, or even shorted in the markets where LTCM was prominent, which in turn depressed prices and led to further losses for the hedge fund. If the perception had instead been that capital would be forthcoming, or if the letter had been successful in its (fairly transparent) pitch of new opportunities, the resulting actions would have been different. The failure might have been averted, and new opportunities could indeed have been seized.

LTCM's founder John Meriwether reflected after the calamity, quoting his colleague Victor Haghani, "The hurricane is not more or less likely to hit because more hurricane insurance has been written. In the financial markets this is not true. The more people write financial insurance, the more likely it is that a disaster will happen, because the people who know you have sold the insurance can make it happen."

In the case of LTCM, investors were correct in their assessment, even if their actions based on that assessment helped precipitate the end result. But the interaction between beliefs and actions need not have anything to do with objective truth. What matters are the individuals' subjective views and interpretations. In 1948, the sociologist Robert K. Merton coined the term *self-fulfilling prophecy* for this interaction: "The self-fulfilling prophecy is, in the beginning, a false definition of the situation evoking a new behavior which makes the original false conception come true." In other words, saying it can make it so. A public pronouncement might lead others to act in a way that will lead that pronouncement to be true, even if there's no basis in fact. The sarcastic website Gawker proclaims, "Today's gossip is tomorrow's news." In financial markets, that is too often the case.

History is rife with examples of bank runs precipitated by depositors' or investors' beliefs, whether unfounded or not, that an institution might be in trouble. In 2008, the boss of Lehman Brothers, Richard Fuld, blamed his firm's implosion on those circumstances. In 1907, fear that the Knickerbocker Trust was foundering caused the entire financial system to become unglued until J. P. Morgan gathered enough capital to hold it together.[2]

Extending this to Soros's take on reflexivity, market expectations—even incorrect expectations—can cause market activity that changes reality to match them, rather than expectations moving to conform to reality, as standard economics would have the causality go.

Reflexivity refers to a dynamical system where there is feedback between the participants and the environment. By this broad definition, reflexivity has been applied in many settings, extending beyond economics to sociology, biology, and even philosophy. And by this definition, agent-based models are inherently reflexive models, at least when they are applied for the tasks where they have a particular advantage.

Reflexivity in the more general sense is the inevitable result of feedback in a dynamical system that has links between agents' actions and the state of the environment. Within the human context, we call it experience, and experience as it leads to changing world views. In a mechanical system this type of feedback is not common. There may be interactions and there may be feedback but it doesn't alter the essential organic structure of the system or, put another way, it doesn't continually alter the structure of the system based on the feedback in a non-predetermined way. This type of feedback is something that is innately human. It is more than negative feedback or positive feedback; it is feedback that changes the environment and the nature of responses and, given the changes in the environment, finally changes the system itself.

Agent-based models operate in a reflexive world. Period by period, agents observe the environment and determine their actions accordingly, with a result that leads to the environment that is revealed for the next period. The environment includes the effect of each agent's action on the other agents. The relationship between reflexivity and agent-based modeling is readily seen by comparing the characteristics of an agent-based model from chapter 9 (agents, environment, heuristics, interactions, and dynamics) with this list by Eric Beinhocker of the essential elements for a model to incorporate reflexivity:[3]

- There is an environment in which agents are each pursuing some objective.
- The agents interact with the environment, and they can alter the environment by their actions through what Soros calls a manipulative function.
- The agents have what Soros calls a cognitive function through which they observe the environment and reassess their position relative to their objective.
- Each agent has a model that relates and coordinates the cognitive and manipulative functions; they have an understanding of the way they alter the environment that relates to their objectives.

Beinhocker notes that although these elements are necessary for reflexivity, they are not sufficient. We need two additional elements, which add further intricacy to the relationship of agent-based models and reflexivity:

- The agent operates in a complex environment. The complexity in the model comes from two directions: the interactions between the various agents, and the nonlinear feedback of the system.
- The heuristic that drives the actions of the agent can change in response to interactions between the agent and its environment. Thus, there is a feedback between the perception of the environment and the agent's internal model.[4]

Limits to Knowledge and Fallibility

What about Soros's second key condition for reflexivity: fallibility? It is true that the human world is by its nature filled with fallibility, but even without fallibility people might not appear rational because it makes sense not to be rational at the moment. (Thus heuristics.) They might miss what is going to happen as a result of their actions because of emergence that they cannot anticipate, even if they had a team of scientists, philosophers, and conjurers to see their environment and try to do so. They might appear slow to take the lessons of history to heart, but this is because the lessons of history do not apply if the future is not like the past.

Combine the workings of agent-based economics—updating of an agent's model, complexity, and the dynamics of interaction, and the alterations in the environment—and you have the recipe for a reflexive system: the agent's model allows for learning, but the effect of interactions within the dynamical system makes that learning insufficient, given that the system will have changed by the time that learning can be put into action. Fallibility, operationally if not literally, is the inevitable result. That is, the agent will learn, which is part of the cognitive function, and then adjust its actions, which is part of the manipulative function, but as multiple agents do so, the goal posts move. Thus, constructing such an accurate internal model and improving its performance through learning in a complex environment runs into the limits to knowledge.

But let me add here to the discussion of Soros, but in more plain-spoken terms, that we are also fallible in the more commonsense way that we all possess an invariable human quality: we can be stupid. Sometimes we simply do things that make no sense.

There is no accounting for stupid in the rational expectations hypothesis, where everyone is using the same model, and the model they are putting down on paper really is the way the world works. It's okay for there to be errors, but they are benign and well-behaved errors. General equilibrium theory has everyone knowing all the possible states of nature. We cannot be blindsided. And of course, the efficient market hypothesis in its various forms gets the point that people are not doing things that, within the context of the world as constructed, make no sense. It might be that they do not have all the information out there, but they do a good, workmanlike job with the information they do have. We might be a bit off but get things generally right. We don't miss the trail markers by so much that we get lost in the woods.

We need to recognize that as humans we are endowed with stupidity. We go out and do things that really are both inexplicable and damaging where, as we say, there is no excuse. That doesn't exactly square with Leibniz's famous declaration, *Nihil est sine ratione* (there is nothing without its reason), and eighteenth-century rationalism. Stimulated by that conviction, science energetically explores the *why* of everything, such that whatever exists seems explainable and thus predictable, calculable. The man who wants his life to have a meaning forgoes any action that hasn't its cause and its purpose.

But in literature there is a different recognition. Kundera credits the great nineteenth-century French author Gustave Flaubert with discovering stupidity, noting, "I daresay that is the greatest discovery of a century so proud of its scientific thought." Of course, even before Flaubert, people knew that stupidity existed, but they understood it somewhat differently: it was considered a simple absence of knowledge, a defect correctable by education. In Flaubert's novel *Madame Bovary*, stupidity is an inseparable dimension of human existence; "It accompanies poor Emma throughout her days, to her bed of love and to her deathbed. Stupidity does not give way to science, technology, modernity, progress; on the contrary, it progresses right along with progress!"

The protagonist of Dostoyevsky's *Notes from the Underground* relishes his stupidity—he is smart enough to know he is being stupid, but sees stupidity and whimsy as a statement against a world that has submitted itself to mathematical determinism. The unnamed underground man writes, "twice two makes four, and such positiveness is not life, gentlemen, but is the beginning of death." Mathematical determinism arrests human desire and imagination: "a man in the nineteenth century must and morally ought to be pre-eminently a characterless creature." The underground man moves from being a petty bureaucrat to leading a life of embittered fantasy, but he insists on the right to desire what is stupid and whimsical and injurious because "it preserves for us what is most important and precious—that is, our personality and our individuality." The underground man believes he is standing up for the essence of humanity against the scientific rationalism that depicts human beings as machines of perfect calculation.[5]

Inexperience and stupidity, however defined, color the course of our human existence. We cannot look back without shaking our heads at the prospect espoused by economics, that we landed where we are through the grace of a stochastic intertemporal optimization. What can economics do with this essential point of humanity, fallibility?

Warfare and Strategic Complexity

We have radical uncertainty by living in the real (human) world. We also create this uncertainty through our actions, sometimes intentionally as we seek an advantage. Take this account of a battle during China's Warring States period:

> In 341 B.C., the Ch'i State being at war with Wei, sent T'ien Chi and Sun Pin against the general P'ang Chuan, who happened to be a deadly personal enemy of the latter. Sun Pin said: "The Ch'i State has a reputation for cowardice, and therefore our adversary despises us. Let us turn this circumstance to account." Accordingly, when the army had crossed the border into Wei territory, he gave orders to show 100,000 fires on the first night, 50,000 on the next, and the night after only 20,000. P'ang Chuan pursued them hotly, saying to himself: "I knew these men of Ch'i were cowards: their numbers have already fallen away by more than half." In his retreat, Sun Pin came to a narrow defile, which he calculated that his pursuers would reach after dark. Here he had a tree stripped of its bark, and inscribed upon it the words: "Under this tree shall P'ang Chuan die." Then, as night began to fall, he placed a strong body of archers in ambush near by, with orders to shoot directly they saw a light. Later on, P'ang Chuan arrived at the spot, and noticing the tree, struck a light in order to read what was written on it. His body was immediately riddled by a volley of arrows, and his whole army thrown into confusion.[6]

In warfare, as in finance, uncertainty is not exogenous, simply sitting out there as part of the world. In war, as in finance, we create it ourselves, deliberately. People game the system; they deliberately change the rules and assumptions, and they do this in ways that were not anticipated (and thus could not be modeled) beforehand. Granted, finance is ostensibly circumscribed by the rules of law, but so is war, in its conventional sense, circumscribed by the rules of the Geneva Convention. Yet as Sun Pin's deception demonstrates, military history abounds with examples of "asymmetric warfare," with an adversary not playing by your rules or your game. These tactics can often confuse, deter, and even defeat a superior force. In the United States, the Vietnam War remains a painful example of a fight with an adversary that refused to comply with the American playbook of large armies fighting fixed battles. More recently, we've witnessed the suicidal tactics that ISIS employed in conquering huge parts of Iraq and Syria. Strategic complexity, whether deliberate or the product of the tactics employed, can change everything.

THE STRATEGIC GAME OF ? AND ?

This concept was brilliantly exploited by John Boyd, an extraordinary military strategist, unassailable fighter pilot, and, rare in the U.S. military, an iconoclast of the first order. To demonstrate, he titled one of his talks "The Strategic Game of ? and ?" to convey the essential point that warfare is not a game.[7] Or if you want to think of it as a game, it is a game that is ill-defined, with rules that are, to put it gently, subject to interpretation: "If it works, it is obsolete. Yesterday's rules won't work today."[8] This point was also made by the great nineteenth-century German field marshal Helmuth von Moltke: "In war as in art there exist no general rules; in neither can talent be replaced by precept."[9] That is, plans—and models—don't work because the enemy does not cooperate with the assumptions on which they are based. In fact, the enemy tries to discover and actively undermine his opponent's assumptions.

For Boyd, fomenting confusion is the key to tactical dominance: "The warrior's object is to create pandemonium, chaos, disorder—and you sweep out the debris." His philosophy found its first success in air-to-air combat, where it allowed technically inferior aircraft to dominate the skies. Rather than simply operate efficiently in the given environment, he taught pilots to "generate a rapidly changing environment" to suppress or distort the opponent's observations so that he could not adjust to these environmental changes, reducing him to "confusion and disorder," so that he would accumulate errors "because of activity that appears uncertain, ambiguous or chaotic."

The germination of Boyd's ideas came from the combat record of the U.S. F-86 Sabre against Russian MiG-15s during his time as a fighter pilot in the Korean War. The F-86 Sabre was more vulnerable than the MiG-15 because of its larger turn radius. Yet it had a ten-to-one kill ratio over the better-performing MiG-15. Many attributed this to superior training for the American pilots.

Boyd recognized there was something more going on, and he homed in on the jet's agility. The F-86 Sabre responded to the pilot's commands quicker than the MiG because it used hydraulic as opposed to the manual or hydraulic-assisted controls of the MiG-15. As a result, in the words of one of Boyd's acolytes, "an F-86 that was losing the fight—with a MiG about 40 degrees [off] his tail—could start a turn in one direction, then, as the MiG followed, reverse the turn. . . . The maneuver might gain the F-86 pilot 10 degrees almost immediately, putting the MiG 50 degrees off." Doing this maneuver repeatedly would push the MiG further and further out of sequence, and finally the F-86 could make its way into a firing position behind the MiG. The F-86 pilot also used less effort on the controls, so as he put the MiG through these maneuvers he would exhaust the enemy pilot, adding further disorientation. He realized that it was superior transitions and the confusion those transitions created in the opponent that mattered for air superiority, rather than outright speed or turn radius.

After the war, Boyd helped to create the Fighter Weapons School at Nellis Air Force Base in Nevada. He was nicknamed "Forty Second Boyd" because he had a standing bet that from a starting position with an opponent on his tail he could outmaneuver the "enemy" and be in a position to shoot him down in less than forty seconds. In six years and more than three thousand hours of combat training, he never lost the bet. And he usually won in ten to twenty seconds.

His observations from the Korean War and his dogfight experience at Nellis coalesced into his key principal of combat, the famous OODA loop: observe, orient, decide, act. The OODA loop, or Boyd Cycle, is a statement of strategic reflexivity. Just as Soros notes that "human beings are not merely scientific observers but also active participants in the system," for Boyd we act with deliberation in moving the course of the system to our advantage. He put this notion in stark terms—terms that translate for the practitioners into life or death: "We want to get inside another guy's tempo or rhythm, where we pull him down. . . . [W]e have to make a decision as to what we're going to do, and then implement the decision. . . . Then we look at the action, plus our observation, and we drag in new data, new orientation, new decision, new action, ad infinitum."

In war, the key to victory is creating both complexity through the confusion sown by quick changes and the tight coupling that prevents successful adjustments to those changes. The objective is to move to unanticipated new environments, thereby creating endogenous uncertainty. In finance, we have seen this through the arms race of leapfrogging others in trading speed in high-frequency trading, and in adding the fog of complexity to the environment through derivatives. In the 2008 meltdown, that complexity could arrive in the form of things like synthetic collateralized debt obligations—derivatives based on derivatives.

If we are going to use the analogy of war in economics and finance, the battlefield where Boyd's dictum most applies is the realm of information. One tactic in this battlefield is to create informational asymmetries. If the market is becoming efficient, if information is immediately accessible to everyone at the same time, then either create new private information or else speed up your access to the public information. Derivatives play a role in the first approach, with investment banks such as Goldman Sachs creating information asymmetries by constructing financial instruments such as credit default swaps that they understand better than the buyers. For the second approach, consider the news feeds that are pushed to high-frequency traders with millisecond response times.

Another tactic is to deny the market information by destroying it. One such maneuver has been called algorithmic shredding, where an algorithm breaks down trades into confetti-like pieces that obscure information that might otherwise be broadcast to the market.[10] At the same time, those doing the shredding employ more sophisticated methods to track the pattern of trading as it moves from one venue to the next in order to reconstruct vital details about the preshredded trade. Or you can distort information, as occurs with the predatory trading that pushes prices down even further when the market is already weakened, in order to force others into liquidation. We will see in the next chapter that this was a key factor in the unraveling of the financial system in the 2008 crisis.

BOARDS DON'T HIT BACK

Complexity in the information battlefield, the willful creation of complexity—complexity that is peculiarly human in origin—and the resulting endogenous uncertainty all spell trouble for the foolhardy armed only with the standard model that dominates today. Yet they keep trying to apply it, even to the point of approaching economics as if it were a branch of physics.

Would that it were that simple. In the Bruce Lee movie *Enter the Dragon*, Lee faces his archenemy in a fight. To intimidate him, his opponent holds up a board and splits it in two with his fist. Lee watches passively and says, "Boards don't hit back." That gets to the reason physics does not work in finance, and not for lack of trying: markets *do* hit back.

Wall Street employs loads of physicists for their otherworldly math skills, but the markets are not physical systems guided by timeless and universal laws. Markets are systems based on gaining an informational advantage, on gaming, on action and strategic reaction, and thus a space that can never be expressed with a fully specified model or with well-delineated possibilities. There is feedback to undo whatever is put in place, to neutralize whatever information comes in.

The natural reply of the physicist to this observation is, "Not to worry. I will build a physics-based model that includes feedback. I do that all the time." The problem is that the feedback in the markets is designed specifically not to fit into a model, to be obscure, stealthy, to come from a direction where no one is looking. That is, the radical uncertainty is endogenous. You can't build in a feedback or reactive model, because you don't know what to model. And if you do know—by the time you know—the odds are the market has shifted. That's what makes a trader successful—he can see things in ways most others do not, anticipate in ways others cannot, and then change his behavior when he starts to see others catching on.

I have seen this issue repeatedly in risk management, and it is one reason any risk management model will not cover all risks. Once the model is specified, the traders will try to find a way around it. Are you measuring interest rate risk? Well, fine, then I will do a trade that is interest rate neutral but bets on the slope of the yield curve. Now you're measuring yield curve risk? Fine, then I will do a trade that is both interest rate and yield curve neutral, but rests on the curvature of the yield curve—a butterfly trade. And as this game is being played, the complexity and thus endogenous risk is increasing with each iteration. One of the problems with the standard risk measures is that they become exposed to multiple dimensions for such gaming, and for gaming in a way that is harder to detect. In fact, it was largely reliance on these measures (such as value at risk) that allowed for the ballooning of risks in the banks pre-2008.

Not by chance are so many people trying to add complexity to the markets. Whatever rules are put in place, whatever metrics devised, traders will ferret out workarounds. In a nuclear power plant, if you replace a poorly designed valve with a new and better-designed one, the new valve doesn't try to figure out ways to make you think it is closed when it is really open. Traders will do that.

Complexity and Radical Uncertainty

We can move from simple mechanical systems to complex systems of non-linear feedback, to complex adaptive systems, where the agents alter their behavior based on changes in the environment, to complex reflexive systems, where the feedback goes in both directions—that is, where the environment changes the behavior of the agents, and where the behavior of the agents also changes the environment—and finally to strategic complexity generated by adversarial thinking such as that manifested by Boyd's OODA loop for tactics in warfare. So we have a spectrum of complexity along the lines of that in figure 10.1. Reflexivity lies near the end of the spectrum because it deals with the interactions taking place in observing the environment, taking action, and regrouping based on the resulting changes in the environment and the experiences that ensue. Even further along the spectrum is strategic complexity. This is the complexity that is created deliberately as in the case of war. Because it is inherently a human enterprise (though various other species have their own ways of creating complexity as a defense mechanism), it still has reflexivity as part of its complexity, but is adding a level through deliberate action, and thus can be expected to compound the complexity further.[11]

Computational irreducibility, emergent phenomena, and non-ergodicity will all become more manifest as we move along the spectrum. They are, so to speak, side effects of complexity. We might likewise think of radical uncertainty as a side effect of complexity, so that the further we move along the spectrum the more likely radical uncertainty will become manifest in the dynamics. But given its ethereal nature, we can think of radical uncertainty in other ways as well. We can also think of radical uncertainty as a type of complexity. From the standpoint of computational irreducibility, we might look at radical uncertainty as occupying a position that is beyond the edge of the complexity spectrum, at least beyond the "visible" complexity spectrum that we can observe and analyze. Radical uncertainty is the dark matter of complexity. We cannot see it, we cannot even detect it, we cannot measure it in terms of informational irreducibility, but we know it is there because every now and then it hits us between the eyes.

To see how we can put radical uncertainty into a complexity context, let's revisit Conway's Game of Life. It is a stripped-down, rudimentary form of an agent-based model. Life has a set of agents, the black, living cells, which observe their environment each period. Their environment is limited to the adjacent cells, much as the agents in a traffic model will see only the

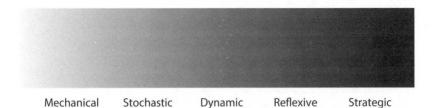

Mechanical   Stochastic   Dynamic   Reflexive   Strategic

FIGURE 10.1. **The complexity spectrum.** The spectrum of complexity ranges from deterministic mechanical systems, to stochastic systems, to types of dynamic systems, such as nonlinear and adaptive, to those that have reflexivity, and finally to systems with strategic complexity, such as those dictated by warfare. Moving from left to right on the spectrum increases the likelihood the system will exhibit the characteristics of computational irreducibility, emergence, non-ergodicity, and radical uncertainty. Or we might place radical uncertainty beyond the "visible spectrum" shown here. *Adapted from Beinhocker (2013).*

cars surrounding them. They take action in response to their environment based on a heuristic—namely, they count the number of living cells around them and live, die, or reproduce accordingly. And those actions change the environment and subsequently have consequences that extend to other agents.

The Game of Life is a complex system that exhibits computational irreducibility, emergence, and non-ergodicity.[12] But radical uncertainty? That seems to be a stretch, given that it operates on a well-defined grid, where any cell can only be black or white, where in principle we can describe every state that can occur.

To understand how radical uncertainty can exist in the Game of Life, consider a related question (actually, in important ways an identical question): Does the fictional Library of Babel eliminate radical uncertainty? In the Library of Babel we have a detailed description of anything that can occur, anything that is possible. It contains things that can occur in our present day, can occur at any time in the future, and all things that have occurred in the past—both in our world and in any other world. Every experience you might have and every reaction that you or anyone else can have to that experience is written in prose and in poetry and as a historical account. In other words, there is no state of the world that has not been recounted. Can we argue that there is no radical uncertainty because, in principle, we can envision a Library of Babel in which every possibility is known? Can we do so even though the library contains more books than could be packed into the known universe? We can't, because "in principle" is not in reality.[13]

So now take the Game of Life. Let's say we want to consider, for any arbitrary initial state, where we might be some number of periods down the road. If the grid is, say, 5 by 5, we have 25 cells, and we can determine every possible state by having a computer run through all the combinations of white and black cells. Essentially we have every binary number that is 25 digits long. We can then run the game forward starting with every possible combination, and then know all the ways the world can progress if we start in that configuration. But what if we have a grid that is ten thousand cells on each side, or ten million on each side? Life has been run on a grid larger than that. Enumerating all the possible states can be made as momentous a task as filling the volumes of the Library of Babel. Indeed, the number of volumes in the Library of Babel might pale by comparison. So although in principle we can know every possible state, in reality we cannot. That's life.

Complexity and the End of Theory

This is the nature of economic theory: axioms that are extended out using deductive methods to present a general mathematical approach that attempts to mimic the methods of physics, methods for a mechanical world. And this is where economic theory runs aground: when the world of complexity intrudes and we can't reasonably use the simplifying assumptions the theory requires; we can't reasonably view the world as mechanistic, timeless, and universal; and we can't aggregate everything into a representative agent.

Complexity does intrude. As we march down the path of increasing complexity, one by one the pillars supporting neoclassical economic theory give way. As we move along the complexity spectrum from mechanical through stochastic, dynamic, and reflexive to strategic, we enter a world that has more and more in common with the actual world that we as humans inhabit, and as we do so we face a world that is increasingly buffeted by the enemies of economic theory, by the four horsemen. The deductive, axiomatic methods that underlie neoclassical economics decline in relevance. As we embrace complexity we come to the end of theory.

Agent-Based Models for Financial Crises

11

The Structure of
the Financial System:
Agents and the Environment

John Houseman, playing his Academy Award–winning role as the law professor Charles W. Kingsfield Jr. in *The Paper Chase*, introduces students to his class this way: "I train your minds. You come in here with a skull full of mush; you leave thinking like a lawyer." My objective in the next chapters, though perhaps without the same panache or authority, is to show how I think about the financial system from a practical standpoint using an agent-based approach. Applied to finance, the agent-based approach encompasses the financial structure of agents and their heuristics, the market environment within which they operate, and the outcomes that result from the interaction of the agents with the environment. In the following two chapters I will show how this works, but I am not going to be advocating for a specific model, laid out, parameterized, and solved, because if there is any area where the capacity to "roll your own" exists, it is with agent-based modeling's agile approach.[1]

To give you a sense of where I'm going, I'll draw an analogy between the sources of a stampede as people escape from a fire and the components of a market crisis. A stampede's outbreak is an unpredictable emergent event, the sort of thing that has become the bread and butter of agent-based models.

If you are a fire marshal trying to manage this risk, the critical question is whether the space is too crowded, and this depends on three things: the number of people in the space, how many people can exit per minute based on the number and size of egress, and the time available to exit based on the flammability of the space. Modeling the number that can exit per minute is difficult, because we are not looking at people walking through the exit in an orderly way. There is the potential for panic and stampedes. So we need to model this based on how people behave in a crisis—a role for agent-based models.

Using this as an analogy for the financial system, market concentration measures the number of people meaningfully in the market, liquidity determines the rate at which people can exit, and leverage or, more generally, the potential for forced selling determines the flammability of the market and thus the number of minutes available to exit. Oh, and rather than people dying, prices drop. But for financial markets, things get more complicated. The exits to a building do not shrink just because people are pushing through them, whereas in financial markets they do—during a crisis, liquidity dries up.[2] The material in the building does not change to something more flammable if the exits are smaller, whereas in financial markets the drop in liquidity can fuel cascades. And the number of people in the space does not increase as the fire becomes more intense, but in financial markets, bystanders and those who are in other markets get caught up.

So I will present the makings of an agent-based model that incorporates the critical components of concentration, leverage, and liquidity. But the first ingredient in an agent-based model is the environment in which the agents interact, and which they affect by their actions.

The Environment

There is a lot of plumbing under the streets of New York City, where I reside. If the streets were to disappear, I would be tripping over gas lines and electrical conduits. Pipes carrying water from the New Croton reservoir (completed in 1906) weave under the streets of Manhattan. If I traveled to midtown, I would have to stay clear of steam pipes that carry heat from power plants to various buildings, not to mention the pipes that carry the condensation from the steam, as well as sewage pipes. We don't see this maze of plumbing; we don't even think about it until a break in a water main creates a flood, a gas leak causes an explosion, or the sewage system backs up in our basement. Then we are reminded of the complexity that literally lies just below the surface.

Likewise, when we get to the modeling of financial crises, it all has to do with plumbing. If you want to follow a crisis, you need to follow the money, and the money flows through the plumbing. It stops along the path to be processed into assets, to be delivered to those who need funding to transform into securities, to be sent as collateral. If one of the pipes gets clogged or breaks under pressure, we have the makings of a crisis. If it fails to feed what is downstream, or backs up to spill into other systems, that crisis will spread.

If we keep things abstract and general, the mechanics of a crisis are not so difficult. But abstraction doesn't really get us very far. We need to get ourselves a schematic of this plumbing and start from there. For an agent-based approach, or for that matter most any simulation approach, the key is setting it up correctly, which means understanding the structure: where the agents are operating, their environment, their heuristics, and the resulting dynamics, all specific to the financial system. If you don't start here, you're spinning your wheels.

Figure 11.1 lays out the structure of the financial system, showing the intricacies of the plumbing that connects the various components of the system—the hedge fund, the cash provider, and the like. In this figure, the components are centered around the bank/dealer, and the bank/dealer itself has a number of subcomponents. For all its detail, this schematic is simplified in a number of ways, the most obvious one being that there is only one of each type of component in this schematic. In reality there are many bank/dealers, hedge funds, and so forth.

The fastest way to gain an appreciation for the real world of the financial system and the degree to which economics has abstracted it away is to walk through the labyrinth as we are doing here. Nothing occurs by a wave of the hand. Funds travel through the plumbing as they go from one place to the other, usually with intermediate stops. Cash is borrowed, assets are bought and then used as collateral, sometimes the collateral is used a second time to borrow even more.

And the pipes don't simply shuffle assets from one institution to another. Things change, much as the flows within a chemical plant are altered as they pass into the various processing units.[3] Flows going from depositors to long-term borrowers are subject to a maturity transformation: the standard banking function of taking in short-term deposits and making longer-maturity

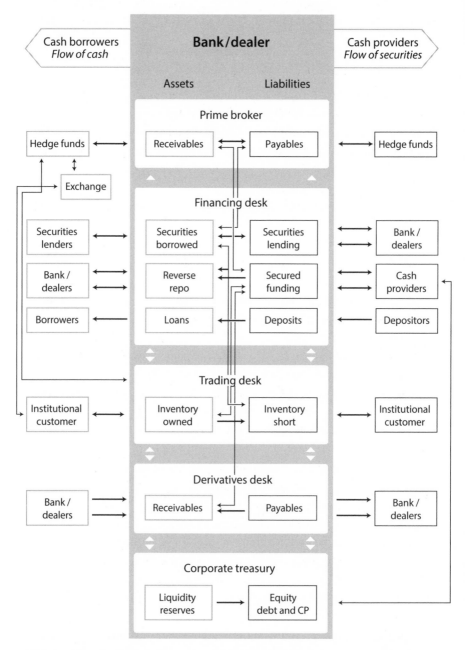

FIGURE 11.1. **A map of the financial system.** This figure provides detail on the agents within the financial system, along with the flow of funds, collateral, and assets, as well as the internal workings of a bank/dealer as an intermediary. In the corporate treasury function, the abbreviation CP stands for commercial paper. This is simplified in that it shows the detail and flows between only one bank/dealer and other entities. In actuality, there will be a network of many bank/dealers and other entities. *Adapted from Aguiar, Bookstaber, and Wipf (2014) and Aguiar et al. (2016).*

loans. The flows of funding from cash providers through secured funding and prime brokers to hedge funds are making a credit transformation: the less creditworthy hedge funds receive funding from lenders who have an appetite only for very low credit risk. The flows between the financial institutions on either side of the bank/dealer's trading desk are subject to a liquidity transformation: less-liquid assets, such as mortgages, are structured into debt instruments with liquid tranches, and market making provides liquidity. And the participants in the derivatives area are subject to risk transformations: the return distribution of assets is changed, such as by issuing options.[4] Interactions matter, and so the institutions that are connected to the various pipes alter the flows.

THE WHITE NIGHT GOES DARK

There are three types of flows in the financial system: assets, funding, and collateral. Figure 11.2 represents these three types of flows in a multilayer schematic that continues along the lines of the one-layer schematic of figure 11.1.[5]

The top layer in figure 11.2 is for asset-trading activities and flows between asset managers and the security markets. It includes mutual funds, hedge funds, the trading and investment arms of insurance companies and pension funds along the periphery, linking with the exchanges and market makers in the core. The middle layer is for the flow of funding. The bank/dealers are at the core of funding flows.[6] Collateral is presented as the bottom layer: collateral arrangements, the transformation of collateral though upgrades and reuse, the risk management of collateral based on haircuts and quality.[7] These features are not apparent when considering collateral flows as simply the opposite of funding flows.

This multilayer exploded view of the financial system lays bare vulnerabilities that are not apparent in the one-layer representation of figure 11.1, ones that we can understand only now because of the events surrounding the White Night, *Notte Bianca*, in Rome in 2003.

On September 27, 2003, Rome turned into a multivenue carnival. Shops, clubs, and bars stayed open all night. Museums, cinemas, theaters, and art galleries ran into the wee hours of the morning. There were circus acts and other performances, music on the streets. This cultural event was modeled on the festival organized the year before in Paris—which has spread to many other cities since. The mayor of Paris joined Rome's mayor, Walter Veltroni, at a performance of *Romeo and Juliet* at the Globe Theatre

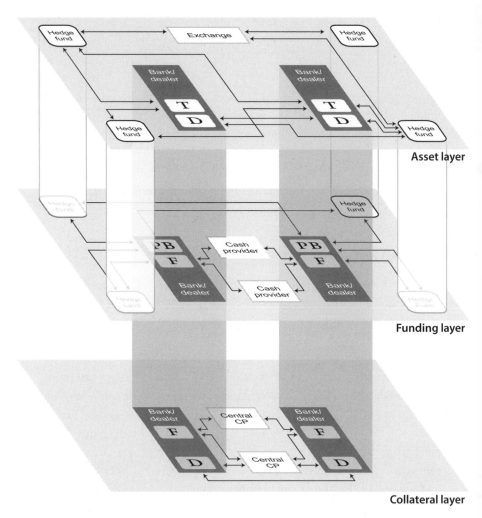

FIGURE 11.2. **A multilayer view of the financial system.** This multilayer schematic has layers for assets, funding, and collateral. Some financial entities participate in more than one layer, resulting in dependency and connectivity between the different layers. Particularly notable are the bank/dealers, which participate in all three layers through the activities of their various subunits. The abbreviations under the bank/dealers are T for trading desk; D for derivatives desk; F for financing desk; and PB for prime broker; on the collateral layer, Central CP is for central counterparty clearinghouse. *Adapted from Bookstaber and Kenett (2016).*

in the Villa Borghese park. They then went to a performance of *Tosca* and a concert by Nicola Piovani near the town hall. The streets were filled with a million revelers.

Then, at 3:27 AM the lights went out. A blackout enveloped Italy and parts of Switzerland, touching fifty-six million people. Any other day, a power outage at three in the morning would have had little immediate effect, but on the White Night, thirty thousand people were stranded on 110 trains, others caught in the subways. And it was raining. As a *New York Times* reporter covering the event described it, "a ghostly legion of wet and bedraggled nocturnal revelers found themselves stranded on the streets."

Twenty-six minutes earlier, heavy winds had created a flashover between a conductor cable and a tree on one of the main electric transmission lines, the Lukmanier line, that runs between Switzerland and Italy. After spending ten minutes unsuccessfully trying to restore the Lukmanier line, the Swiss network operator alerted his Italian counterpart to lighten the load on the San Bernardino line, because the physics of electrical flows dictated that the electricity would jump to and overload that transmission line. But this fail-safe maneuver was prevented by another line-to-ground fault at 3:25 AM that led to the San Bernardino line shutting down as well. There then followed sequential failures of other transmission lines in the border region, resulting in a catastrophic blackout throughout Italy at 3:27 AM.

The propagation of grid failures generally occurs due to a cascade of overloads that triggers breakers from node to node in the network. The operators on the Swiss and Italian sides of the border were frantically dropping loads across lines and trying to restart, but the devices refused to switch and reopen the breakers. What the operators didn't know was that the source of the Italian blackout was different from what their manual of emergency procedures had anticipated. In the Italian blackout, the problem came from the interaction between the electrical network and a second network, a communications network that controlled the operation of the power network. When the node on the Lukmanier failed, it spanned to the communication network by disabling a nearby server. That server failure affected adjacent servers because they depended on the one server as a part of their communication cluster. The power stations that were connected to these servers then shut down due to the loss of their controllers, which in turn affected the servers adjacent to that node.[8]

The failure propagated, hopscotching between one node on the power layer to a node on the communication layer, from that one communication network node to other nodes on the communication layer, and then back to the power node through these servers. That is, the vulnerability was acute because of the interdependence of two distinct networks: the communication network depended on the electric network for power, and the power network depended on the communication network for its instructions and coordination. Making matters worse, the two networks matched up hand-in-glove in their topology and geography: the servers were geographically and structurally similar to their power counterparts.[9] They were perfectly paired for maximum calamity.

AN ENVIRONMENT THAT IS TOO BIG TO FAIL

There is a lesson in the Italian blackout if we want to understand financial crises. The Italian blackout is one of the first examples of a large-scale failure of a multilayer network. In the Italian blackout, networks designed to work separately interrelated: the electrical network that powered other systems, and the communication system that harbored the controllers of the electrical system. Taking a network view of figure 11.2, the various layers are like separate, interrelated networks within the financial system: the channels that provide and use funding, to the ones that use that funding to buy and sell assets, to the flows of collateral that secure the funding. That is, if we cast the system map of figure 11.2 to create a network view of the financial system, we will find the financial system is such a multilayer network.[10]

The multilayer network has implications for systemic risk that are qualitatively different from those for a single-layer network. Perhaps not unexpectedly, the mode of propagation of risk, the path a shock takes, and the value of integration versus segregation of the functions of various agents or nodes all have a different and richer nature as we move to a multilayer view of the financial system.

In the Italian blackout, the flow of communication between servers and from servers to the station control units was different from that of the flows of power along the grid and into the servers. So the links between layers lead to a different functional effect, and lead to a transformation from one flow to another. Reformulated in the context of the financial system, risks in one activity become risks to other activities as they propagate and amplify within and, more important, between the different layers. Funding becomes the fuel for acquiring assets, and the assets become the source of collateral, which in turn is the basis for generating the funding. It is not surprising that the addition of these functional relationships and transformations in the types of flows that arise for interlayer connections create vulnerabilities that do not exist in a plain vanilla, single-layer network.[11]

The multilayer network has important implications for the issue of systemically important financial institutions. We already know that size matters. But to that we can add a critical new consideration: the importance of the institution in spanning layers.[12] That is, if an institution can pass the disruption in one layer through to another layer, it is turning a local, specific disruption into a systemic, multilayer one.

Large banks span three layers, creating shafts for a fire to spread from one story to another. And more than this, at every stage the banks fan the flames by cutting off funding, freezing collateral, and pulling away market liquidity. To reduce their systemic importance—and indeed the systemic importance of any agent—we not only can control their leverage and size, but also reduce the degree of their interlayer spanning. This provides an argument for breaking up the banks. And it also suggests the approach for doing so. Going from a small set of big banks to a larger set of small banks will not do the trick if those smaller banks still span the layers. There will be many smaller shafts to spread the fire from one layer to the next. Rather, the banks need to be broken up to create firewalls between the layers. We cannot have the full-service banks that provide collateral, funding, and market making all within one structure, no matter what their size.

The Agents and Their Heuristics

An agent-based approach starts, naturally enough, with agents. The agents delineated in figure 11.1 are:[13]

> *Bank/Dealers.* The term *bank/dealer* refers to both banks and broker-dealers, most of which have become aligned with banks post-2008. The bank/dealer can be thought of as one of the agents in the financial system, but as we can see in figure 11.1, it itself contains various agents, each performing a different task, interacting with different agents, and operating with a share of independence. Bank/dealer agents include, for example, JP Morgan, Goldman Sachs, and Deutsche Bank, a dozen or two in all.
>
> The agents internal to the bank/dealer can include a prime broker, financing operation, trading desk, derivatives desk, and the bank/dealer's corporate treasury. The prime broker services clients such as hedge funds that are looking for leverage. It also helps hedge funds and other investors that want to short securities. The financing desk is the secured-funding operation; it borrows, using securities as collateral.[14] The funding is passed on to clients, both directly by the financing desk and through the prime broker, and is also used to fund securities owned by the bank/dealer. The trading desk buys and sells based on client demand, setting prices and

managing inventory in its market-making activities. Trading activity includes a wide swath of bonds, from corporate and emerging markets to mortgage instruments to U.S. treasuries and sovereigns, and includes repackaging inventory as securitized products. The derivatives desk executes derivative transactions such a swaps, forwards, and options for itself and for clients. The bank/dealer's corporate treasury raises unsecured funding by issuing equity and debt, and short-term funding such as commercial paper.

Hedge Funds. Hedge fund agents borrow from the bank/dealer's prime broker to support their long and short trading positions. And, of course, the hedge funds trade with the bank/dealer's trading desk, as well as with various exchanges. Hedge funds are on both sides of figure 11.1 because when they are holding assets short they provide funds to the bank/dealer; when they are going long they borrow. Agents in the hedge funds space include Bridgewater, Citadel, and D. E. Shaw. There are several thousand hedge funds in total, though fewer than one hundred of any note.

Cash Providers. Cash providers are agents that include asset managers, pension funds, insurance companies, securities lenders (who receive cash from lending securities), and, most important, money market funds. The cash providers fuel the financial system. Without funding, the system—or any part of the system that does not have funding—comes to a halt in as little as a day. The collateral passes from the borrowers to the cash providers, usually with the bank/dealer as an intermediary.

Securities Lenders. Like the cash providers, the securities lenders provide the bank/dealer with securities and funding. Large securities lenders often lend securities to the bank/dealer and also reinvest the cash in the form of secured funding that they provide to the bank/dealer.[15]

Institutional Investors. The institutional investors encompass a wide swath of agents, ranging from asset managers to pension funds, sovereign wealth funds, and insurance companies. As we will see in the next chapter, these agents are critical for providing liquidity to the market. Because of their tendency to become embroiled in forced selling, and thus to have a special role in fostering crises, we have hedge funds as a specific agent type, but hedge funds really are a special class of institutional investor that can borrow money to put on leveraged positions, take on short positions, and enter into illiquid and unusual investment opportunities.[16] So they have a lot of freedom, though that freedom can lead to peril.

I've organized figure 11.1 to highlight two aspects of the market that are critical for crises. One is to show that banks are multifaceted and can come at the market in a number of ways. Another is to highlight the flow of funding from the cash providers through the bank to the users. Directly or indirectly, nearly all the functions in the financial system draw on funding, and on collateral as well, because in the case of secured funding, the pathways are two-way streets: when there is funding in one direction, there is a flow of collateral in the other.[17] This is why the interest rate and credit markets are so critical to crises. We have seen twenty-point down days for equities without much in the way of long-term effects. The same is not true for the markets that are integral to funding.

Each agent observes its environment and takes action accordingly. In practice, we will be dealing with actual agents: bank/dealers such as Goldman Sachs, Morgan Stanley, or Citibank; hedge funds such as Citadel, Bridgewater, or D. E. Shaw. Each has a different business model, a different level of risk taking, and a different culture. Some of this will be spelled out in the governance structure and policies and procedures, some will be communicated to their investors.[18] And during times of crisis, some of the heuristics are hard wired, without any ability for the agents to alter their course; most notably when it relates to issues of margin calls or forced liquidations due to reduced availability of funding.[19]

Each agent has its own set of heuristics. These will vary from one agent to the next, but generally speaking, the heuristics will be along these lines: the prime broker limits the funding it provides based on the collateral it holds and the haircut required by the cash provider; the trading desk will make a market based on the internal limits it is given for inventory, where those limits will depend on the availability of funding and the willingness to hold risky inventory; hedge funds maintain a target leverage—too high and there is the risk of margin calls and forced liquidation, too low and their returns suffer; and cash providers lend based on the dollar value of the collateral and a haircut based on the perceived creditworthiness of a borrower and the liquidity of the market.

The actions of the agents based on their heuristics can be broken out into Soros's cognitive function, where the agent takes in the environment (from the world to the mind), and the manipulative function, where the agent executes on its decisions and alters the environment on that basis (from the mind to the world). For example, take a hedge fund. Each day it determines the appropriate amount of each asset to hold and, by implication, the amount of leverage it should take on, which is the cognitive function. It then uses this to determine whether it will need to buy or sell each asset, and this decision will affect the environment. This is the manipulative function.

Figure 11.1 is a concrete application of the "we are in the real world" point. When we look at this figure, the theoretical, abstract constructs behind economics pale. How can economics expect to deal with a crisis when it does not look at the plumbing that feeds and propagates the crisis? The objective is to understand the actual financial system in which we reside. The model must be relevant and revealing, not simply built in a way that is rational, consistent, and beautiful to the mathematically inclined. We cannot divine the behavior of a hypothetical financial system any more than a chemical engineer can assess a spill by starting with "assume there is a chemical plant." He must analyze the plant itself. Lars Syll, a professor of economic history and prominent critic of mainstream economics, asks why economists "consider it worthwhile and interesting to make evaluations of real economies based on abstract imaginary fantasy worlds," which he likens to "telling physiologists to evaluate the human body from the perspective of unicorns."[20]

Dynamics

Now that we have laid out the environment through the system map and the agents of the system, we can start the engine, turn the model on, and see how the dynamics unfold. In market crises there are two types of dynamics: asset-based fire sales and funding runs, or funding-based fire sales.[21] And each feeds into the other.

Asset-based fire sales focus on the interaction between institutional investors, particularly leveraged investment firms such as hedge funds; their funding sources, notably the bank/dealer's prime broker; and the asset markets where the forced sales occur. As shown in figure 11.3, this sort of fire sale occurs when there is a disruption to the system that forces a fund to sell positions. This disruption can occur through various channels: a price drop and resulting drop in asset value, a decrease in funding or an increase in the margin rate from the prime broker, or a flood of investor redemptions. In any of these events, the fund reduces its assets, causing asset prices to drop, leading to further rounds of forced selling.

Market price

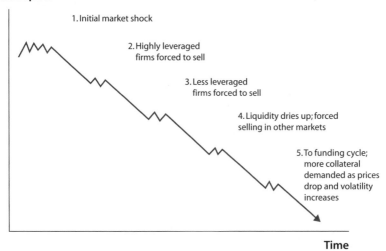

1. Initial market shock

2. Highly leveraged
   firms forced to sell

3. Less leveraged
   firms forced to sell

4. Liquidity dries up; forced
   selling in other markets

5. To funding cycle;
   more collateral
   demanded as prices
   drop and volatility
   increases

Time

FIGURE 11.3. **Asset-based fire sale dynamics.** An asset-based fire sale begins with a shock to an asset market that leads to a sudden large price drop. Firms that are leveraged are forced to sell to meet margin requirements. As the forced selling sustains downward pressure on prices, margin calls feed back to magnify the effects, forcing additional rounds of selling. The firms that are under pressure also sell positions they hold in other markets, creating contagion in the price decline. The drop in the value of collateral that has been posted with assets in the affected markets can lead to stresses in funding. *Adapted from Office of Financial Research (2012).*

Funding-based fire sales focus on the interaction of the bank/dealer with its cash providers. As shown in figure 11.4, it is triggered by a disruption in funding flows as might happen if there is a decline in the value of collateral or an erosion of confidence. This reduces the funding available to the trading desk, and its reduction in inventory again leads to a further price drop, so a funding-based and an asset-based fire sale can feed on each other. For example, a funding-based fire sale might precipitate an asset-based fire sale (the funding restrictions for the bank/dealer can reduce the funding available to the hedge fund through the prime broker, leading to asset liquidations) and vice versa. A drop in collateral value caused by a shock to asset prices or an increase in the collateral haircut will feed into a fire sale. Thus, although we have these two types of fire sales related to two of the three layers of figure 11.2, fire sales can also be instigated by the third of the layers, the collateral layer.

These dynamics are driven by the anvil and hammer of leverage and liquidity. Sudden redemptions can also do the job, but usually it is the effect of leverage that forces selling. And it is illiquidity that causes prices to drop;

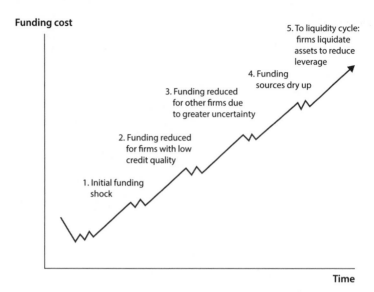

FIGURE 11.4. **Funding-based fire sale dynamics.** A funding run often begins with concerns about counterparty creditworthiness and a drying up of liquidity. These increase funding costs, placing strains on vulnerable firms. The rise in funding costs creates concerns about counterparty risk for less vulnerable firms. The higher funding costs lead firms to sell positions, and the resulting drop in asset prices can turn the funding run into an asset fire sale. *Adapted from Office of Financial Research (2012).*

creating the cascades that turn a simple, one-time shock into something far worse. If the markets are highly liquid, selling can be accommodated without a notable price decline, and there will be no cascades or contagion. If there is little leverage in the market, there will not be a need for substantial deleveraging even in the face of a market event. Because forced deleveraging leads to asset sales, and asset sales lead to price declines (which then leads to further deleveraging), both leverage and illiquidity are essential components of a market crisis. That is, with perfect liquidity, the forced selling from leverage will not lead to a price cascade; with no leverage, even an illiquid market will not lead to a fire sale because there will be no forced selling.[22]

I'll illustrate the objectives of the model by showing how the model can trace a shock as it reverberates through the system.[23] The model can be applied to a system with many agents, but here I will apply it to a tractable network of three assets, two hedge funds, two bank/dealers, and a single cash provider that treats each bank/dealer separately. Figure 11.5 shows how the various agents in the model relate. In this figure, bank/dealer 1 and hedge fund 1 hold equal weights in asset 1 and asset 2, and bank/dealer 2 and hedge fund 2 hold equal weights in asset 2 and asset 3. The cash provider supplies funding to the bank/dealers, which in turn supply funding to the hedge funds.

Even in this simple specification, which is a stripped-down version of figure 11.1, the interactions of the agents and how those interactions are affected by changes in the parameters remain complex. Figure 11.5 illustrates the point that the pipes between agents can tie to any of several functional units; for example, a bank/dealer can tie in to another bank/dealer as a derivative counterparty or as a security lender. In the first case, they would be subject to credit shocks, while in the second, they would be subject to funding shocks. Figure 11.5 shows the progression of one simulation run of the agent-based model. Each stage in the figure, which is a snapshot of the model at different points in the progression from the initial shock, is depicted by showing which agents influence other agents. A new pathway of effects is indicated by a black line, and continuation of a shock along a pathway is indicated by a dark gray line.

In stage 1, an initial shock in asset 1 affects hedge fund 1 and bank/dealer 1 because they have exposure to asset 1, and the shock also affects the cash provider through the bank/dealer because the collateral it is holding drops in value.

In stage 2, the effects of the initial shock propagate to affect asset 2, because both hedge fund 1 and bank/dealer 1 sell positions in their portfolio to meet margin calls. Asset 2 also drops in price. This has the same sort of effect on hedge fund 2 and bank/dealer 2 as the shock in asset 1 had for hedge fund 1 and bank/dealer 1. And asset 1 will drop further due to continued pressure on hedge fund 1 and bank/dealer 1. The cash provider has its collateral drop even further, and because bank/dealer 2 has used its assets as collateral, it is now also affected by reductions in funding from the cash provider.

By stage 3, asset 3 is embroiled in the effects from the initial shock, because hedge fund 2 and bank/dealer 2 have exposure to asset 3, and in the face of forced selling will start to liquidate their holdings of that asset. Also, with funding restricted for the two bank/dealers, a new channel of contagion opens up. The credit relationships between the bank/dealers weaken. Bank/dealer 2 sees the weakening of bank/dealer 1 from the drop in its asset holdings and the reduction in funds. As the crisis evolves through further periods, the credit concerns might move in the other direction as well. Imagine that you are a hedge fund that invests only in asset 3. You don't have

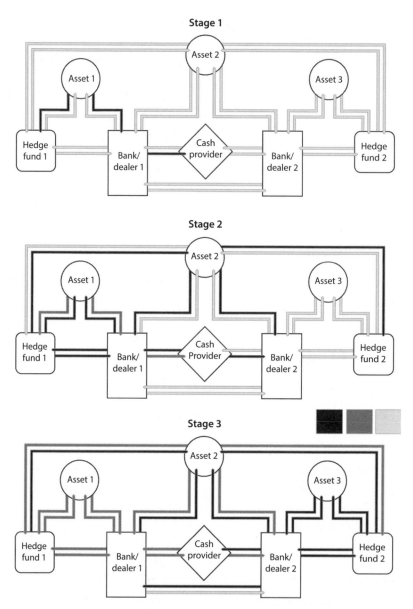

FIGURE 11.5. Stages in the propagation of a market shock within an agent-based model. In stage 1, a shock occurs in asset 1, which affects the agents holding that asset. Hedge fund 1 and bank/dealer 1 reduce exposure, which leads to selling of both asset 1 and asset 2, and the cash provider reduces funding due to a drop in the value of the collateral it holds. The result is a reduction in the price of asset 2, which affects those holding that asset, namely hedge fund 2 and bank/dealer 2. These entities do not hold asset 1, but do hold both asset 2 and asset 3. Their subsequent selling leads to a drop in asset 3. The weakness of bank/dealer 1 also leads to interbank credit risk. The dark lines indicate the agents of the system that are embroiled in the particular stage; the intermediate shaded lines indicate agents that continue to be involved from an earlier stage; the light lines indicate agents that have not yet become involved.

any exposure to asset 1, where the initial shock occurs, and you don't even have exposure to assets that are also held by funds that hold asset 1. Yet you end up seeing your portfolio drop as a result of the shock. That is real collateral damage!

The propagation analysis of liquidity, leverage, and allocations presented here is based on a price shock as the triggering event. An agent-based model can readily also allow for shocks based on a reduction in funding by the cash provider, a drop in creditworthiness of the bank/dealers, and a redemption shock to the hedge funds. Each will have its own course for propagating through the system, and these various shocks can occur in sequence. For example, in addition to the asset shock, we could insert an exogenous funding or credit shock in one of the periods. In such cases, the progress of the dynamic will generally be extended. As we will see in section V, for the 2008 crisis these channels were important.

12

Liquidity and Crashes

In one news segment on *Saturday Night Live*, the newscaster announces, "And today on the New York Stock Exchange, no shares changed hands. Everyone finally has what they want." The punch line raises a legitimate point: Shares are always trading. We are never satisfied with what we have.

The principal reason that prices vary, especially in the short term, is the demand for liquidity that results from our apparent fickleness. If you want to buy or sell a stock—or if you have to—you are a liquidity demander. And what you are demanding when you demand liquidity is to do this quickly, and with low transaction costs. It is in the froth of liquidity where most trading profits are made. Not only does the demand for liquidity move prices, but the breakdown of liquidity is one of the primary drivers of crashes, as well. I assign the dynamics of liquidity to three types of agents: liquidity demanders, liquidity suppliers, and market makers.

To illustrate this breakdown, let me run through two of the major market dislocations in the U.S. equity market, one that chopped 20 percent off the stock market in one day, and the other that rapidly reduced the price of some S&P 500 stocks to a penny a share in a few minutes.

The Environment

The financial environment includes a means of egress for the financial markets: liquidity. Liquidity is a door that can yawn wide open. Or it can close shut. And, consistent with the dictum that the markets operate to extract the maximum pain, when investors really want to get out, that is what happens. And when investors need to get out but cannot do so readily, they need to get out all the more. And the door shuts tighter. We can see this in action by looking at two of the most noted liquidity events in the U.S. equity markets in recent years: the portfolio insurance–induced 1987 crash, and the Flash Crash of 2010.

THE CRASH OF OCTOBER 19, 1987

On October 19, 1987, the S&P 500 suffered its worst one-day drop in history, down more than 20 percent. This was not the result of a rational reaction to new information, as the efficient market theory would imply. It was the result of a portfolio strategy that sucked the liquidity from the market. We all kept on trying to sell when no one was there to take the other side of the trade. That strategy was portfolio insurance—a strategy that I helped popularize when I was at Morgan Stanley. (Yeah. My bad.) I was in the middle of executing this strategy when the market became unhinged.[1]

Portfolio insurance was not really an insurance policy—though calling it that was a great marketing hook—but rather a dynamic hedging strategy that attempted to create insurance-like protection. The strategy had all the potential pitfalls of any hedge. For portfolio insurance—or for that matter any other hedging strategy—to work, the market must be liquid. If a hedge cannot be readily adjusted, then all bets are off. By October 1987, the scale of portfolio insurance had reached such proportions that there was not enough liquidity to go around. If one small portfolio uses this sort of strategy, liquidity will not be an issue. If everyone is trying to do it, it can become a nightmare, a little like everyone on a cruise ship trying to pile into a single lifeboat: it won't float. On Monday morning, October 19, 1987, everybody who was running a portfolio insurance program pulled out the computer runs from the previous Friday's record 110-point decline. And those runs said to head for the hills.

The portfolio insurance hedgers traded in futures, and that morning, starting even before the equity market opened, in aggregate they sold nearly a half billion dollars of S&P futures, some 30 percent of the public volume. Futures prices dropped precipitously. Ultimately, what we sold in futures had to find its way into selling of the equities themselves through the New York Stock Exchange (NYSE). So the individual stocks finally registered the full brunt of the selling coming from the futures pit in Chicago.

The traders in the S&P pit are mostly market makers who thrive on having quick reactions and speed of execution. By contrast, equity investors who frequented the NYSE were not particularly focused on speed, nor were they concerned with the minute-by-minute movement of the market. Equity investors were not glued to their screens, ready to react en masse with the same speed as the market makers, and certainly not with the speed of the computers that were firing out the hedging orders.

Naturally enough, the market makers in the futures pit lowered prices to elicit the other side of the trade. A falling price is normally the dinner bell for buyers. But during a crisis, it doesn't work that way. There's a limit to how much more interest a price cut can attract, at least if you're trying to do it in short order. No matter how quickly the price fell, the decision making by the equity investors, the buyers, took time; unlike the quick-twitch futures pit traders, they made portfolio adjustments only after reasoned consideration. The increasingly aggressive price drops backfired. Many potential buyers started to wonder what was happening and backed off completely.

The root cause is what I call a heterogeneous decision cycle—the time frame for deciding what to do in the futures market is substantially different from—namely, shorter than—that in the equity market. We could see the effect on our trading floor. One of our institutional clients in Boston was bullish on IBM and had discussed adding more of the stock to his substantial portfolio. His salesman tried to grab him as IBM started to tank, but he was in a meeting. A second call failed to locate him. We could imagine him heading off to grab some coffee and leaf through his morning faxes, unaware of the chaos that was unfolding in lower Manhattan. Back at the NYSE, a day's worth of activity had happened in what seemed to be ten minutes. Our IBM specialist was starting to panic. A flood of sell orders was coming in and there were nowhere near enough buyers to take them off his hands. With price as his only tool, he took IBM down another other point, and then two more points, to try to dredge up some buyers. The portfolio manager in Boston finally got back to his desk, saw the beating IBM was taking, and gave us a call. If IBM had been off a half point or a full point, he would have put in an order. But with stocks in free fall he hesitated, waiting instead to get a read on what was going on with IBM and the market generally.

Because this client worked for an asset management firm with a long-term investment horizon, he could put on a position just as easily tomorrow as today. He watched the market's cascade with something approaching detached curiosity. As shares fell further, from 5 to 10 to 20 percent, he felt some panic. But for the moment, he and many of his counterparts were on the sidelines. Meanwhile, for the specialist, more shares piled up in inventory with each passing minute.

The result was a disaster. The potential liquidity suppliers and investment buyers were being scared off by the higher volatility and wider spreads. And, more important, falling prices were actually inducing more liquidity-based selling because the more prices fell, the more hedging came out of the prewired portfolio insurance algorithms.

Liquidity dried up because of the difference in time frames between the demanders and the suppliers. By the time equity investors could have reacted and done some bargain hunting, the specialists had moved prices so precipitously that these potential liquidity suppliers were scared away.[2] The key culprit was the different trading time frames between the demanders and the suppliers. If the sellers could have waited longer for the liquidity they demanded, the buyers would have had time to react and the market would have cleared at a higher price. Instead, $500 billion in market value was erased in a couple of hours.

THE FLASH CRASH OF MAY 6, 2010

On May 6, 2010, the U.S. equity markets suffered what became known as the Flash Crash. The market dropped more than 7 percent in a matter of fifteen minutes. Some stocks dropped to a penny a share; others rose to $100,000 a share. These extreme prices occurred for somewhat arcane reasons, but those really were the prices at which you would have had to sell or buy at that moment.

They wouldn't seem to be related, but the Flash Crash had echoes of the 1987 crash. The Flash Crash was another crisis of liquidity, one in which liquidity demand came in faster than the supply—the same sort of time disintermediation as occurred in 1987. The difference was in the available computer power. With the wonders of high-frequency trading, this crash occurred in minutes rather than over the course of hours.

There has, not surprisingly, been a lot of ink spilled over the Flash Crash, with various congressional hearings and a months-in-the-making report from the Securities and Exchange Commission and the Commodity Futures Trading Commission (the SEC for the equity markets, the CFTC for the futures).[3] These agencies were caught flat-footed because they had no access to the trade-by-trade or order-by-order data, nor did they have the hardware to analyze the millions of data points even if they had had access. Indeed, when the *New York Times* came to the SEC to find a high-tech setting for a photo of Gregg Berman, the SEC's point person for the report, the best they could do was the Trading and Markets Division's market room, a twenty-by-fifteen-foot room armed with a bunch of PCs, a set of TV monitors, a Bloomberg terminal, and a fax machine!

I was at the SEC at the time, and was involved in analyzing the Flash Crash early on. One pretty simple take—one that didn't get highlighted in the final report—is that the problems all started with the SEC's rule for decimalization of the equity markets in 2001, and reminded me of the game show *The Price Is Right*.[4] (Which may explain why this point didn't make it into the final report.)

THE PRICE IS RIGHT: THE SHRINKING MARKET MAKER IN THE EQUITY MARKET

I watched *The Price Is Right* in its first incarnation in the early 1960s, when my grandmother would have the show blaring from the living room while she did her household chores. In *The Price Is Right*, the winning contestant, the one who gets the motor home, the twelve-piece dining room set, or the trip to Hawaii, is the one who bids the closest to the suggested retail price of the merchandise without bidding above it. If the contestant's bid is just one dollar above the price, he is out of luck. One strategy contestants used, which through my ten-year-old eyes seemed like playing dirty, was for contestant No. 2 to bid one dollar more than the first contestant. If the first contestant bid $23,000, the next one bid $23,001. If the first contestant underestimated the price by even one dollar, he couldn't win. He was essentially taken out of the game.

Suppose you had to put up your own money to make a bid under those rules. If you knew someone could step in front of you at one-dollar increments, you probably wouldn't participate. The game would fall apart. To make the game work, the spread between bids would have to be wide enough to give people a chance. A general rule of thumb might be to have the bidding increments be related to the contestants' uncertainty about the price of the merchandise. If they hardly had a clue and thought the price might be anywhere between $20,000 and $50,000, then maybe the bid increment should be more like $5,000 than $1. The point is that there is some notion of a reasonable bid increment, and bid "dollarization," allowing bids to be in dollar increments, ruins the game. No one plays, or if they do play, they won't play for more than a nominal stake.

This is akin to what has happened in the equity markets. There is a notion of a reasonable spread, related to price volatility and liquidity. The volatility measures the risk something bad will happen before the trader can unload his inventory, and the liquidity determines the time it will take to unload. If a trader is willing to put up a good size order at this spread, but the trading increment is less than that, he can end up much like the first contestant in *The Price Is Right*. He might be bidding with a ten-cent spread, only to see someone step in front of him at nine cents. And what is good for the goose is good for the gander, so someone else will step in at eight cents, and so on, until you get someone sitting at a spread of a penny.

Wall Street gets a bit more complicated than *The Price Is Right*, because if things go badly for a trader sitting at $.09, he can lean on the person bidding at the $.10 spread, turning around to put his position to him. Again, this will occur all the way down the line, but only if the trader at the tighter spread has a smaller position than the guy he is leaning on. So the bid size will be smaller and smaller as you run down the increments from $.10 to $.01. The increments will be smaller, but the need for speed will be greater. Anyone sitting at $.01 does not have much of a margin for error. He will be a Nervous Nellie, pulling away and handing the position over to the next person in line at the slightest hint of a problem. It can turn into a game of hot potato, with speed all the more critical for the ones operating at the thinnest margins. Just as with *The Price Is Right*, if the increments are too small, no one will be willing to put any real money into the game. Knowing he is being leaned on by those with smaller bids, the person sitting at $.10 will exit the market. A domino effect will take place all the way down the line.

The point is that with decimalization we end up with a smaller order book. The person who normally would be willing to trade in size at a reasonable spread pulls away, and the traders down the line need to get faster and faster trading platforms. You can run through the order book like crashing through thin ice. The mitigating factor is that the high-frequency traders will come in to grab you before you sink. But if there are not enough of them, or if they cannot react fast enough, you fall beyond their grasp until you hit bottom.

So how do we get from *The Price Is Right* to a smaller order book to the stock of Procter & Gamble sinking from $60 to $40, or Accenture nearly evaporating as it fell from more than $40 to one penny a share—in one minute? Let's say there are 50,000 shares of market orders in some stock down 10 percent from the current price. Some shock occurs—and in the case of the Flash Crash, it seems that the shock came from the S&P Mini futures contract—and the price of the stock drops to hit those market orders. The order book is thin; there are not 50,000 shares of bids anywhere near forty dollars a share. So the price drops instantly to $39. Still not enough orders. It keeps running through the order book until there is nothing there. If things didn't go at a millisecond pace, someone would come into the market when it is 10 or 20 percent down. But there is literally no time for anyone to think. In fact, there is no time for programs to fill in the order book as the market orders run their course. The computers are on autopilot, based on algorithms, which include, among other things, a program to shut off if the market seems to be acting strangely. And a price drop of 10 percent or more in a stock in a matter of minutes qualifies. The next stop is down to the next bid, which is at the "stub," a penny a share. This stub bid is there because market makers have to post some bid and offer, and if they really are not interested, they will bid at a crazy price, like a penny a share, and offer at some other crazy price, like $100,000 a share.

The mechanics of portfolio insurance and the Flash Crash are similar. Portfolio insurance is a hedging program, a dynamic one that adjusts based on the value of the portfolio. It's like having a preprogrammed stop loss, where a certain amount of your portfolio is sold based on the portfolio value. The Flash Crash was also the result of preprogrammed selling, this time due to old-fashioned market stop loss orders. In 1987, the specialists were not well capitalized and fled in the face of the onslaught of sell orders. In 2010, no market makers were even expected to stand in front of the selling, and because of decimalization, there was a thin order book. One way to scare up orders was to drop prices precipitously. This then fed back into the computers, which calculated a new, increased hedge—hit further market order stops, so to speak—which then spit out further sell orders to the futures, and the cycle went one more turn. No one could step back and say, "Wait a minute, let's think about this for a bit." That is, it was a tightly coupled process.

High-frequency traders might react in milliseconds, but they still do take time before they can react. A market order does not have to react; it is already preprogrammed. You might wonder why anyone would do a market order; but if you are a retail investor and want to be sure you get out, and believe the market is going to be well behaved, it makes sense. You are concerned about getting out before prices drop 5 or 10 percent; if you get picked off and get taken out a penny or two, it is not anything to worry about.

The combination of all these factors led to a cycle of price drops feeding further price drops, with the only respite coming when regulators hit a circuit breaker.

The Agents and Their Heuristics

So, whether it is 1987 or 2010, we get a similar sequence of events. There is an initial shock and preprogrammed selling gets triggered in the face of that decline. It is worth noting that usually we think of leverage and margin calls as leading to the cascade; here we see that it can come from other quarters. We should therefore ask whether there are strategies that require a predetermined, mechanistic response to market shocks, like portfolio insurance in 1987 or market stop loss orders in 2010. The selling occurred at a faster rate than the investors in 1987 or the algorithms in 2010 could react. That is, the demand for selling occurred more quickly than the price could communicate and attract supply. Interjecting these sorts of strategies can destabilize the system.

It is like this: If you own a store and are trying to push inventory out the door, you drop the price. But if you take 20 percent off, and the inventory isn't gone after five minutes, you don't respond by taking 50 percent off. You know it takes time for people to wander in and decide what to buy; so you wait a while before discounting further. If you are selling shirts, you don't wait as long as if you would if you are selling a Chagall. Lowering prices faster doesn't get you very far. In fact, that is the measure of liquidity—how long it generally takes before a prospective buyer walks in the door after you have discounted the price to make things move. This is a pretty simple point, but it is at the core of why we end up with even the most sophisticated of investors and traders creating crises.

At the core of these two cases are three key types of agents in relation to liquidity:

> *Liquidity demanders* that need to buy or sell. They have a need for immediacy; they care more about time than price, and are willing to move the market price to meet their needs. When the market is in crisis mode, they are forced to sell in order to raise cash, tamp down risk, or meet margin calls.
>
> *Liquidity suppliers* that try to profit from the demanders. They seek to meet the liquidity demand—for a price. There are some short-term liquidity suppliers, such as hedge funds and other speculators,

though sometimes they end up falling into the liquidity demand group. If the liquidity demand is very high, the deep pockets to take the other side belong to investors who have a longer time frame—the asset managers, pension funds, and sovereign wealth funds.

Between the two is the *market maker*. The market maker is the transaction intermediary, the broker, moving the price based on the liquidity demander's needs in order to attract the appropriate amount of liquidity supply. Market makers trade with a very short horizon. They don't want to take on risk; they want to buy in one instant and off-load their position in the next. They make their money off the bid-offer spread and from stockpiling positions in the face of demand by their clients (also called front running, which is allowed in many markets). The risk they face is being flooded by buys or sells without finding anyone to take the other side, forcing them either to hold inventory as the market moves against them or to drop their price and sell at a discount.

Modeling liquidity during market crises is difficult because of the complex, nonlinear dynamics of market participants interacting—people get a little weird. Measuring relatively small transactions does not give us much insight, just as watching snowshoe hares scurry across a frozen lake gives no indication of whether the ice will support a man. That means the successful, liquid day-to-day operation of a market will not provide the necessary insight into the ability of the market to support a sudden on-rush of liquidity demand. Like the sudden breaking of the ice, liquidity can be subject to emergent phenomena, to sudden, surprising changes in the structure of the market.

Part of the complexity arises from the feedback that occurs during periods of market shock and illiquidity. Low liquidity coupled with the forced sales of leveraged investors can cause further drops in price, leading to the cascades and contagion of fire sales, and further sapping liquidity from the market. Thus liquidity becomes an endogenous element of the broader market behavior, and cannot be analyzed without attention to issues of leverage, funding, and the resulting changes in investor behavior.

The complexity also arises from the heterogeneous decision cycles among those in the market, specifically the difference in time frames between the liquidity demanders, who require immediacy, and the liquidity suppliers, who aren't in such a big hurry. The importance of this is stressed by Duffie (2010), who presents a model highlighting the impact of inattentive investors, with particular interest in its implications for the 2008 financial crisis. As Duffie points out, some markets require a week for sufficient supply to arrive to support demand. The difference in timing is a result of the different decision cycle of investors, which influences price since only a subset of investors actively participate in providing a pricing signal to the market. This will have implications for pricing even during typical day-to-day market activity. But it will have particularly adverse effects during times of stress.

A sudden price dislocation can lead to forced selling due to margin calls, redemptions, programmatic selling algorithms such as portfolio insurance, stop losses, or risk parity strategies and other pressures.[5] Such liquidity demanders exhibit greater immediacy. That is, the time frame of the liquidity demanders shrinks, and there is more of a focus on the speed of liquidation than on price. On the other hand, those in a position to supply liquidity aren't under the gun, and continue to be price sensitive; more critically, they don't share the same short-term focus. Many liquidity suppliers are not even monitoring the markets with an eye to trade frequently.

Compounding the time horizon issues of liquidity demanders and suppliers are the impacts that inventory constraints can have. For example, a specialist firm during the 1987 crash could not find buyers, and had a rapid growth in inventory, overwhelming its capital. Investors with ready cash did not immediately materialize to take advantage of the rapidly falling prices; this inaction led to further price drops and triggered even more portfolio insurance selling.[6]

Thus the key points we must understand if we are to successfully wrangle liquidity during market crises include the nature of the demanders and suppliers: what are their decision cycles; how much are they affected by market dislocations; and how critical is the market under stress to their portfolio adjustments? Of the market makers: what is their capacity for taking on inventory; and how long are they willing to hold these positions? And of the cycle of feedback: how are these answers affected by market dislocations; and how do they in turn further affect funding, leverage, and balance sheets?

Dynamics

The environmental factors generally can be thought of as exogenous shocks that can come from anywhere. A good starting place is to examine how the market deals with changes in the liquidity demanders' need to buy or sell. We can see how a simple change, as would occur if there is forced selling because of a market shock, can lead to complex behavior in the market maker's decision to offer short-term liquidity and how the impact of the demand shocks will be affected by the speed with which the liquidity supply finds its way into the market.

In figure 12.1, I have a visualization that illustrates liquidity behavior during a market event, focusing on the interaction of the three types of agents: demanders, market makers, and suppliers. This figure shows the progression of a liquidity event from the point preceding the initial shock to the point of eventual recovery. Each long vertical bar indicates the liquidity supply around the current price. The bar increases in gray scale as it moves away from the current price, indicating an increase in the selling supply as prices rise and buying supply as prices drop. The hashed area is the bid-offer range around the midpoint of the current price, with darker hashes indicating higher market-making capacity.

In the normal market at the left, there is a high level of market-making capacity with a similar level of liquidity supply on both sides. The next panel shows the situation at the start of an event. Liquidity demand starts to enter the market, shown as the second bar, and it begins to draw both market-making capacity and liquidity supply to take on this selling pressure. In the third panel, the flood of liquidity demand reduces market-making capacity. The drop in price increases the amount of liquidity demand but has yet to elicit more liquidity supply. This inflection point, which is called a phase transition in complex systems, suggests the moment where everything comes unglued. The abrupt loss of liquidity supply combines with the disappearance of market-making capacity to create inventory for sellers, resulting in a sudden drop in liquidity.[7] This illustrates the difficulties with determining the extent of the liquidity effect during a market event. The effect is both nonlinear and subject to large error on the downside. Prices continue to drop, and by the time depicted in the fourth panel, liquidity supply starts to react. Finally, in the last two panels, the liquidity supply cavalry has arrived with sufficient force to replenish market-making capacity, and most of the liquidity demand has been filled. Prices finally begin to rise to reflect the ending of the liquidity event.

Three components determine the creation of a liquidity-driven dislocation. The first, obviously, is high liquidity demand—a ton of sellers. The other two are the ability of the market makers to take on inventory, and the time required for the liquidity suppliers to arrive to take on the other side of the trade. For low-volume periods, the number of market makers is the

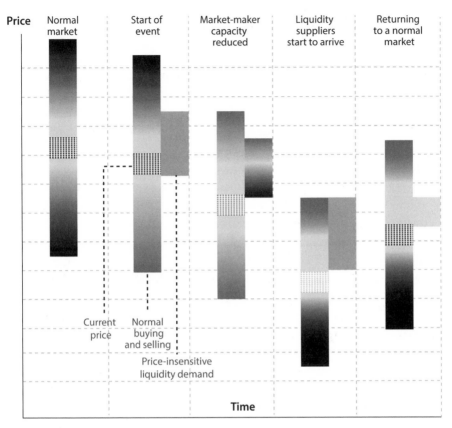

Price | Normal market | Start of event | Market-maker capacity reduced | Liquidity suppliers start to arrive | Returning to a normal market

Current price

Normal buying and selling

Price-insensitive liquidity demand

Time

FIGURE 12.1. **Stages of a liquidity crisis.** The dynamics of liquidity during a market event, with a focus on liquidity demanders, market makers, and liquidity suppliers. The event progresses from left to right. Each long vertical bar indicates the liquidity supply around the current market price. The bar increases in gray scale as it moves away from the current price, indicating an increase in supply. The hashed area is the bid-offer range around the midpoint of the current price, with darker hashes indicating higher market-making capacity. The second panel shows the situation at the start of an event, with event-related liquidity demand entering the market. By the fourth panel, liquidity supply begins to react to the price drop, market-making capacity is then replenished, most of the liquidity demand has been filled, and by the last panel prices begin to rise to reflect the ending of the liquidity event.

most significant determinant of market impact. As we move to periods of high liquidity demand, however, the number of liquidity suppliers becomes primary. In a crisis, everything's in flux: Which agents are under pressure? How concentrated are the various agents to the assets? How do the actions of the liquidity demanders bleed into the ability of the market makers to hold inventory? The evolving interplay of these forces at the time of the event is what matters most.

The Denouement: The Crisis of 2008 and the Threat from Illiquidity

Leverage was pinpointed as the prime mover in 2008, and it remains the focus of academic research and regulatory oversight. But I don't think it will be leverage the next time around. Regulation has moved the risk to liquidity, largely by what it has done to the banks, the key agents involved in market making for the critical rates and credit markets. First, the reforms that came out of the Basel Committee on Banking Supervision restrict the amount of leverage banks can carry. This reduces their capacity to act as market makers. Second, the Volcker Rule, which is part of the Dodd-Frank Act, reduces the incentives for the banks to provide market making. In times of crisis, you need the market makers to buy and hold positions until the liquidity suppliers come in. That is a pretty dicey proposition, because the risk of holding that inventory is very high. But before Volcker and Basel, the banks would do it, because they could make money by trading on their own account against the client flows. If they stepped away, they would find their clients less willing to trade with them when the dust settled, and so they would lose trading revenue down the road. Now they can't trade on their own accounts, so they are more willing to step to the sidelines. I was instrumental in the development of the Volcker Rule, pushing for what is called the market-making exception that allows the banks still to make markets, and I think it or something like it is critical to maintaining financial stability. But like most regulation, especially complex regulations, it comes with unexpected collateral damage. And in this case the damage is to reduce market liquidity.

With this shift from leverage to liquidity, risk has moved into the shadows. Leverage is observable. All you have to do is look at how much money a firm has borrowed, or look at the value of its portfolio versus its capital. But liquidity—that is, the liquidity that really matters, the liquidity that is available when everyone seems to be rushing to sell—is difficult to assess. Most research on asset liquidity focuses on day-to-day market functioning during noncrisis periods, employing measures based on data such as bid-offer spreads and daily volumes drawn from these typical market periods.[8] Such data provide limited insight into the large liquidations during periods of sharp price declines and related fire sale dynamics.[9] If there is one place where a recognition of the agents and their actions—and the use of agent-based methods to determine the effect—is needed, it is in assessing crisis liquidity dynamics.

13

The 2008 Crisis with an Agent-Based View

To put some flesh on the dynamics I presented at the end of chapter 12, it is hard to do much better than the crisis of 2008. It is an embarrassment of riches. The meltdown illustrates how interactions and experience dictate the route of a crisis, and the essential role of reflexivity in creating cascades and contagion. How would an agent-based model have operated during the 2008 crisis?

I was involved in a number of ways with the crisis.[1] First off, I had a sense it was coming. In the first paragraph of my 2007 book, *A Demon of Our Own Design*, I recount my experiences as a risk manager embroiled in various financial crises as a backdrop to my concern that a financial crisis "is going to happen again. The financial markets that we have constructed are so complex" that it is impossible to see where one event will propagate, and it can all happen too quickly for us to respond, so that "apparently isolated actions and even minor events can have catastrophic consequences."

After the book was published and the financial crisis was coursing through the financial system, I testified before Congress several times about a range of financial weaknesses related to it—the roles of derivatives, leverage, complexity, the failures of risk management, and the continuing overhang of systemic risk. Then, as the dust began to settle in 2009, I was recruited by Washington to help restructure the regulatory environment to reduce the prospects for future crises, helping in crafting Dodd-Frank and the Volcker Rule, and setting up the risk management process for the Financial Stability Oversight Council, the senior risk management committee for the financial system, comprising, among others, the secretary of the Treasury and the chairmen of the Fed, the SEC, and the FDIC.

My last role in government was to develop an agent-based model to assess vulnerabilities in the financial system, using 2008 as an object lesson. I left government before the product was realized, and it continues to work its way along. But looking back at the 2008 crisis, it is clear to me that this is the approach to use. If we had looked at the financial crisis through an agent-based model, even as narrative rather than as a blinking-lights simulation, had we been able to use these methods as the crisis ran its course, we would have been able to get ahead of the process and possibly stem its effects. Such a model could show the key agents, the links between them, and the effect of their actions on the environment and then on the actions of others.

Of course, I have the benefit of hindsight. But in this chapter I will show how 2008 could have been structured through, and possibly contained by, an agent-based approach. I will essentially fill in the example at the end of chapter 11 with real agents and actions. The 2008 crisis is complex—it is really a number of crises with their respective agents and environments all rolled into one—and I must pick my spots.

There are the agents and related dynamics in the setting of the stage: the rising leverage, the spate of innovative products that turned pockets of housing troubles into systemic troubles and created a hair-trigger mechanism for defaults. There are the agents embroiled in the climax: the largest bank failures in U.S. history, the drying up of funding that spread to the real economy, and the shotgun weddings between investment banks.[2]

And between the two there is the unraveling of the financial system from early 2007 through mid-2008 as the weaknesses emerged from the shadows and coursed from the small, backwater market of subprime mortgages into the heart of the financial system. I will look at this middle period and the way a storm turned into a hurricane, hit landfall, and directed its path toward the points of maximum damage.

To begin, let's view the financial system through the lens of warfare, taken to the extreme. While working in Washington, I got involved with the Department of Defense on the question: If you were a hostile foreign power, how could you disrupt or destroy the U.S. financial system? That is, how do you create a crisis?

Well, one way to do it begins, as does any strategic offensive, with the right timing. Wait until the system exposes a vulnerability. Maybe that is when it's filled with leverage, and when assets are becoming shaky. Then create a fire sale by pressing down prices to trigger forced selling. (It might cost a couple of billion dollars in the process, but we are talking about war.) At the same time, freeze funding by destroying confidence. Maybe start rumors, maybe pull your money out of institutions with some drama. (And if your ideology extends to making money, short the market before you start pushing things off the cliff.) That, in a nutshell, is what turned the vulnerabilities of 2006 and 2007 into the crisis of 2008, and nearly destroyed our system. And we didn't need an enemy power; we did it all by ourselves.[3]

Cascades, Contagion, and Marks

Before getting into a blow-by-blow account of this period, I should mention that the nature of the cascades and contagion during the 2008 crisis is unusual.

Cascades typically occur because a shock leads a leveraged firm to buckle and be forced to sell. The sale creates downward pressure on prices, leading to further forced liquidations. In the 2008 crisis, the drop in prices and further forced selling did not come from market activity. Prices were marked down by counterparties to levels that bled out key firms and weakened the market, all without any actual selling. The assets were not very liquid, and as things gathered steam, they became less liquid still. There was no market to facilitate what economists call price discovery. Which meant you were at the mercy of the firm lending to you. It was judge and jury; it could pretty much make things up, assert a very low price for the collateral, instigating a margin call, and there was little you could do about it beyond complain and pay up.[4]

This mark-to-market point is a critical one for understanding the development of the crisis. Let's say your bookie demands that you put up $20,000 of collateral for a marker on a $15,000 bet. You give him your gold Rolex watch, worth $20,000. He comes back to you a week later and tells you that you need to put up another $3,000. Why? "People, they aren't so interested in these Rolexes anymore. It's marked down to $17,000." You shell out the $3,000, and a week later he comes back again. "You know that watch. Well, now it is only worth $15,000 so you'll need to scrape up another $2,000." You say, "Wait, I see prices for watches just like it, anywhere from $20,000 to $24,000." He says, "Hey, do you owe them money, or do you owe me money? You've got the marker, I've got the watch, and I say that today it's worth $15,000."

Contagion usually occurs because a firm that is forced to sell due to a price drop in one market is compelled to pull out cash by selling in other markets where it holds positions, so the prices in those markets drop as well. This was not the dominant route of contagion in the 2008 crisis. It was the result of structured products that shared exposure in the subprime market—or were thought to share exposure. Rather than who owned what, the question was what contained what.

To see this, look at the structured financial products coming out of a trading desk in the way petroleum products come out of the distillation tower in a refinery. There, crude oil comes in, and is separated or "cracked" into various grades of products, from heavy heating oil to light naphtha. The raw material for the structured products at the heart of the 2008 crisis was mortgage-backed securities (MBSs), and the distilled products are various grades or tranches of collateralized debt obligations (CDOs), where the grade is determined by the risk of default. Just as any product coming out of the distillation process depends on the crude oil that feeds the process, any CDO coming out of the securitization process will have the markings of the MBS that comprises the feedstock. If the feedstock is tainted or diluted, the structured products will be as well. If the feedstock includes subprime mortgages that rise in defaults, any security that comes out of the process, or that uses those products as its own raw material, will be affected.

Agents

For the agents in 2008, it is a matter of filling in the blanks in figure 11.1. There are banks operating in their various roles; hedge funds; cash providers; and various other financial institutions. There is buying and selling of assets, borrowing and lending, posting or taking in collateral. The agents we all know; at the end of the day, it is a small group: the banks are JP Morgan and Citigroup; the broker-dealers (which, if they survived, became banks down the road) are those that are in the thick of trouble—Bear Stearns and Merrill Lynch. And causing the trouble all around, Goldman Sachs. The two hedge funds that set it all off are housed in Bear Stearns Asset Management; the financial institutions are AIG and some others that in the grand scheme of things had bit parts, a few monolines and a few mortgage firms. And there are the rating agencies that helped nudge things over the edge: Moody's and S&P.

Subprime mortgages—a sliver of the mortgage market—started it all off. Then as things gathered steam, anything that smelled of subprime became garbage: CDOs on subprime and then on anything with mortgage exposure; asset-backed commercial paper backed by mortgage securities; structured investment vehicles (SIVs) that might have mortgage exposure; and credit default swaps (CDSs) meant to insure against firms with these various sorts of exposure—CDSs held as investments, as inventory, and as collateral.

The Ball Gets Rolling

THE PREDATORS' BALL

Hedge funds have looked for a free pass on the 2008 crisis, because it centered on the banks.[5] But the first shot fired came from two hedge funds at Bear Stearns Asset Management (BSAM), and things fell apart quickly from there. These were the Enhanced Leverage Fund and the High-Grade Fund, both of which invested mostly in mortgage-backed securities and CDOs based on subprime mortgages.

Soon after its launch in 2006, the Enhanced Fund ran into trouble as a benchmark index for its holdings, the ABX BBB−, fell 4 percent in the last quarter of 2006, and another 8 percent in January 2007. February was even worse—the index tumbled 25 percent. Investors began to leave both funds. By the end of April 2007, the two hedge funds were down 50 percent. The flood gates of investor redemptions were opening.

As things worsened, lenders evaluated the collateral posted by the funds and began to issue margin calls. The first step in this process was valuing the collateral. For liquid, frequently traded securities like public equities this is easy to do. You simply check the market price. But the soup of securitized products like collateralized mortgage obligations did not trade frequently, so value was based on dealer marks, which are estimates of where the dealer thinks the security would trade. These marks are critical for the system, because portfolios and thus earnings and even the viability of the firm depend on their value, as does the collateral that is securing their loans. Marking securities to market is largely an exercise in goodwill. There is nothing to bind the mark; the dealer does not have to buy at that price; there is no recourse even if a dealer pulls a number out of a hat. This is a flaw in the system that became a recurring problem. In particular, Goldman Sachs marked its mortgage-based securities far lower than those of other dealers. This created crippling effects for many of its clients, the first in line being the two BSAM hedge funds.

On April 2, 2007, Goldman sent marks to BSAM as low as 65 cents on the dollar, which meant that some of the hedge funds' securities were being valued at a discount of 35 percent. These were substantially lower than marks coming from other dealers, but were added into the average of the dealer marks that were used for pricing the portfolios. On May 1, Goldman pushed its marks down even more, to as low as 55 cents on the dollar. This led the reported value of the Enhanced Leverage Fund for April, which had been marked down 6.6 percent already, to be revised down 19 percent. Anticipating the onslaught of this revision, BSAM immediately froze redemptions. The death spiral commenced.

After BSAM froze redemptions, Merrill Lynch seized $850 million of collateral that had been posted against its loans. What Merrill did with this collateral was critical for the market. Firms with exposure in subprime were holding their breath. They all knew that prices were collapsing, but until there were trades at those prices they did not have to mark down their positions. There was a quiet pact across the broker-dealers to hold off selling into the market. But eventually someone wants to get his money and breaks rank. Merrill began to sell. Now there was a market price for marking positions, spreading the impact beyond the BSAM hedge funds.

The illiquid market, further stressed by these events and already anticipating a flood of selling of the hedge funds' positions, was primed for a classic fire sale. Prices continued to crater, creating another round of margin calls and increasing the clamor for investor redemptions. By the end of July 2007, the run on the BSAM funds, as well as the shutdown in funding, forced both to file for bankruptcy.

Rather than contain the damage, the collapse of the two funds spread it. Pushed along by exquisitely timed but long overdue downgrades and negative watch warnings on structured products, the ABX BBB– index fell 33 percent in July. The forces that brought down the BSAM hedge funds broke into the broader market. Investors in commercial paper, who had abandoned BSAM early on, started to pull away from other borrowers. Repo lenders tightened credit extension to other borrowers by increasing the haircut on subprime collateral, increasing the margin requirements on institutions with mortgage exposure, and shrinking loan terms, especially for firms that were considered potentially problematic. Other firms that had used mortgage-backed securities as collateral faced greater demands, and had to sell liquid assets to meet these demands, which became a conduit for contagion.

Stage 1 of figure 13.1 traces out the pathways for this period in the evolution of the crisis, which occurred between April and June, 2007. The dark lines are the agents of the system that were embroiled in this stage.

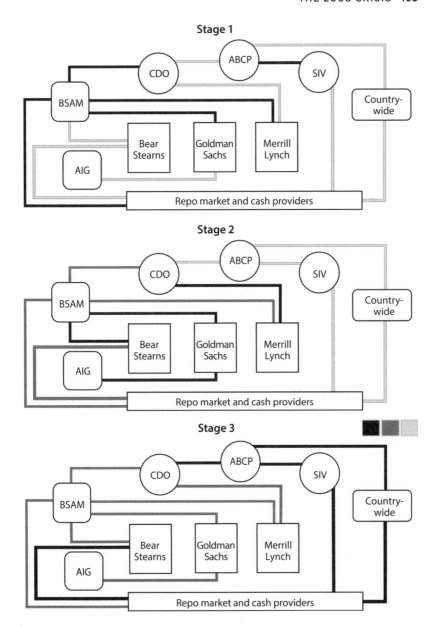

FIGURE 13.1. **Stages of propagation during part of the 2008 crisis in an agent-based model setting.** Stage 1 shows the period April–June 2007, focusing on the failure of the BSAM hedge funds. Stage 2 shows the period June–July 2007, with AIG and the CDO market becoming a focus. Stage 3 traces the pathways of the crisis from August through the fall of 2007, as contagion spreads to other markets, and hits the funding sources from various directions. The dark lines indicate the agents of the system that were embroiled in the particular stage; the intermediate shaded lines indicate agents that continue to be involved from an earlier stage; the light lines indicate agents that have not yet become involved.

MORE OF THE SAME

On July 26, as the BSAM funds were in their death throes, Goldman next set its sights on one of its major clients, the giant insurance company turned derivatives house, AIG. Goldman held $21 billion of AIG's credit default swaps, a form of insurance against downgrades in credit.[6] Goldman began to work its mark-to-market voodoo again, marking AIG's CDOs as low as 80 cents on the dollar, far below the consensus of the other broker-dealers. Merrill Lynch, for example, valued the same securities at 95 cents or higher. On one particular CDO, Goldman used a price of 75 cents on the dollar, while other dealers valued it at 95 cents. The view at AIG was that Goldman was pursuing a strategy to "cause maximum pain to their competitors."[7] One AIG trader, while acknowledging that the marks could be "anything from 80 to 95," recalled that Goldman's marks were "ridiculous."[8]

In all of this there were no shots fired, so to speak, no trades taking place. In fact, Goldman, perhaps somewhat cynically, offered to sell AIG securities at their low mark, knowing that AIG would never take Goldman up on the offer, because doing so would put a market price out there, and force AIG to mark its entire portfolio at the disastrously low prices. With Goldman leading the pack, other firms piled on. SocGen came in with a margin call based on a mark that was provided to it by Goldman.[9] The dance of low marks and demands for margin—with Goldman sending a formal demand letter every day—continued for fourteen months, in the end pulling tens of billions of dollars out of AIG and leading to the breathtakingly large bailout of the firm.

Stage 2 of figure 13.1 traces out the pathways of this next stage of the crisis, which occurred in June and July, 2007. As in the other two stages, the dark lines are the agents that started to become involved in this stage. The intermediate shaded lines are those from stage 1 that continue to be involved in this stage.

LOOKING UNDER EVERY ROCK

Contagion arose as the market began to look for possible subprime exposures lurking in other assets. It found them in the asset-backed commercial paper (ABCP) market, a key source of short-term funding for many firms. ABCP is a way firms can borrow against the collateral that backed the commercial paper, and much of that collateral was mortgage-based securities, including subprime.

One of the largest borrowers in this market was the German bank IKB.[10] Goldman, which had helped raise capital for IKB's commercial program, suddenly withdrew. This was the starter's gun for a broader-scale abandonment, and Deutsche Bank cut off its credit lines. IKB's difficulties led the ABCP market to freeze up. And this was not limited to ABCPs backed by mortgages. No one was splitting hairs; if it was ABCP, it was considered toxic. Which proved disastrous for firms that relied on the ABCP market for their funding. Most notable in the line behind IKB was Countrywide Financial, one of the leading subprime lenders. In early August, Countrywide found that it could not roll over its commercial paper, leading to downgrades, investor panic, and a run on the bank. On one day alone, August 16, customers pulled out $8 billion.

IF IT MOVES, KILL IT

In August, another fire break was overrun with the market for SIVs. Though there were some SIVs with some subprime exposure, generally SIVs had little to do with the mortgage market and were not subject to the short-term vagaries of the market. They were funded mostly through medium-term notes that were liquid, and unlike many of the mortgage products, the fact that they traded frequently meant that they could be marked to actual market trades. But at this point, a whiff of mortgage exposure was enough.

With funding already restricted in the repo market by higher margins and demands for higher-quality collateral, with the ABCP market seizing up and SIVs dead in the water, the fall of 2007 reached a panic point when money market funds started to face problems. SIVs were a particular issue here, because these were held widely by money market funds. The money market funds were a prime source of the raw material—they were the ultimate cash provider—that found its way through the SIVs and other instruments.

Another funding source that got clobbered came through trouble with monoline insurers. The two largest monoline bond insurers, MBIA and Ambac, had taken $265 billion of guarantees on mortgage-backed securities and related structured products. These and other monoline insurers had no capital cushion to speak of; they had a "zero loss tolerance" business model. Any losses, and they were gone. This spurred an unusual contagion: the monolines also provided protection to auction rate securities (ARSs), securities that fundamentally were unrelated to the mortgage market. These reset by auction every few weeks, but in February 2008, the concern with the monolines led these auctions to fail, and as a result the borrowers were trapped, their liquidity gone, and rates that usually were in the 3–4 percent range reset at 10–20 percent.

Stage 3 of figure 13.1 traces out the pathways of this stage of the crisis, which occurred in the period from August through the fall of 2007. (Because of space concerns, the figure does not include the path from the monolines to ARSs.)

The Beginning of the End

With markets in a tailspin, firms that had large inventories of CDOs and other mortgage-related products were seeing losses that were beyond their comprehension. The largest were Citigroup and Merrill Lynch, which had to write down $24 billion and $25 billion, respectively.[11] Within days of each other, the CEO of Merrill, Stanley O'Neal, and that of Citi, Chuck Prince, resigned.

The stage for the panic in the fall of 2008 was set where things began: at 383 Madison Avenue, the headquarters of Bear Stearns. The parent company of Bear Stearns Asset Management and its two ill-fated hedge funds, Bear had upped its equity investment in the more troubled fund, the Enhanced Leverage Fund, and as funding dried up, the firm became the sole repo lender to the High-Grade Fund, loaning it $1.6 billion. When Bear took the funds' exposures onto its own book, the market dislocations passed through to it. So it sat in the crosshairs of its lenders. And Bear Stearns was already heavily exposed to the same subprime garbage that had led to the demise of the two hedge funds. Mortgage securitization was the biggest piece of the Bear Stearns fixed-income operation, and the firm was one of the top underwriters of CDOs. After the two BSAM hedge funds declared bankruptcy, the credit rating firm Standard & Poor's placed Bear Stearns on a "negative outlook," citing the failed funds, the company's mortgage-related investments (many of which S&P had blithely rated AAA), and its relatively small capital base.

Bear had traditionally used unsecured commercial paper for much of its financing, but with rising concern from cash providers, this funding route closed down. Bear instead became critically dependent on the repo market for a day-to-day flow of funding, and relied on the collateral from its prime brokerage business to fuel that lending.[12] Other banks began to refuse Bear Stearns as a counterparty, stoking concerns about default. Hedge fund clients using Bear Stearns as their prime broker became concerned that Bear would be unable to return their cash and securities, and started to withdraw. Some repo lenders were unwilling to lend to Bear even against U.S. treasuries as collateral. From the time of the hedge fund failures and related actions, the do-or-die issue for Bear Stearns was retaining the confidence of its sources of collateral and funding. That was it; there was no fundamental solvency problem with Bear beyond that.

That confidence was broken by none other than Goldman Sachs. When a firm wants to get out of a derivatives position, it is typical in the derivatives business to assign that derivative in a procedure called a novation. On Tuesday, March 11, 2008, a small hedge fund, Hayman Capital Partners, decided to close out a $5 million derivatives position it held against Goldman. Bear Stearns offered the best bid, and so Hayman planned to assign the position to Bear, which would then become Goldman's counterparty. Hayman notified Goldman, and Goldman wrote back, "GS does not consent to this trade." It was all but unprecedented for a counterparty to reject a routine novation; and at $5 million, this was peanuts. The next morning, Goldman simply said, "We do not want to face Bear."[13]

When news hit the street that Goldman had refused the transaction with Bear, the game was over.[14] All confidence was gone. On Thursday, March 13, Bear reported to the SEC that many of its operations would not be open for business the next day. It was a breakdown for the firm, and ultimately for the financial system. With the demise of Bear Stearns and the related runs by repo lenders, hedge fund customers, and derivative counterparties, whatever had remained of funding liquidity dried up for the broader market. The two clearing banks for the repo market, JP Morgan and BNY Mellon, which were on the hook for credit events that happened intraday, began demanding overcollateralization, and higher-quality collateral, and simply would not ensure access to the repo market for counterparties who seemed to be at risk, no matter what their collateral. In this world, if you had leverage that required short-term funding, if you had assets that could not be liquidated, if you had high exposure to the markets that had collapsed, you were the walking dead.

The End of Theory

14

Is It a Number or a Story?
Model as Narrative

I'm a frustrated novelist. It's an interest that surfaces from time to time. My first attempt, in the 1980s, was a thriller that portrayed a world without physical currency, where all transactions were done on a system called transNet, and where the central plot revolved around a group bent on destroying the records of that system, throwing the world into chaos. (In other words, Bitcoin gone rogue on a global scale.) There was a backup copy of transNet held in vaults deep under the mountains in Utah (where Mormons keep copies of their genealogical records), but the plot included the erasure of those records once they surfaced. If anyone is interested, I could dust it off and try to finish it, but now the plot would not be so original. Not that originality means much for thrillers.

I undertook my most recent effort a few years ago, when I was spending four days a week in an apartment in Washington, D.C., while doing a stint of public service. By this time, I recognized that I couldn't compose a thriller because I am too literal-minded. Whenever thriller-type actions or plot turns are called for, I instead think through why this stuff is not entirely plausible, and each step toward plausibility is a step away from a good story. So I turned to writing a more high-arch novel about the boundaries of our knowledge. It tells of a man in two relationships, one with a woman who apparently is rooted in reality but actually is not, and the second with a woman who is otherworldly and with whom he has to convert an indistinguishable mix of fantasy and reality into something tangible and trusting. Given my literary references thus far, you might guess that I patterned it after Kundera. I had the characters, and I had the theme, which in Kundera's view is more critical than the plot. But I couldn't work out a plot, which is not a good place to find yourself if you are writing a novel.

So I engaged a real novelist to help me figure out how to get a plot going. She told me that there are two ways to develop a plot. One is to outline the entire plot from start to finish, and then fill in the blanks—characters, dialogue, that sort of thing. The other is the road-in-the-headlights approach, where you know basically where you are going, but you navigate each twist and turn in the road as it happens. Thrillers tend to go with the second approach. From a novelistic standpoint, they depend on a sort of "I didn't see that coming" radical uncertainty for the plot, even though structurally they are ever so predictable.

Similarly, there are two ways to develop a model. One is to map out the world in a mechanistic way and have a model that (you hope) will predict the course of the story from start to finish. The other is to build a model that is flexible and unanchored, that adjusts with each unexpected twist in the road. Crises are like thrillers, in that you can't envision where things might end up until they are nearly on top of you. The road-in-the-headlights approach is the way to go.[1]

I have argued that we need a departure in the way we build models. But we also need a departure from the way we employ a model, any model, in the deliberation of financial risk. Whatever the value of the output of economic models, they are not particularly useful because they do not relate to how crises actually unfold. They also do not relate to the way decisions are made over the course of a crisis, which gets to another reason the novel is a good point of departure. When I've been in the middle of a crisis like the 1987 crash, I am sitting around a table with the various characters working through a story line; as a crisis evolves we are trying to fit a narrative to the events and develop a good, supportable plot line going forward. The effective model is a tool for developing these qualitative narratives, not a machine that spits out numbers onto the table. In the narrative mode, the agent-based model conforms with the investment approach to decision making and the deliberations during crisis events.

The point isn't to crank out and act on a number. It is to set up a model to see what light can be shed on a real-world problem, and to see if it can fit a larger, intuitive narrative about what is going on. The decision makers pose a narrative and then test it for believability—is the plot line a reasonable one? In a sense, every time we run the model, we are generating a possible, plausible story of how a crisis might unfold. And in a crisis, when the engineering mindset no longer serves, what matters is whether the story makes sense. The point about agent-based modeling is not to throw out a number, but to guide and support this collective narrative.[2]

This is the secret for having a model to deal with the last of the four horsemen, the planet of inexperience, for having a model that overcomes the problem of how to model something that you assert at the outset you cannot model. In a world of radical uncertainty, narratives unfold in concert with the dynamic. Each chapter builds on the previous one. The agents, the environment, the heuristic may all change. And every story is different.

If You Can Model It, You're Wrong

Models are pointless under these circumstances; I am not proposing a specific model to deal with crises. I am putting forward a process, a paradigm that, at any point in time, will be manifest as a model for that period. But as the crisis unfolds and components of radical uncertainty appear, the model will shift with the emerging reality. There is no solution or answer. We operate in a world of inexperience and are guided by a model couched in ambiguity. That is why I am opposed to an axiomatic doctrine of economics. As Keynes wrote, "We are merely reminding ourselves that human decisions affecting the future, whether personal or political or economic, cannot depend on strict mathematical expectation, since the basis for making such calculations does not exist; and that it is our innate urge to activity which makes the wheels go round, our rational selves choosing between the alternatives as best as we are able, calculating where we can, but often falling back for a motive on whim or sentiment or chance."[3]

Let's turn again to warfare, where radical uncertainty is the stock in trade, and to the military strategist John Boyd. He gave a warning at an address to the Air War College: "The Air Force has got a doctrine, the Army's got a doctrine, Navy's got a doctrine, everybody's got a doctrine." But of his own work, he said, "doctrine doesn't appear in there even once. You can't find it. You know why I don't have it in there? Because it's doctrine on day one, and every day after it becomes dogma." If you have to write down a doctrine, "assume it's not right. And look at a whole lot of other doctrines" so that you do not become a disciple of any one doctrine. Instead, "you can lift stuff out of here, stuff out of there."

His message is: "If you got one doctrine, you're a dinosaur. Period." And if you've got one model, you are a dinosaur. Period.

Such is Boyd's mode of thinking, which the military theorist Antoine Bousquet summarizes as a belief in a "perpetually renewed world that is 'uncertain, ever-changing, unpredictable' and thus requires continually revising, adapting, destroying and recreating our theories and systems to deal with it." Grant Hammond, the author of *The Mind of War*, expresses it this way: "Ambiguity is central to Boyd's vision . . . not something to be feared but something that is a given. . . . We never have complete and perfect information. We are never completely sure of the consequences of our actions. . . . The best way to succeed . . . is to revel in ambiguity."[4]

Economic models are designed to do away with ambiguity. Certainly, it will be a rocky path to publication for someone who proposes a model that is rife with ambiguity and can't get to a clear answer. But we should admit things into the model that are not themselves explained by the model, and that change in ways that cannot be predetermined within the structure of the model. More broadly and profoundly, the model itself should not be fixed; it will change as the environment changes, and will change in ways that cannot be anticipated. (If it could be, then that would simply redefine the model.) This gets to the nature of Boyd's "Game of ? and ?" and the related concept of reflexivity. You can never write something down (or program it up) and say, "This is it; this is the model." We cannot have a fixed, self-contained model of a social system.

Someone clever might say that if we have variability in the model we use, then we can develop a model for our models, and then that is actually our model. How do we answer this; how do we get outside of ourselves to be able to know the model we will have, and keep that different from some model that determines what model we will have? It is radical uncertainty that prevents us from creating a model of all our future models. We cannot know or even anticipate some things until they are sitting in front of us.

And yet, I seem to have put forward a model that traces all of this. So if everybody uses that model, will the emergent phenomena and other aspects disappear? Won't we be back in the rational expectations world, albeit arguably with a better model? And if we don't do that and a model is available for everyone who deals with these issues, then aren't we assuming that people are stupid? We can then get back to business, restate the point of demanding rationality, rigor, and consistency, and simply move that argument to the current model.

In any nontrivial setting of even minimal complexity—which means almost any real-world economic situation—the true underlying model will not be given a priori to the agents, knowledge of initial conditions and parameters will be limited, data will be finite and noisy, computing power will be finite, and the agents doing the observing will also be participants in the system. This means that in almost any real-world situation, the internal models of agents must be fallible. And that fallibility is also part of the system that the agents are trying to understand. We thus have the self-referential, recursive loop that is at the center of Soros's concept, which Eric Beinhocker illustrates: fallible agents try to understand and act in an environment of fallible agents trying to understand and act in an environment of fallible agents trying to understand. . . . Predicting the future path of such a system then requires perfect knowledge of the agent's own fallibility and the fallibility of all other agents—perfect knowledge of fallibility is truly a contradiction in terms.[5]

Yet, it is precisely these limits to knowledge and the fallibility that they imply that the rational expectations hypothesis (REH) in economics assumes away.[6] Under REH, we all live in a simple world without either interactive or dynamic complexity and we all act perfectly rationally whatever the economic situation. Some may argue that REH incorporates reflexivity because it models two-way feedback between agent beliefs and the world. But REH does not incorporate any fundamental limits to knowledge in complex environments, the inevitable fallibility and heterogeneity such limits introduce, or the deep indeterminacy that reflexive interactions between fallible agents create.[7]

This point requires us to once again reflect on the real world rather than an abstract one. People do not use the same model, and they do not universally accept the agent-based modeling methodology. So it will not be the case that many people employ this model. But if people do, then that model can be used as part of their heuristics. And that will then change the model itself. This gets back to some extent to the point that if you know the model you are wrong. And you get into the loop of: I know the model, but he knows that I know the model and so he changes his model, in which case I have to change my model. Couple that with the uncertainty that we have in terms of knowing other people and you have a situation where you cannot all be sharing the same model. Another way to think about it is that it will most likely be the case that there is no fixed-point solution. The assumptions that are necessary for such a solution are extremely restrictive and would be unlikely to be met in real life. Also, there is a level K problem. People do not think through level after level in the "I know he knows that I know" loop.[8]

This is along the lines of Frydman and Goldberg's imperfect knowledge economics, which dismisses mechanistic and predetermined models and the neoclassical construct that market participants steadfastly rely on one forecasting strategy. Instead, "profit-seeking market participants revise their forecasting strategies at times and in ways that they themselves, let alone an economist, cannot fully foresee—especially given that institutions, economic policies, and other features of the social context that underpin movements of fundamentals also change in non-routine ways."

Yet, look at the efforts of the academic industry, spilling over to the regulators, to analyze the potential for future crises. What are they up to? Right now, having dug our way out of the 2008 crisis, they are by and large preparing for the next crisis by trying all sorts of leverage-related measures and analysis. Why? Because leverage was identified as the culprit the last time around. Look around and you will see a burgeoning industry of models and systems developed by various academics to produce measure of systemic risk. They all mix bank leverage with some other special sauce, run everything backward and pinpoint many months in advance the banks that ended up being enveloped by the crisis. Well, guess what. Take away the special sauce, build a model based only on leverage—or simply make a chart of leverage—and you get pretty much the same result, because we know that in the specific case of the banks in the specific case of the 2008 crisis, ultimately leverage was that culprit.

Perhaps it was natural for Jevons and others to have reached into the toolkit of the methods used for the natural world to build the underpinnings of economics. Insofar as how we behave looks like other natural phenomena or the workings of the mechanics of physics, it can carry over well enough. In what way are our human interactions different from the coursing of celestial bodies? In what way are people different from machines? It is that our actions and feedback change the world, and do so in part by changing the way we look at the world, changing the problems posed and the models to address those problems.

So we need to have models that do not close, that are perpetually incomplete, accommodating the limits of our knowledge. Methods that require closure, or that act omnisciently—and being subject to error around the edges still defines the world from an omniscient viewpoint—miss the fundamentals of humanity. If we inhabit a day-to-day world, then this miss might not matter. On the other hand, if we are looking at the time scale of societies and civilizations, or at the scale of dislocation of a world gone to the dogs from war, pestilence, or famine, these fundamentals come to the fore. Financial crises are a tame version of the latter. By whatever cause, once we are off the rails, we are facing a system that has uncoupled, where the approaches that work in normal times are not off by just a few degrees.

Once we reach the limits to knowledge in dealing with humanity, with people, in the scale that admits changes in the model or changes in how we view the world, we have lost both the ability to create a model and the repeatability of an experiment. That is, we cannot look at the behavior in past crises as determinate of the future. This means, among other things, that we cannot test in the standard econometric way.

Which gets us to the issue of testing and estimation. I am presenting the concept of agent-based models, and specifically how it relates to crises, as a paradigm rather than an engineering how-to treatise. That allows me to bypass the difficult aspects of how you estimate the parameters of the model, and how you test it empirically. How do you do that if there is no model, if the world you want to model will not look like the past? A model result is not reproducible if crises do not repeat, if people change over time based on experiences, or if the agents of the model affect the world and alter it in unanticipated ways, any more than you can repeat a strategy for battle, because having done it once, the enemy will react differently and in an unanticipatable way.

We move through the world traveling along a single path. When we look at history as a guide for crises, we get only that one path. That path is not repeatable. And if we had a time machine to go back and try another path (and, needless to say, could take actions to alter the world without having all matter and antimatter collide, which as I understand it is the general risk that this poses), we cannot go on board at any arbitrary point and see the same story unfold from that point onward. Let's state that the world is not ergodic. This means, among other things, that we cannot test crisis-related models in the standard econometric way. If we want to understand a crisis, we have to construct a story, and we must be willing to do so in the "road in the headlights" fashion: ready to change the narrative as the story line develops. A change in narrative means a change in model, and the model changes are not simply a matter of revising the values of various parameters, be it by the statistical tool of Bayesian updating or whatever. It might be a change in heuristics, in the types of agents in the system.[9]

The Model Builder as Pragmatist

At the outset, I argued that we need to add humanity to the process, that this leads to radical uncertainty of the kind that is swept under the rug in today's mathematical, axiomatic neoclassical economic model. The best reflection of humanity comes through literature, not logic. Models need to be like novels, molding to twists and turns and unexpected shifts. The key actors and their approaches to the environment change, just as in literature we see one person go from evil to good and another from optimistic to embittered as events unfold.

One of the great modernist novels of the twentieth century, *The Man without Qualities* by Robert Musil, gives us as the protagonist a man who could well be a refugee from the axiomatic world of the standard economic model: Ulrich is a mathematician in the midst of an existential crisis, questioning his vocation, removing himself from the formality of logic and moving into "a web of haze, imaginings, fantasy and the subjunctive mood." For Ulrich's frame of mind, Musil coins the term *essayism* and calls those who live by it *possibilists*.[10] Musil sought to describe with essayism a "solution in the absence of a solution"; trying things out one way and then another, following one fork in the path and then doubling back to the other, not seeking out the rigor and decisiveness of mathematical proofs but instead approaching the world with a sense of limited knowledge, an aloofness to any certification of what is real or true.[11] The possibilists act with "the capacity to think how everything could 'just as easily' be, and to attach no more importance to what is than to what is not." The scholar Ross Posnock has remarked that Ulrich's mindset forms "a modernist paradigm for new ways to be human, one that extends backward and forward, echoing Emerson, Nietzsche, William James, pragmatism, Bergson, . . . and existentialism."[12] I'll stop at pragmatism.

For the pragmatist, in the view of the controversial neopragmatist Richard Rorty, the "claim that we now have an interpretation of the world which gets it right," is nothing more than "a self-deceptive way of praising the interpretation which chimes with our hopes and fears, rather than with somebody else's."[13] He writes that the pragmatist thinks that calling "a belief 'true' is no more than to say it is good to steer our practice by." There is no "big synthetic practice called 'being rational' or 'seeking Truth.'" There is no "Reality as It Is in Itself." And, I would add, certainly not when dealing with human nature, certainly not through puffing up so thin a part of human nature as economics, and certainly not in the face of the radical uncertainty surrounding a crisis.

Mine is a pragmatic rather than theoretical or axiomatic view. It is one shared by the philosopher of science Thomas Kuhn (1962), who uses the term *normal science* to describe the sort of work most science is engaged in. Normal science aims to extend and refine the existing paradigm. The paradigms we have in science now are not closer than earlier paradigms to an ideal or perfect paradigm; science is not heading toward a final paradigm that is superior to all others. There is not some ideal paradigm that can govern all of science. In this sense, science is pragmatic.

There are many worlds that might have occurred. There are many ways to evaluate those worlds. And there are many paths the world can take. Pragmatic thinking employs any number of tools rather than putting all our chips on "the combined assumptions of maximizing behavior, market equilibrium, and stable preferences, used relentlessly and consistently." Boyd said that "if you're in an equilibrium condition, you're dead."[14] Orientation, the second of his four-stage OODA loop, "isn't just a state you're in; it's a process. You're always orienting." I am arguing against the equilibrium condition and for a process, one that has feedback that requires constant reorientation. It is agile modeling: the model is reoriented over the course of the process. The model changes with time and circumstance. There is no machine, there is no black box, there are no formal principles, no provably correct answers, no solution. What there is, is a process where we can have a model at any point in time that can illuminate and augment our narrative. What von Moltke observed for war and art is also true for the complexity of crises: talent cannot be replaced by precept.

Agile Modeling

There are two ways to catch a fly ball—the easy way and the hard way.

The hard way to catch the ball is to measure the velocity and spin of the ball immediately after it leaves the bat, understand the medium through which the ball will travel—air resistance and wind velocity—feed these into a differential equation, which itself is the product of a centuries-old mathematical enterprise, plug it all into a computer and then identify the exact spot on the field that corresponds in real life to the coordinates of the output. (And don't forget to yell, "I got it.")

The easy way to catch the ball is the way ballplayers actually go about the task. If the ball is already high in the air by the time you react, fix your gaze on the ball, start running, and adjust your running speed so that the angle of gaze remains constant. This is called the gaze heuristic.[15] A player who relies on the gaze heuristic can ignore all the variables that underlie the physics of generating a baseball's trajectory; he can ignore the question of why and how the ball has ended up going where it's going, and pay attention to only one variable. He will not know where he and the ball will end up until he is at that spot, but when he does get there, the ball will be there as well. This gaze heuristic is also used by animal species for catching prey and for intercepting potential mates. Bats, birds, and dragonflies maintain a constant optical angle between themselves and their prey—as do dogs when catching a Frisbee.[16]

The heuristic we use for catching the baseball is philosophically distinct from the mathematical approach, and this philosophical distinction extends beyond how we catch a baseball to how we run our lives, interact socially, and in general how we operate as humans. The difference between these approaches is the difference between the philosophical foundation of the natural sciences and the (correct) philosophical foundation for the social sciences. More to the specific point, it is the reason agent-based models are the correct approach to use to deal with financial crises, and economic models are not.

DEDUCTIVE AND INDUCTIVE APPROACHES

The hard way to catch the ball is deductive. Deduction starts with general propositions or axioms, and applies logic and mathematics to derive principles from them. It might be that the axioms are proposed based on a view of how the world works, but the results do not depend on that.[17]

The easy way to catch the ball is inductive. Induction looks at specific cases, and generalizes from them. The end result of those generalizations can be the formulation of a deductive argument, but more generally induction is like learning from experience.[18] Whereas the deductive approach is built on mathematics and formal logic, the inductive approach is more of a hodgepodge, a broadly interdisciplinary approach that might make use of statistics and mathematics, might get its bearing through historical study and literature, or might use heuristics that are only loosely tied to observation and past experience.

The critical distinction between the deductive and inductive approach is that deduction can solve a problem, in the sense that you can know the result based on the mathematical proof or applying the results of a formula. Deduction leads to general solutions, to mathematical shortcuts for solving a problem. With induction you do not (and perhaps cannot) take such a shortcut; you can only know the result by seeing things through to the end. A computationally irreducible problem can be tackled only through an inductive approach, but other problems, ones that can conceptually be solved using deductive methods, can also be solved inductively, as the baseball example illustrates. The deductive approach that would solve for all the variables the instant the bat strikes the ball can shortcut the process of watching the ball in flight. (Although that would surely take the fun out of it.) The inductive approach comes from the heuristic, which can determine the point where the ball will land only by following the unfolding of the event. You've got to play the game.

Life is inductive. You know where we are going only once you arrive. Economics uses a deductive approach; the agent-based model is inductive. With an inductive approach there is continued revision of the model, not just revision of the estimates for parameters, but the nature of the heuristics and the network of interactions—or at least it is natural to have such revision, while for a deductive approach revisions suggest that either the axioms or their implications manifest through the mathematical development are wrong.

The deductive, analytical approach, though requiring a lot more information, can tell you the instant the ball is hit where it will land. It gives you a predetermined model. With the inductive, heuristic algorithm you know where things will end up only by executing the act of catching the ball, in either a real or a simulated setting. You can't know the spot where you'll catch the ball until you run through that world, until you experience the flight of the ball up to the point it lands in your mitt. On the other hand, if there is a shift in the wind that was not known to the deductive player, his calculation will be off, whereas there is a chance the inductive player will still succeed. If there is some measurement error, the inductive approach will be more robust.

The inductive approach depends on context—it is not going to work (or cannot be demonstrated to work unless it can be cast into a deductive proof) in every case. Rather, with the inductive approach, we do not try to solve the problem at the start based on axioms and logical deductions for all time and all people. We move forward and essentially live our lives as the world unfolds. It is environmentally based, so as the environment changes, we take it into account. Environment is specific to the context, because we allow the context to unfold.

ECONOMICS AND THE DEDUCTIVE APPROACH

Enamored as they are with deductive methods, economists continue to take omniscience as the starting assumption: that we catch the ball the hard way. *The Selfish Gene*'s Richard Dawkins describes our baseball player (and I suppose, by extension, bats, birds, and dragonflies): "he behaves as if he had solved a set of differential equations in predicting the trajectory of the ball. . . . At some subconscious level, something functionally equivalent to the mathematical calculations is going on."[19] It is very mysterious—at "some subconscious level" we are doing something "as if" we are solving a differential equation. We don't do this. We don't even try.

Economics has chosen a paradigm that seeks to solve at the beginning the way things will wind up at the end. It tries to figure out where the ball will land as soon as it leaves the bat. Economics solves the problem in a general setting based on a set of rules that constitute the way people act. It does this because from the time of Jevons it has used the methods of what he and others of his generation called mechanical science.[20] Economics thus does not allow for the midcourse corrections of the outfielder or changes in the environment that come about from the complexity of interactions, the core of what makes a crisis a crisis.

Economists like Gary Becker regard a valid scientific theory as a representation of the truth—a description of the world that is independent of time, place, context, or the observer. To do so they apply a deductive approach, built on axioms that provide a truth for the markets, a truth that applies for economic beings as well as us humans at any time and any place on Earth. By contrast, the bottom-up approach of looking at how people interact and seeing where that drives the world employs an inductive process. It uses experience and observation; it might use mathematics, but, as with historical analysis, it might proceed through narrative. This is a pivotal difference between the methods of economics and the methods I espouse: understanding crises is as much an exercise in pasting together a story line as it is developing a theoretical structure. Borges said, "Reality is not always probable, or likely. But if you're writing a story, you have to make it as plausible as you can."[21] When we face a crisis, we corral our experience and intuition to create a narrative, and ask, simply, do we buy the story? So a new concept: *agent-based narrative.*

ECONOMISTS, DEDUCTION, AND THE REAL WORLD

One of my sons studied mathematics and computer science at Yale, and because at that school even the most vaunted faculty member teaches undergraduates, he had the privilege of taking his freshman calculus class under one of the world's great mathematicians. He was soon dismayed to find that in one homework assignment and test after another he was getting zero points for some of his proofs and full credit for others. No partial credit. For this professor, either a proof was right or it was wrong. He could not see, either for his own work or for that of his students, that there could be a proof that was wrong, but just a little bit wrong or close to correct. A proof was a proof, and if it wasn't a proof, then it wasn't.

This ultimately is the basis of the deductive approach. You cannot be only somewhat right, and you can find many ways to be completely and precisely wrong. When applying deductive thinking to economics, the neo-classical economist usually sets up an "as if" model based on a set of tight axiomatic assumptions from which consistent and precise inferences are made. The beauty of this procedure is, of course, that if the axiomatic premises are true, the conclusions necessarily follow. But in a world of humans, the premises are not true—no premise is going to be provably true. So the method is wrong.

Because the deductive approach draws conclusions from axioms, its relevance depends on the universal validity of the axioms. The operations within the natural world that are rooted in physical mechanics, that are timeless and universal, can meet the requirements for applying these deductive methods. But not so for the human. For example, Soros argues that because reflexivity leads to indeterminacy, one cannot create axiomatic theories of human social systems. Reflexive systems are time- and context-specific, not timeless and universal. We have to at least justify our disregard for the gap between the nature of the real world and the theories and models of it. Keynes (1938) wrote that economics "is a science of thinking in terms of models joined to the art of choosing models which are relevant to the contemporary world."

If the human world is fraught with inconsistency and indeterminacy, why should we use models from the natural realm that are designed to be rigorous and all-encompassing? An economist might argue that we have to make simplifying assumptions in order to create rigorous, mathematical models. But then we must ask why these models should be constructed in this manner, and whether they apply or are simply an intellectual exercise that reaches no further than a cartoonish, two-dimensional world.[22]

INDUCTION AND CRISES

If you were a dinosaur (granted, a very thoughtful one), the crisis you might have wished you could model would have been the mass extinction during the latter part of the Cretaceous Period. Needless to say, this was a one-time epochal event, for which there was not much historical basis for extrapolation from your daily dino world.

In the 1980s, too far after the fact to be of much use for the dinosaur—if anything at all could have been of use—Luis and Walter Alvarez hypothesized that a huge meteor hit the Earth about sixty-five million years ago, causing a massive explosion and dramatic weather changes that coincided with the extinction of the dinosaurs. Key to proving this hypothesis is the presence of unusually high levels of some rare chemical elements such as iridium in layers in the Earth's crust that are about sixty-five million years old. These chemical elements tend to be found in meteors in much higher concentrations than they are near the surface of the Earth. This observation is strong evidence supporting the Alvarez theory that a meteor hit the Earth around that time.

With the Alvarezes and the dinosaurs we are looking at a specific case, not trying to build an elegant general model. We are not inferring to a generalization, but rather to a hypothesis about a structure or process that would explain the data.[23] We are not looking at the individual cases and trying to go from there to a general theory. What we are doing is more akin to writing a story than building a theory. I do not believe there can be a general theoretical approach for understanding crises, whether it is built up using axioms or through the formal process of inductive logic. The approach for determining the cause of the extinction crisis for dinosaurs will not carry over to create a theory that also works for passenger pigeons. Like financial crises, every extinction can be explained ex post, and many could be forecast based on the propagation and cascade of events, but they do not follow some general theory, and starting with axioms is not going to get you where you want to go.

The basic message is that when there is a high degree of complexity, you have to figure it out as you go along.

15

Conclusion

I began with the observation that we are human, that we are colored by the essential human qualities of our experiences and interactions. The dimensions of complexity erupt from this simple base—complexity that demands the use of agent-based models. I could hardly conclude otherwise: we are human, and a financial crisis is ultimately a human event. Not only do crises emerge because of the complexity that comes from being human, but they also exact a human toll: a young family in Las Vegas loses their home, a single mother in Des Moines loses her job. The film based on Michael Lewis's book *The Big Short*—which nails the ins and outs of the financial crisis, albeit with personalities that are amplified a few notches—gets these human effects. After dealing with the banks, the rating agencies, the mortgage brokers, the hedge fund honchos, and the complexity cooked up by the financial engineers, the movie's final scene shows a van at a gas station. The driver, a rugged man, now homeless, stands beside the vehicle. His two children crawl up into the clothes and furniture packed into the back. He hugs his wife reassuringly, and gazes past her with an expression that conveys the defeat and uncertainty of their world gone wrong.

You can go through dozens of books on the crisis and miss this critical human dimension. But this is where any paradigm for dealing with crises must reach. And agent-based economics presents a paradigm that does.

This is the way it has to work: we need agent-based economics to create a weather service for the financial markets. We need to forecast the tropical storms of financial dislocation. Will a storm turn into a hurricane? What path will it take? How bad will things get? The forecasting doesn't need to be tremendously precise at the outset. With more data and detail about the agents, our modeling will improve over time. Whatever we can do with this modeling approach is better than where we are now; it is greater than zero. Today we enjoy ten-day weather forecasts, but when the modern methods for weather forecasting first became operational it took twenty-four hours to run a forecast for the next day's weather.[1] The forecast just kept pace with the weather it was forecasting!

And we can get more than a forecast. We can't do anything about the weather, but we *can* alter the course of a financial storm. The agent-based approach can form the foundation for dampening crises. Financial crises ensue with cascades fueled by forced selling that in turn saps liquidity from the market. At its core, a crisis progresses because liquidity demand outruns liquidity supply. Selling drops prices, and the drop in prices forces more selling, accelerating as liquidity and funding dry up. One certainty: there is plenty of capital out there to provide that liquidity. Unfortunately, with the speed of the selling and the uncertainty that it engenders, that capital stays on the sidelines.

The key to dampening any crisis is to pull that frightened, and frozen, capital into the process. That will happen only if those investors understand the dynamics behind the cascades so that they aren't going to, as the saying goes, catch the falling knife. Agent-based modeling is the guide. With better understanding of how the crisis will unfold, where the dominos will fall, and how bad it might become, more liquidity can flow into the market.

Who can bring that capital to bear? Maybe the regulators. But where *are* the regulators in all of this? One big problem is that they have many agendas, and are shackled by their own rules and statutes, which slows their response and limits the tools they can use. Remember, too, that the regulators are singing from the same hymnal as the academics. The academics feed the regulators with the standard model and the regulators accept it as a given. Why wouldn't they? They're cut from the same cloth. The Federal Reserve has enough Ph.D. economists to staff a dozen universities. I've devoted some chapters to discussing the limitations of the standard economic model that dominates academics; the same can be said about the model the financial regulators use. In economics, unlike politics, it's a single-party rule.

The point is that you can't appreciate the dynamics of a crisis and its human component if you are sitting at the New York Fed, working at a white board at 33 Liberty Street, where the discussion is abstracted from the world of many varied human participants, where the discussion begins, "Assume a consumer X with a consumption function $f()$; an investor Y with a portfolio optimization $g()$; a financial system with N banks." That doesn't sound like you, does it? There is no central control room for monitoring and directing the markets and the emergence of a crisis, any more than there is for directing a school of fish or maintaining order for pilgrims during the Hajj. To abstract from the crowd, to ignore the various human inputs, is to miss the essence of the problem. Invested in the old model, they're fiddling with dials that they can turn up to 10 when it seems that they need to get to 11. There is no 11 on that dial, and even if they could turn it up, they would still be out to sea.

Asset Owners Are People, My Friend

Life would be easier—and it would be fitting—if those who are part of the problem were also part of the solution. Yet in financial crises that is not the case. The leveraged investors will always be leveraged, and if not fueling the cascade through their forced selling, they will be pulled to the sidelines lest the raging fire reach their powder kegs. The banks will always be tucking in their tails as the crisis progresses, hoarding their capital, restricting lending, and pulling back from making markets. These are defensive strategies imbedded in their business models and their mindsets. Asset managers, though with sizable capital and immune from the effects of leverage, will always be bound up by their investor mandates.

But there is another class of investors who can be the lifeguards at our financial shores, able to pull us to safety: asset owners. You can run through all the books on the crises, reread your economics textbooks, and the odds are you will not find the term *asset owner*. A bit strange, isn't it, considering that asset owners are the source of vast amounts of capital? Everything starts with the asset owners. They include retail investors like you, but on a larger scale they are institutions such as global pension funds with oceans of capital under management. In some countries there is a centralized pension fund, called a sovereign wealth fund, such as Norway's government pension fund with assets of $850 billion, or the Abu Dhabi Investment Authority with some $800 billion. Such funds are behemoths, but they hold their citizens' savings; in a financial sense, they are you and me. The hedge funds, money managers, and banks all feed off these asset owners. The asset owners are rarely leveraged and do not have short-term demands for returns—they are looking out for the needs of their constituents years into the future, as they should.

So, consider this. Take the largest of the asset owners, arm them with agent-based methods that give them a window into the dynamics of a crisis, and have them engage in a strategy to keep capital at the ready. Why? So that when a crisis is gathering steam, when prices are down 10 or 20 percent, possibly headed to 30 percent off, they start to buy. When the dust settles, whether in weeks or months, they will have made a sizable return. And they are earning it. They are making that return because they are providing a valuable social service: their investments are providing the liquidity supply the market is screaming for.[2] Their capital will dampen the cascade, reduce the systemic risk, and speed the realization of their return—reflexivity in action.

In today's world this is a bold strategy. Asset owners are understandably conservative, and because they have such long horizons and need to put so much capital to work, they tend to be slow and deliberate in their investment decisions. To enter the fray during a crisis, to risk catching that falling knife, is not their typical approach. For a chief investment officer to even suggest doing so risks being seen as imprudent. So this is a strategy that requires forethought and careful analysis. The battle strategy must be laid out, the plan approved and put in place before the crisis hits. What makes my proposal different today from what it might have been in the past is that through agent-based methods, and the broad accessibility to data to populate it, we now have the machinery in place to understand the origins and course of many types of financial crises, namely, those that are based on the combined elements of leverage, concentration of assets, and growing illiquidity.

Revolutions

Over the course of the Industrial Revolution, capital became dominant and people became one more factor in the production function. The political economy of Smith, Ricardo, and Mill gave way to the mathematical neoclassical economics that dominates today. How has that worked for us? In ever more complex and broad-based financial crises, not well.

This is where we are now: the pipes connecting markets and institutions—and the markets and the institutions themselves—are again being ripped up and rerouted. It is in part the result of government regulation that has redefined the roles and the power of banks, with other institutions scurrying to fill in the gaps or, worse, with critical functions left wanting. It is in part a rethinking of the economic and financial assumptions that have steered us from as far back as the end of World War II—the questioning of the path of integration, open trade and borders, and globalization. There are emerging risks emanating from the fracturing of petrostates as the world attempts to decrease its dependence on oil. China is a new power in the financial markets, with regional territorial ambitions. In all of this, we are seeing not only pathways for financial vulnerability and crisis but also the multiplying effect of a growing link between financial and geopolitical risks.

This time—every time—it really is different. We are not stepping into a smooth, equilibrium sort of world where the agents and institutions will behave the same way in the future as they have in the past, or even where the agents in our financial system will be those of the past. We have had one hundred fifty years of neoclassical economics. We need to look elsewhere if we are going to be successful in understanding and containing complex, dynamic financial crises.

If we build a highway for self-driving cars, we don't need to use an agent-based model (so long as there are no human drivers or pedestrians on it). If we construct a network of distributed databases sharing and updating information, we don't need to use an agent-based model. We don't need an agent-based model for a mechanical, predetermined world. We do need an agent-based model, however, when we move from robots to people. And so we need agent-based models to understand and deal with crises. This model is needed when we have agents—people—who are largely autonomous in making decisions, based on their own particular approaches to the world, and what they do changes the world. It is needed when people are operating as individuals, without a central planner who sees and controls everything, people who are not necessarily behaving like economic automatons. Because people don't. It is needed when people learn, when their actions affect the world and one another in ways that can be understood only as we follow them along the path. It is needed when we move from a mechanical world to one with human complexity and reflexivity.

In such a world, one where we have people who work from experience and context, who interact with and affect one another in the way people really do, we must start with these agents. If we aggregate up, we assume away the problem and we miss the periods of emergence that define crises. As economics moved from the political economy of Smith through Mill into the mathematical world of the natural sciences, it left these behind. That works well only if everyone is "like a goddamn robot."

I have outlined a new paradigm for looking at financial crises and for giving us the ability to defuse them. The agent-based approach respects the nature of people. It recognizes the interplay between our interactions and the environment. It operates without the fiction of a grand leader, or a representative consumer or investor who is as unerringly right as a mathematical model can dream. This approach does not force fictional but convenient mathematical constructs that assume everyone will keep running on the tracks. It allows for construction of a narrative—unique to the particular circumstances in the real world—in which the system may jump the tracks and careen down the mountainside, and this narrative gives us a shot at pulling the system back safely. Agent-based models are the guide. A better understanding of how the crisis will unfold, where the dominos will fall, and how bad it might become can allow more liquidity to flow into the market. In short, agent-based economics arrives ready to face the real world, the world that is amplified and distorted during times of crisis. This is a new paradigm rooted in pragmatism and in the complexities of being human.

ACKNOWLEDGMENTS

Two institutions, and in particular three conferences sponsored by these institutions, have played an important part in inspiring me to write this book: The Economy as a Complex Adaptive System II, a conference hosted by the Santa Fe Institute in 1993, which introduced me to agent-based modeling, and the Annual Conferences of the Institute for New Economic Thinking in 2014 and in 2015, which spurred my thinking on such far-ranging topics as the concept of reflexivity and the value of literature in understanding the human aspects of the economic world, and which also gave me encouragement in knowing there is a groundswell of others who are questioning the current economic paradigm. I am indebted to the U.S. Treasury and the Office of Financial Research for support and to my colleagues there with whom I have collaborated during my research on applying agent-based models to understand our financial vulnerabilities and systemic risks.

I wish to thank those who have read through various drafts of the manuscript and have provided valuable editorial assistance along the way: David Bookstaber, Jennylyn Garcia, Janice Horowitz, Steve Ross; my editors at Princeton University Press, Seth Ditchik, Peter Dougherty, and Joe Jackson; and Madeleine Adams and Bill Saporito for developmental and manuscript editing.

Finally, I thank my wife Janice and daughter Anna for making the wooden "Shhhhh" sign for me to post on the door when I was at work on the book.

NOTES

Chapter 1: Crises and Sunspots

1. See Watson (2014), 75–76: Lucas (2009) suggested that it was unfair to hold economists to account for the financial crisis when their demand-and-supply vision gave them no vantage point to comment on such possibilities in the first place. He wrote that the simulations of equilibrium-oriented macroeconomics were not presented as an "assurance that no crisis would occur, but as forecast of what could be expected conditional on a crisis not occurring" (Lucas 2009, 67). Thomas Sargent agreed, dismissing the critics for their "foolish and intellectually lazy remark[s]" and saying that their concerns "reflect either woeful ignorance or intentional disregard for what much of modern macroeconomics is about" (Rolnick 2010, 28). British bankers offered apologies for their role in the crisis when they appeared before the Treasury Committee in early 2009, but it appears the economists who shaped the field have shared no such compunction. Of course, the politicians and the regulators also offered no apologies and, in fact, took bows for having saved us all.

2. Kay (2012), 87.

3. Irving Fisher (1892, 109) wrote, "Before Jevons, all the attempts at mathematical treatment fell flat. . . . [T]he mathematical method really began with Jevons in 1871." Alfred Marshall's writings also had the indelible mark of Jevons' theories, though Marshall was never as willing as Fisher to recognize Jevons' contribution. Still, Joseph Schumpeter (1954, 837) wrote, "No unbiased reader can fail to perceive . . . that Marshall's theoretical structure, barring its technical superiority and various developments of detail, is fundamentally the same as that of Jevons, Menger, and especially Walras."

4. See Schivelbusch (2014).

5. Hobsbawm (1999), 87–93.

6. Mill (2004), 418.

7. In Hutchison (1972), the four pillars of Mill's theory are the wages fund, the labor theory of value, the natural wages doctrine, and the Malthusian constraints on population.

8. Over the ensuing one hundred and fifty years, capital has moved front and center, but—given the technology firms that make up an ever-increasing part of the economy—that is becoming a questionable perspective. How many companies have reached a multibillion-dollar level with only a few computers and the proverbial four guys in a garage?

9. Wells (1849), 169.

10. Tames (1971), document 163: Canon Parkinson "On the Present Condition of the Labouring Poor in Manchester." Also see Hobsbawm (1999), 65, 73.

11. See a discussion in Schabas (1990), 34. Bentham (2007, 30) lists seven circumstances that affect the measurement of pleasure and pain:

> IV. To a *number* of persons, with reference to each of whom the value of a pleasure or a pain is considered, it will be greater or less, according to seven circumstances: to wit, the six preceding ones; *viz.*

> 1. Its *intensity*.
> 2. Its *duration*.
> 3. Its *certainty* or *uncertainty*.
> 4. Its *propinquity* or *remoteness*.
> 5. Its *fecundity*.
> 6. Its *purity*.

And one other; to wit:

> 7. Its *extent*; that is, the number of persons to whom it *extends*; or (in other words) who are affected by it.

12. Jevons (1871), 34–35.

13. For a biographical treatment of Jevons and references to the quotations in the following paragraphs, see Schabas (1990) and Mosselmans (2013).

14. He wrote in *The Principles of Science*, "Can the reader say what two numbers multiplied together will produce the number 8616460799? I think it unlikely that anyone but myself will ever know." This became known as Jevons' number and was finally factored in 1903: 8616460799 = 89681 × 96079.

15. It was also a demand that we "cast ourselves free from the wage funds theory, the cost of production doctrine of value, the natural rate of wages, and other misleading or false Ricardian doctrines." Jevons (1871), 67.

16. The two most notable of these are Carl Menger in Austria and Léon Walras in France. Jevons had no contact with Menger, but did come in contact with Walras at the University of Lausanne. Walras had independently arrived at a similar analysis and also advocated the use of calculus. Jevons accepted Walras as an ally and promised to spread the news of his *Elements of Pure Economics*, though in the end he did so only halfheartedly.

17. Jevons and Foxwell (1884), 4.

18. A treatment of Jevons' interest in crises and his pursuit of sunspots as the explanation is in Poovey (2008), especially 275–83.

19. His reasoning in considering sunspots has a logical structure that echoes in the scientific methods of economics even today. He wrote (Jevons and Foxwell 1884, 194–95):

> It is a well-known principle of mechanics that the effects of a periodically varying cause are themselves periodic, and usually go through their phases in periods of time equal to those of the cause. There is no doubt that the energy poured upon the earth's surface in the form of sunbeams is the principal agent in maintaining life here. It has lately been proved, too, beyond all reasonable doubt, that there is a periodic variation of the sun's condition, which was first discovered in the alternate increase and decrease of area of the sun-spots. . . . Little doubt is now entertained, moreover, that the rainfall and other atmospheric phenomena of any locality are more or less influenced by the same changes in the sun's condition. . . . The success of the harvest in any year certainly depends upon the weather. . . . Now, if this weather depends in any degree upon the solar period, it follows that the harvest and the price of grain will depend more or less upon the solar period, and will go through periodic fluctuations in periods of time equal to those of the sunspots.

20. Kundera (2003), 164.

21. Lucas (2009).

Chapter 3: Social Interactions and Computational Irreducibility

1. "On Exactitude and Science," in Borges (2004).

2. Put more concretely, if a problem is computationally irreducible, the only way to figure out what is going to happen is to simulate each step. This is an inductive process (but not the sort of inductive process that then can be generalized into a deductive result), where computing $f(n)$ requires following approximately the same path as computing successively all the values $f(i)$ from $i=1$ to n.

3. Wolfram (2002).

4. Šuvakov and Dmitrašinović (2013) used computer simulations to tweak the initial conditions of the families of the existing solutions until a new type of orbit materialized.

5. Unlike some other dynamical systems, such as Conway's Game of Life, which I will discuss shortly, computational irreducibility is not a theoretical limitation for the three-body problem. That is, an analytical solution is not excluded as a possibility. It just seems not to be something we can figure out.

6. Jevons (1918), 760.

7. Saari (1996), 2268.

8. See Scarf (1960). These points are presented in Ackerman (2002).

9. Conway's Game of Life was popularized by Gardner (1970).

10. The grids are finite, so along the edges and corners there are only three to five neighboring cells. However, the analysis ignores the edge and corner cases.

11. There are other configurations that commonly occur, such as oscillators, which have cells that go on and off over a cycle of periods; still lifes, which do not change from one period to the next; guns, which shoot out gliders or other types of spaceships which then travel along the grid; and puffer trains, which move like gliders while leaving a trail of black cell "smoke" behind.

12. The gliders and spaceships are critical components of the ability of Life to act as a computational engine, because they can transmit information from one place to another.

13. For example, a world with regularity conditions, such as twice differentiable functions, and single representative agents to represent all consumers or investors. And when the problem cannot be compressed and it is necessary to move beyond a one-period model, mapping out a largely predetermined path (such as with predetermined intertemporal utility functions and probability distributions), or keeping the journey to two or three steps.

Chapter 4: The Individual and the Human Wave: Emergent Phenomena

1. Helbing and Mukerji (2012) present an analysis of crowd quakes or crowd turbulence, where there is no event triggering a mass panic but rather a domino effect from something as innocuous as people stumbling. In another article, Helbing, Farkas, and Vicsek (2000) show how simple measures can lead to a reduction in the turbulence that creates emergent stampedes. Something as simple—and counterintuitive—as placing a pillar three feet from the exit can dramatically reduce injuries in a fire. In a simulation with 200 people in a room with 45 seconds to escape, 44 people escape and 5 are injured when there is no column, whereas with a column 72 people escape and no one is injured.

2. By moving closer to one another, the fish also might be mistaken for one large entity. One article that provides more detail on the rules of fish and birds is Hemelrijk and Hildenbrandt (2012).

3. He won an Academy Award in 1998 for "pioneering contributions to the development of three-dimensional computer animation for motion picture production."

4. One of the key researchers in the field of cellular automatons, Stephen Wolfram (2002), has exhaustively studied a range of two-dimensional cellular automaton structures, some of which are computationally irreducible and create an endless variation in results based on the alive-or-dead state of only three adjacent cells

5. Keynes (1973), 249.

Chapter 5: Context and Ergodicity

1. Wittgenstein (1984), 3e.

2. A mathematical presentation of ergodicity is in Gray (2009), chapters 7 and 8. Ludwig Boltzmann, the founder of statistical mechanics, coined the term *ergodic*. If a dynamical system is ergodic, you can pick some random point and follow its path, and over time that point will pass arbitrarily close to every other point in the space. If we take the average of this point's path over a long enough time period, it will be representative of the whole population of the space. The average for the point's path is called the time average for that point. The average of all the points in the space is called the space average. So if a dynamical system is ergodic, the time average will equal the space average. Bringing this down to Earth, if we have a dynamical system that is ergodic, then a sufficiently long time series will describe the properties of the overall system. And because any other point will also pass over every point in the system, that time series will give us the same statistical properties as the path of any other point. In particular, the time series of our past observations—which we can think of as our observation of the path on one point, that is, of the world we have known—will tell us the statistical properties of the future path. If a process is not ergodic, then the past we have observed might not be at all representative of what will occur in the future. The world we have known might miss important possible characteristics of events that might occur, or miss the complexity of these possible events.

3. For the issues with ergodicity for additive versus multiplicative processes, see Peters and Adamou (2015).

4. As does science in general. The scientific view on ergodicity (though he doesn't use that term) is discussed by Yale professor Denis Hollier (1989, 55, 60–61) in his treatment of the work of George Bataille. Hollier contrasts the way history is lived, where we do not know how it will turn out, with what Bataille calls the "ancient geometric conception of the future," which gives us "assurances in advance through science about the future, without running any risk, reducing the future to no more than the reproduction of the present." By constructing the future the way an architect oversees a project, we put on the formal "mathematical overcoat" that stops time. Bataille argues for a revolutionary movement that liberates the future from the prison of science. Submitting the future to planning and projects diminishes the present. This is the context for Bataille's statement, "The project is the prison."

5. Lucas (1981), 223–24.

6. See Humphrys (2008).

7. Humphrys (2008), 242–43.

8. Which gets us to the Turing test. To determine when a computer had met some level of competing with human intelligence, Turing suggested that a computer hide behind one curtain, a person hide behind a second, and the tester pass questions through the curtain to each. If a person cannot distinguish the responses of a computer from those of a human, then at least in this limited respect the computer has attained humanlike intelligence.

There already is an annual Turing test, the Loebner competition, in which a set of judges spend a few minutes conversing (via keyboard) with computers and with people, and then must decide which is which. It is not a great test to get at the objective Turing had in mind, however, because it is a competition rather than a normal human environment. The judges are trying to weed out the computer through types of questions and cadence of conversation, not engage in the flow of normal, real-world conversation. And the computers try to game the test by keeping their responses simple, answering slowly so there are fewer chances for the judges to make observations over the fixed time period, and keeping the conversation vacuous. A more reasonable Turing test would be to invite a computer into a round of dinner conversations where the human subjects are not made aware that this is occurring. (They would all have to be remote conversations, for obvious reasons.) After the fact, subjects are told that some of their companions might have been computers, and only then are they asked to rank the guests by "humanness."

MGonz has the rudiments of passing the Turing test, but it sets the bar far lower than the Loebner competition. It is a sort of remedial test, of a one-liner, invective-laden variety, where the objective is to rant while ignoring anything the other person is saying. If a program can induce us to sink to the level of insult and profanity of MGonz, it can pass the Turing test. (And we may indeed be sinking to that level, not by becoming more verbally abusive, but by becoming less verbal, period; moving toward the vacuous and noncontextual as we embrace new modes of conversation.) But it is not depth of content that differentiates humans from machines. A computer can already beat us in terms of content. One human in a previous Loebner competition was pegged as a computer because she knew more Shakespeare than the judges thought was humanly possible, but not more than what they thought was possible for a computer.

For a discussion of the MGonz, the Loebner competition, and the Turing test more generally, see Christian (2011).

9. For example, of their many works, see Tversky and Kahneman (1974). Also see Kahneman (2011).

Chapter 6: Human Experience and Radical Uncertainty

1. The term *radical uncertainty* is taken from Knight (1921, 233) in his famous passage that distinguishes risk from uncertainty: "Uncertainty must be taken in a sense radically distinct from the familiar notion of risk, from which it has never been properly separated. . . . The essential fact is that 'risk' means in some cases a quantity susceptible of measurement, while at other times it is something distinctly not of this character; and there are far-reaching and crucial differences in the bearings of the phenomena depending on which of the two is really present and operating. . . . It will appear that a measurable uncertainty, or 'risk' proper, as we shall use the term, is so far different from an unmeasurable one that it is not in effect an uncertainty at all."

Keynes (1937, 212–23) gives his take on radical uncertainty: "By 'uncertain' knowledge, let me explain, I do not mean merely to distinguish what is known for certain from what is only probable. The game of roulette is not subject, in this sense, to uncertainty; nor is the prospect of a Victory bond being drawn. Or, again, the expectation of life is only slightly uncertain. Even the weather is only moderately uncertain. The sense in which I am using the term is that in which the prospect of a European war is uncertain, or the price of copper and the rate of interest twenty years hence, or the obsolescence of a new invention, or the position of private wealth-owners in the social system in 1970. About these matters there is no scientific basis on which to form any calculable probability whatever. We simply do not know. Nevertheless, the necessity for action and for decision compels us as practical men to do our best to overlook this awkward fact and to behave exactly as we should if we had behind us a good Benthamite calculation of a series of prospective advantages and disadvantages, each multiplied by its appropriate probability, waiting to be summed."

Lucas (1977, 15) also gives a sense of radical uncertainty by considering the decision process of someone with psychotic behavior: "Even psychotic behavior can be (and today is) understood as 'rational,' given a sufficiently abnormal view of relevant probabilities." However, this "will not be of value in understanding psychotic behavior. Neither will it be applicable in situations in which one cannot guess which, if any, observable frequencies are relevant: situations that Knight called 'uncertainty.'" When there is radical uncertainty, "economic reasoning will be of no value" (Lucas 1981, 224).

2. There are two ways to think about radical uncertainty: you do not know the probabilities, or you do not know the states of nature, that is, the sort of things that can occur. See Epstein and Wan (1994), and Epstein, Marinacci, and Seo (2007), for definitions and descriptions of these two ways of looking at radical uncertainty, and in particular for the implications of not knowing all the possible states, what can be termed unforeseen contingencies. See Ellsberg (yes, the Ellsberg of Pentagon Papers fame) (1961), for an early treatment of ambiguity in the probability of known states, which is a common—but I believe less convincing—approach to radical uncertainty.

These two notions are qualitatively different, and the second is more extreme. To get a sense of the distinction and the qualitative difference, consider these two scenarios:

1. I am in a battle, and I know the possible states, namely, I know that the enemy might try to breech the defenses at location A, B, or C. But I have no idea of the odds of which one they will try. I still can defend myself by putting troops at each location. At the least, I know the sorts of things that might happen and can worry about them with some definition.

2. I am in a battle, and I have no idea what the enemy might do or the types of weapons they have. I cannot even begin to conceive of all the possible states because I live in the year 100 BC and the enemy has been transported through time from the year AD 2010. So forget about not knowing the probabilities, I don't even know where to assign the probabilities. (And imagine my surprise when bombs start dropping from the air.)

These scenarios show the difference between not having an inkling about a state and assigning a zero probability to (or having ambiguity about the probability of) a known state. If I assign a zero probability to the enemy coming through location A, I have information and can do something about it. I can name the state; imagine my relief in knowing I don't have to worry about it. Or, even if I have no idea about the probability assigned to the state, at least I have something better than unanchored anxiety, fearing that something will happen but not knowing what it might be. That is different from discovering what I could never have imagined, that bombs start falling from the air. I would not react to that by saying, "Look at that: there is a state to which I assigned zero probability."

In statistical mechanics, the third Shannon-Khinchin axiom states that adding a state with zero probability will not change the model. Mathematically, this corresponds to defining the otherwise undefined expression $0*\ln(0)$ as 0. Some sort of axiomatic approach is needed because otherwise I am in a situation of needing to include everything that cannot happen in my description of a system!

We can consider radical uncertainty to be present in this case where the system cannot be described, when the choice to define $0*\ln(0) = 0$ is not valid. For the radical uncertainty that comes from not knowing all the states, the mathematician simply shrugs his shoulders and says, "I don't know what to do here," while the scientist then defines a mathematically nonexistent object in a way that allows him to carry on.

3. Russell (1995), 66.

4. These recollections are from Russell (2000).

5. Rucker (2005, 157) gives an intuitive proof of Gödel's impossibility theorem, and provides this simple explanation:

> The gimmick in Gödel's proof is very similar to the gimmick in the famous Liar paradox of Epimenides: "I am lying," says Epimenides. Is he? Or, as in "What is Truth," define B to be the sentence "B is not true." Is B true? The problem is that B is true if and only if B is not true. So B is somehow outside the scope of the applicability of the concepts "true" and "not true." There is something viciously meaningless about the sentence B, and one is inclined just to try to forget about it.
>
> But Gödel's G sentences cannot be so lightly dismissed. With his great mathematical and logical genius, Gödel was able to find a way (for any given $P(UTM)$ actually to write down a complicated polynomial equation that has a solution if and only if G is true. So G is not at all some vague or non-mathematical sentence. *G is a specific mathematical problem that we know the answer to, even though UTM does not!* So UTM does not, and cannot, embody a best and final theory of mathematics.

6. Beginning in the 1980s, the symbolic capabilities of Wolfram's programming language, Mathematica, has moved us down this road.

7. The printing problem was the one posed by Turing in demonstrating undecidability. The better-known halting problem is attributable to Martin Davis (1958, 70).

8. Lloyd (2007), 36.

9. See Dawson (1997), 68–74.

10. The reason for this, viewed from the standpoint of classical physics, is that accurately measuring the position of an electron requires illuminating the electron with light of a very short wavelength. The shorter the wavelength the greater the amount of energy that hits the electron and the more accurate the measurement, but the greater the energy hitting the electron the greater the impact on its velocity.

11. There is yet another limitation to knowing the present sufficiently to forecast, first propounded by Edward Lorenz (1963), and popularly illustrated by the "butterfly effect." Lorenz showed that for many nonlinear systems even the slightest error in measurement will be compounded over time to cause a forecast to veer increasingly off course.

12. Soros (1987). Also see Soros (2013) and related articles in that issue, and the first two lectures in Soros (2010).

13. And we can add to this Robert K. Merton's (1948) concept of the self-fulfilling prophecy, which I will discuss in chapter 10.

14. Popper (1957), 18.

15. Kundera (2003), 132–33.

16. The discussion here is based on Posnock (2008). In his exposition of Kundera's novel, Posnock points out that though one was shaped by twentieth-century communist Czechoslovakia and the other by the nineteenth-century democratic United States, Kundera's concept is mirrored in Ralph Waldo Emerson's (1993) essays "Circles" and "Experience." In "Circles," Emerson writes that, as is the case with Tomas and Teresa, the "results of life are uncalculated and uncalculable," and we wish to let go of control; we have an "insatiable desire" to "do something without knowing how or why." The opening line of Emerson's essay "Experience" echoes Kundera: "Where do we find ourselves?" His immediate answer is as if we are awakening from a dream to still be in a dream. There "is no end to the illusion," and our human condition is one of continual surprise.

17. "The Library of Babel," in Borges (1969).

18. The length of the individual books does not pose a constraint on this unbounded knowledge—a discourse requiring more than 410 pages will be contained in a multivolume set.

19. Actually, there are some things you won't be able to find anywhere in those volumes, which gets back to the problems with Hilbert's proposed program. We know there is a mechanical procedure for filling all the books in the Library of Babel. It might take a very long time, but it can be done with a routine, mindless process, the process of a "computer," and it finally is a task that we know can be completed. If we do that, will we be able to find somewhere in those books the proof for any mathematical statement, demonstrating that it is either true or false, or in the terms of the field, that are decidable? We already know from Gödel that there are some problems for which there will not be a proof to be found anywhere in those volumes.

20. The discussion of Borges' Library of Babel is based on Bell-Villada (1981). The mathematical characteristics of the Library of Babel are presented at length in Bloch (2008).

21. I will treat this topic further in chapter 10, when I discuss complexity and informational irreducibility.

Chapter 7: Heuristics: How to Act Like a Human

1. The examples cited here are taken from Bookstaber and Langsam (1985), and Gigerenzer and Gaissmaier (2011). Also see Bookstaber (2007), 235–37.

2. This behavior is also called learned helplessness. See Seligman (1972).

3. This example is taken from Bookstaber (2007), 230–31.

4. For the "as if" argument, see Milton Friedman's (1953, 21) famous billiard example. The "subject to our constraints" argument suggests Herbert Simon's (1947) satisficing approach.

5. Sargent (1993), 2.

6. Heuristics often bypass one of the primary dictums of optimization, that there should not be a persistent bias in an optimal method. Most any estimation method tries to minimize some measure or error subject to having no bias. That is, there is not a notion of a variance versus bias trade-off. If there is any bias at all, that is problematic because no one should be consistently missing the target by shooting to the left—all you have to do is adjust the windage on the sights, and you will get closer to the target. But heuristics can introduce a persistent bias, and this is viewed by those steeped in optimization methods as cognitive illusions. Yet, as discussed by Gerd Gigerenzer and Henry Brighton (2009), when survival is at stake in a world that is not ergodic (when, so to speak, the target might move or a new target might become more critical), ignoring information that would correct the bias in the current worldview will make sense if in doing so the overall variance is reduced.

7. Our capitalist system is with the blackworms and whiptails—it is asexual. We go with winners and prune away anything inefficient in the current environment. I will not treat this point further, but it is another route we could take in thinking about why we end up in so many crises.

8. A technical point while I'm on the topic: the mechanism by which genes are expressed is known as epigenetics, a system of molecular processes that tell specific genes when to turn on or off. The reason we humans can share so many genes with other species is that, although the genes might be the same, the sequences making up switches, and thus the nature of the genes' interaction, have evolved to be different. Small changes in switches can produce very different patterns of genes turning on and off during development. The diversity of organisms is largely due to evolutionary modifications of switches, rather than genes. This is also the reason that large changes can happen so quickly (at least relative to evolutionary time): the genes stay the same but switches change. These changes can occur in the parts of DNA long thought of as "junk" and are the major force in evolution, rather than the rapid appearance of entirely new genes. We might think of the genes as the grids in the Game of Life, and the switches as the rules determining which of the cells of the grid are on and off.

9. One of the first to explore this possibility was William James, who wrote, "In the practical use of our intellect, forgetting is as important a function as recollecting" (referenced in Schooler and Hertwig 2005, 679). In this view, forgetting is the mental mechanism behind the selectivity of information processing, which in turn is "the very keel on which our mental ship is built" (ibid., 679–80).

10. Kundera (1988) writes that "the will to forget is an anthropological one: man has always harbored the desire to rewrite his own biography, to change the past."

11. "Funes the Memorious," in Borges (1969).

12. I benefit in my accounts of Funes and of Luria and S. from Bell-Villada (1981). For the quotations from Luria in the rest of this chapter, see Luria (1968), 12, 64, 65.

Chapter 8: Economics in Crisis

1. Becker (1976), 5.

2. Jevons (1871), sections IV.60–62.

3. As discussed in Schabas (1990, 92–94), Jevons himself uses aggregation to refer to the average man as an analogue to the use of the center of gravity, where (quoting from Jevons 1874) "one point may be discovered in a gravitating body such that the weight of all particles may be regarded as concentrated in the point, and yet the behavior of the whole body will be exactly represented by the behavior of this heavy point."

4. There are theoretical objections to the use of the representative agent. Saari (1995, 228–29) considers the problem from a mathematician's perspective and concludes that "the source of the difficulty which is common across the social sciences is that the social sciences are based on aggregation procedures. . . . [T]he complexity of the social sciences derives from the unlimited variety in individual preferences; preferences that define a sufficiently large dimensional domain that, when aggregated, can generate all imaginable forms of pathological behavior." Kirman (1989, 137) argues, "The problem seems to be embodied in what is an essential feature of a centuries-long tradition in economics, that of treating individuals as acting independently of each other," that is, ignoring the human fact of interaction. Also see Rizvi (1994), and Martel (1996). Also, Kirman (1992) shows that there is no representative individual whose demand function generates the instability found in the core theory of equilibrium economics, the Sonnenschein-Mantel-Debreu general equilibrium theorem. A critique of economic models employing representative agents is in Syll (2016), 23–27.

5. Keynes, letter to R. F. Harrod, July 4, 1938.

6. Wallace (1980), 24.

7. Clower (1989), 23.

8. Shackle (1972), 102.

9. In many fields, the elite players cannot fully access their own knowledge about how they're doing what they're doing. Self-ignorance is common to many human abilities, from driving a car in traffic to recognizing a face. In games such as chess or go, elite players seem unable to fully access the way they make decisions. This is summarized by the philosopher and scientist Michael Polanyi (1974), "We know more than we can tell."

10. See, for example, Singer and Bolz (2013).

11. Most notably, dynamic stochastic general equilibrium (DSGE) models.

12. Syll (2016), 1. Also see Farmer and Geanakoplos (2009).

13. Solow (2010), 13.

14. "Tlön, Uqbar, Orbis Tertius," in Borges (1969).

15. This returns us to Ireneo Funes. Ireneo cannot reason because he is too bound up in reality, incapable of breaking away from the onslaught of facts to think abstractly, to think induc-

tively about the specifics of the situation, whereas those on Tlön do not reason about reality because they do not live in the real world.

16. See Bell-Villada (1981), 135–41.

Chapter 9: Agent-Based Models

1. See Zheng et al. (2013) for a survey of agent-based models in transportation. The survey references several well-known agent-based transportation modeling platforms, including the Transportation Analysis and Simulation System, and the Multi-Agent Transport Simulation Toolkit. In recent years, there has been a range of new agent-based traffic and transportation applications related to modeling and simulation, traffic control, traffic management frameworks, dynamic routing, congestion management, and fleet management, with applications extending from automobile traffic to rail and air. Agent-based traffic applications include CTMRGS in the United States, CLAIRE in France, TRYS/TRYSA2 in Spain, and CARTESIUS in Germany.

2. This traffic rule is termed Rule 184 in the lexicon developed by Stephen Wolfram, with application to traffic flow by Wang, Kwong, and Hui (1998). For an in-depth survey of cellular automaton traffic modeling and associated statistical mechanics, see Maerivoet and De Moor (2005), and Chowdhury, Santen, and Schadschneider (2000).

3. See Krugman (2009).

4. Evans and Honkapohja (2005), 566.

5. Lucas (1981), 8.

Chapter 10: Agents in the Complexity Spectrum

1. Within the complexity spectrum, some examples of complex systems are given by Page (2011), Beinhocker (2013), Farmer (2002), and Arthur (1999). Complex systems can include feedback, nonlinear interaction, and tight coupling, which prevents adjustments to the effects of the process in the same time scale as the process.

2. Merton (1948) illustrates this with an example of a fictional bank, Millingville Bank, which faces a run because of the cycle of increasing withdrawals based on an incorrect assessment of its viability. He concludes that the "parable tells us that public definitions of a situation (prophecies or predictions) become an integral part of the situation and thus affect subsequent developments. This is peculiar to human affairs. It is not found in the world of nature, untouched by human hands. Predictions of the return of Halley's comet do not influence its orbit. But the rumored insolvency of Millingville's bank did affect the actual outcome. The prophecy of collapse led to its own fulfillment."

3. Beinhocker (2013), 331–32.

4. The changes in the heuristics might extend beyond changes in model parameters or weights to the rules themselves.

5. Posnock (2008), 71; Dostoevsky (2015).

6. Sun Tzu (2009), 129–30. This is used to illustrate Sun's principle: "Thus one who is skillful at keeping the enemy on the move maintains deceitful appearances, according to which the enemy will act."

7. See Coram (2002), Ford (2010), and Hammond (2001) for treatments of John Boyd's exploits and military theories.

8. Ford (2010), 50.

9. Quoted in Smith (2008), 95.

10. See Dark Pool Comment Letter by Steve Wunsch to the U.S. Securities Exchange Commission, File No. s7-27-09, January 14, 2010.

11. See Anderson, Arrow, and Pines (1988), Arthur (1999), Beinhocker (2006); Farmer (2002), and Miller and Page (2007).

12. We have already discussed that the Game of Life is computationally irreducible, in chapter 3 when we first introduced it to illustrate that characteristic. The Game of Life can operate as a Turing machine, and the individual cells or agents, which go about their simple tasks with an awareness of just their neighbors and only flicker to be alive or dead, contribute to emergence. Life is strongly dependent on the initial conditions, and often has periodic behavior depending on the initial conditions, so it cannot be ergodic.

13. And what do we say about a person who gets it right, who predicts a crisis? If the volumes in the Library of Babel could raise a hand when the world unfolded according to their writing, we would find a sage for every event. Some volume will always be right. And others will be close enough.

Chapter 11: The Structure of the Financial System: Agents and the Environment

1. There are, of course, various detailed models that people have "rolled." By far the best source for these, and for a broad compendium of work in the field, is the website Agent-Based Computational Economics maintained by Leigh Tesfatsion of Iowa State University, http://www2.econ.iastate.edu/tesfatsi/ace.htm. And, naturally, ever-improved models will emerge as agent-based modeling becomes increasingly mainstream.

2. Though, granted, an exit can close up during a fire if people are crushed by the stampede and fall at the exit.

3. Bookstaber et al. (2015) draws an analogy between the schematic of the financial system presented here and a chemical plant, using a standard risk management method employed in chemical engineering based on signed directional graphs within a financial system context.

4. A description of some of these transformations in the context of the shadow banking system is presented in Adrian and Ashcraft (2012). Berger and Bouwman (2009) look at the related roles of risk and liquidity transformation.

5. More connections allow more spreading of risk and diversification. But they also provide more channels for a shock to spread. A more connected financial system will have lower risk most of the time, but when crises do arise, we will experience more severe consequences—though perhaps less frequently. See Haldane and May (2011), and Acemoglu, Ozdaglar, and Tahbaz-Salehi (2015). There is also the issue of the trade-off between diversification and diversity: investment diversification reduces risk for each firm, but when all firms hold similar diversified positions, the system as a whole may be more vulnerable. The question of whether interconnections amplify or dissipate shocks depends on many factors in addition to the network structure. To what extent are banks leveraged? Do interbank obligations have priority over obligations to the nonfinancial sector in case of default? When a default occurs, what proportion of the nominal obligations are recovered?

6. This is where securities purchased or received from counterparties as collateral are reused as collateral to obtain funding through the repurchase (repo) market, and where securities are obtained through reverse repo and securities lending transactions to fulfill short requirements, provide financing to clients, or for other internal bank/dealer needs (e.g., liquidity investment).

7. Collateral comes into the bank/dealer through a number of channels, and it is then dispatched through a number of other channels: bilateral, triparty, and central counterparty clearinghouse (CCP). The prime broker is the conduit of collateral from the hedge funds; the financing desk for securities lending and repo; and the derivatives desk for futures, forwards, swaps,

options, and related activities. The bank/dealer's financing operation is the engine for key collateral transformations. It is through the financing desk that collateral is reused and where collateral upgrades are managed. Underpinning all this activity is the collateral management function at the bank/dealer, which dictates the level and the quality of collateral that can be used for securities financing transactions and derivatives obligations. Furthermore, a key aspect of the collateral map is the pipelines for collateral flows. Collateral can be passed directly to the funding agent as a bilateral flow; can be held by a triparty agent, where all counterparties have their collateral pooled but where that pooling remains distinct for each borrower; or can be passed to a CCP, where the collateral could pass through to other CCPs.

8. See Bacher and Näf (2003).

9. Boccaletti et al. (2014).

10. Recent surveys of networks in finance include Glasserman and Young (2015), and Summer (2013). In the research to date, there is little analysis of the details of the "plumbing" of the financial system showing the sources and uses of funding, the movement of cash and collateral in opposite directions for secured funding, the durability of funding, and the flows of unsecured funding. Network analysis has treated the nodes—the banks and other financial services firms—essentially as black boxes.

11. When multilayer networks were first analyzed, it wasn't clear how much could be gained beyond having a more faithful description of the underlying structure. Now we know: a lot. For one thing, a multilayer network tends to be more fragile than a set of isolated single-layer networks. Majdandzic et al. (2014), and Zhou et al. (2014) show that the interplay of those vulnerabilities can be more complex. Damage within a multilayer network tends to propagate in three distinct stages: first, a fast and furious buckling of the system; then, a period in which the damage expands slowly throughout, like ice cracking on a pond; and finally, a fast and devastating collapse. The first and last stages are amplifiers, where any damage done will lead to exponentially more damage. For example, the failure of one node will lead to a failure of ten nodes, which will lead to a failure of one hundred nodes. The middle stage is one of damage saturation, where the failure propagates linearly, so, for example, the damage of one node will lead to the damage of one other node. Also see Bargigli et al. (2015).

12. See D'Agostino and Scala (2014), and Buldyrev et al. (2010).

13. One notable agent absent from figure 11.1 is the central bank (e.g., the Federal Reserve), though that would enhance the model from the perspective of policy analysis. Even without treating the central bank as an agent, it can still play a part in the model because we can impose the policy levers of the central bank into the model exogenously. Insofar as the central bank has discernible rules, these exogenous policy effects can be replaced by including the central bank explicitly.

Also absent from figure 11.1 are the exchanges. I consider these as part of the environment rather than as an agent because they are a venue for trading.

14. The collateral in a secured-debt transaction is intended to limit a lender's exposure to a borrower's credit risk. The amount of collateral received by the lender includes a haircut based on the quality of the collateral, which protects the lender if the borrower defaults. If there is a market or product-specific stress, lenders of secured debt may believe the collateral they hold is insufficient to make them whole because of price deterioration in the collateral. This may trigger lenders to request more collateral, or cause them to halt lending altogether. Haircuts can vary depending on the borrower's credit, which makes it more likely for a lender to feel uncollateralized if the borrower is experiencing credit issues. Collateral quality is an important component of secured transactions. Credit and liquidity stress events usually lead to a flight to quality, as investors seek to hold high-quality collateral. This, in turn, means that investors who have extended debt against lower-quality collateral or collateral that has recently deteriorated in value

may no longer feel comfortable lending against this type of asset. However, the level of haircut and credit standing of the borrower will also play a role.

15. In securities lending transactions, the lender receives cash or securities from the bank/dealer in exchange for lending its securities. The borrowing institution must also provide collateral as margin to the investor, otherwise referred to as a haircut, to protect the investor from price fluctuations in the collateral if the borrowing institution were to default. For example, an institution may provide $110 worth of securities to the secured-funding investor in exchange for $100 in cash, which would imply a 10 percent margin or haircut. This transaction may provide financing to the lender, but it is primarily executed to fulfill the bank/dealer's need for securities. The bank/dealer borrows securities through securities lending transactions to cover its own and its clients' short positions.

16. Though, as a practical matter, many apparently unleveraged asset managers have leverage gained through secured-lending transactions and derivative exposure. And even absent leverage, institutions can also be put into forced selling mode, either through redemptions or through violating risk and asset allocation constraints.

17. To keep from getting too far into the weeds, I haven't included some of the details of the flows of funding and collateral through other intermediary agents, such as triparty agents like Bank of New York Mellon Corporation, JP Morgan, and Euroclear (though JP Morgan and BNY Mellon will appear when I discuss the 2008 crisis); repo central counterparties like Fixed Income Clearing Corporation, LCH.Clearnet Group Limited, and Eurex Repo; and clearing exchanges like CME Group Inc., Intercontinental Exchange Group, Inc., and Eurex Clearing.

18. We are asking not about trading strategies but rather about contingency plans in the face of a crisis. Early applications of agent-based models to finance focused on the market dynamics of trading firms as agents. Although interesting exercises, these models could not be put into practice because the actual trading methods were both proprietary and ever-changing based on market conditions.

19. In which case the agent's Sorosian subjective reality will be the same as its objective reality, and a key condition for reflexivity for that agent will be absent. However, the agent's actions will still alter the environment, and might have an impact on the subjective reality of others.

20. Syll (2016), 73.

21. Models of these dynamics are discussed variously as fire sales, funding runs, liquidity spirals, leverage cycles, and panics (Shleifer and Vishny 2011, Brunnermeier and Pedersen 2009), leverage cycles (Adrian and Shin 2013, Fostel and Geanakoplos 2008), and panics (Gorton 2010).

22. Although I am focused on forced selling due to leverage, there are other avenues for forced selling, such as risk limits that force selling when breeched (and that will be more likely to be breeched when there is a market shock and volatility increases), and preprogrammed selling strategies, such as portfolio insurance, which I will discuss further in the next chapter.

23. The model I am applying here is based on the one developed in Bookstaber, Paddrik, and Tivnan (2014).

Chapter 12: Liquidity and Crashes

1. Bookstaber (2007), chapter 2, discusses the portfolio insurance episode in more detail.

2. So, contrary to common notions, in this instance the price drop was occurring not because of heavy volume but rather because the volume could not be found.

3. For example, Kirilenko et al. (forthcoming), and Commodity Futures Trading Commission and Securities and Exchange Commission (2010).

4. Decimalization, a sort of metric system for setting stock prices, mandated that stocks had

be priced down to the penny as opposed to being priced at fractions, like 55⅛ and such, as they had been historically.

5. Margin calls and forced sales are the most broadly treated motivation for a demand for immediacy in the face of a market drop, but several papers show other pathways for a drop in liquidity with a decline in asset prices. Morris and Shin (2004) show that gaps in liquidity can emerge when traders hit price limits, with the effect of one investor's actions then feeding back to affect the decision of other investors. Vayanos (2004) argues for a similar dynamic through the path of anticipated mutual fund redemptions: investors redeem from mutual funds when asset prices—and hence fund performance—drop to a low enough level, so when the mutual fund thinks it is close to a point where redemptions will start to occur, it will take actions to increase fund liquidity. Kyle and Xiong (2001) show how a decline in prices can lead to liquidations because of decreasing absolute risk aversion.

6. Bookstaber (2007). Market breakdowns after the collapse of Long-Term Capital Management in 1998 (Lowenstein 2000) and during the 2008 financial crisis have similar story lines. Large declines in asset prices were exacerbated by sales from leveraged investors (and borrowers), overwhelming the balance sheets and capacity of traditional market makers. The result was accelerating price declines, more deleveraging, and, in the worst cases, a breakdown of market functioning. These breakdowns can occur based on common factors as well as the assets themselves, as demonstrated by the rapid drying up of liquidity and price declines due to rapid forced selling by a group of leveraged equity funds that were following similar factor-based strategies in 2007 (Khandani and Lo 2011).

7. Nonlinear drops in liquidity in response to increased liquidity demand are fairly common in the literature. For example, Kyle and Obizhaeva (2011a, 2011b), who also provide a summary of other models of market impact, employ a cubic relationship. Broadly speaking, the market impact is represented in their model and in other academic models as a smooth function, but in the case of an agent-based model, this need not be the case; there can be the sudden discontinuous drops common to phase transitions.

8. The analysis of market liquidity has generally focused on day-to-day liquidity during normal periods in equity markets. It has discussed the relationship between price impact and transactions volume. Much of this work and discussion derives from Kyle's (1985) seminal paper, where he builds a dynamic model of trade with a sequential auction model that resembles a continuous market, where he uses three agents: a random-noise trader, a risk-neutral insider, and a competitive-risk natural market maker. By doing so he is able to create a market model by which questions about liquidity and information could be tested.

Price impact is assumed to follow stable proportionality rules, market impact being proportional to the square root (Bouchaud, Farmer, and Lillo 2008, Hasbrouck and Seppi 2001) or cube root (Kyle and Obizhaeva 2011a, 2011b) of transaction size. Stable, proportional relationships also broadly underlie the literature on liquidity measures ranging from standard measures such as turnover and bid/asked spreads to more sophisticated measures that seek to address relationships and common factors of liquidity across markets. Gabrielsen, Marzo, and Zagaglia (2011) classify many of these liquidity measures: volume-based, such as the turnover ratio; price variability–related, such as the variance ratio; and transaction costs–related, such as the bid/asked spread.

9. Bookstaber, Paddrik, and Tivnan (2014) present an agent-based model for fire sales that projects the dynamics of market shocks on the path of leverage, funding, and capital, tracing the cascades and propagation as the initial shock works its way through the system. That fire sale model represents the market impact of the forced selling by a simple linear relationship. Tirole (2011) shows many facets of market structure that can lead to illiquidity, ranging from the market-oriented, such as fire sales and market freezes, to those related to balance sheet and fund-

ing, to those that go to the heart of a firm as a going concern (i.e., solvency and bailouts). Brunnermeier (2009) provides historical context for many of the facets of liquidity in the 2008 crisis. He discusses channels for a drop in liquidity originating from a drop in bank capital, occurring because of a drop in the price of assets they hold; because of reduced willingness to fund or make markets because of uncertainty concerning future access to capital; or because there are outright runs on banks, such as occurred with Bear Stearns and Lehman. The effect through any of these channels is a liquidity spiral, a fire sale that creates a downward cascade in prices and funding, further dampening liquidity.

The interaction of funding and asset liquidity is discussed by Amihud and Mendelson (1988, 1991); Brunnermeier and Pedersen (2009) provide an integrated framework for the two.

Chapter 13: The 2008 Crisis with an Agent-Based View

1. Though I avoided being on the receiving end. In 2008 I was at Bridgewater Associates, a large hedge fund, which passed through unscathed.

2. The broker-dealer Lehman is the best-known failure, but there were also the two largest bank failures in U.S. history, Washington Mutual and Wachovia (which fell into the arms of Wells Fargo with its last dying breath). In terms of the broker-dealers, Merrill Lynch was absorbed into Bank of America, and Bear Stearns was sold to JP Morgan for peanuts.

3. If I were trying it today, I would use a relatively sleepy approach: inject errors into the books and records of the major banks and investment firms slowly over the course of weeks or months. Once the errors were evident it would take a major project to go back day by day and unravel the mess, and, with no one sure who owns what, in the meantime the financial system would grind to a halt. Interestingly, moving to block chain technology for the books and records is a way to defeat this scenario.

4. If there were price quotes from multiple dealers, a firm might be able to argue successfully for using an average or midpoint price, but with few firms making quotes, a very low mark from one still had a significant impact on the average.

5. Memo to the "I'm not making this stuff up" department: There have been many books written on the crisis, running from boardroom intrigues to broad economic studies. Andrew Lo (2012) reviews twenty-one books related to the 2008 crisis. But you have probably missed the best of the bunch. The one that gives the best picture of the crisis—and no wonder: the authors looked at millions of pages of documents, many of them confidential documents of various firms, and interviewed more than seven hundred people (who were reminded that it is a federal offense to lie during the interview), including the heads of the major firms and basically anyone who was involved in the crisis (me included)—is the report of the Financial Crisis Inquiry Commission (FCIC). With Gregory Feldberg overseeing the research and as the key author, the report is comprehensive and surprisingly readable. In tracing the dynamics of the crisis, I am relying on that report, particularly part IV: "The Unraveling" (Financial Crisis Inquiry Commission 2011, 233–386).

I also rely on another must-read page-turner that you've probably missed: the Levin-Coburn Report (U.S. Senate, Permanent Subcommittee on Investigations 2011). It focuses on the mix of nefarious deeds and rank incompetence of key players in the crisis—Wachovia, Goldman, Deutsche Bank, the now-defunct Office of Thrift Supervision, and Moody's—to put forward a real-life thriller of intrigue, deception, and from-the-boardroom nuggets. Like the FCIC report, it is the product of thousands of confidential documents from all the major firms, and hundreds of interviews under oath. Its background of footnotes covers more than five thousand pages!

6. The focus on AIG has been on its derivative business, but it also experienced strains from the securities lending business that was centered in its life insurance subsidiaries. AIG loaned out

securities to generate cash, which was mostly reinvested in residential mortgage-based securities. As the market faltered, counterparties demanded payments to offset the shortfall between the cash collateral provided and the diminished value of these securities. The term of the mortgage-based securities was longer than that of the securities loans that generated the cash for these reinvestments, so AIG's securities-lending program depended on borrowers' continually rolling over their loans. In August 2007, AIG's securities-lending program began to experience problems with the borrowing. To address this, it loaned out additional securities to generate cash, stopped reinvesting the cash collateral it received in anything other than cash equivalents, and sold securities from the collateral investment pool that it could sell at no loss or a small loss. The additional lending increased the size of the securities-lending program from $70 billion in August 2007 to its all-time high of $94 billion in October 2007. AIG repaid redeeming borrowers with the proceeds of the new securities-lending transactions, a situation one AIG executive likened to "a giant Ponzi scheme." Over time, as borrowers suspected trouble, they demanded more collateral, to the point where AIG was paying borrowers more for the cash collateral than it received on its investment of that cash.

7. FCIC (2011), 269.

8. FCIC (2011), 244.

9. See FCIC (2011), 269.

10. IKB was also one of the victims of Goldman's built-to-crash structured products, being an investor in Abacus 2007-AC1. The Levin-Coburn Report (U.S. Senate, Permanent Subcommittee on Investigations 2011, 474–624) presents in brutal detail Goldman's activities in constructing these securities. Along with the Abacus 2007-AC1 deal held by IKB, it focuses on Hudson 2006-1 and Timberwolf I. The report also discusses similar activity by Deutsche Bank.

11. Other firms did not escape unscathed: Bank of America, Morgan Stanley, JP Morgan, and Bear Stearns all had losses in the $3 billion to $10 billion range.

12. To see the risk of using short-term funding, think about what would happen if your mortgage were set for a one-week term; every week you had to reapply, and if everything checked out you would get the next week's financing for your home. If on any week the bank declined the loan—maybe you lost your job, or the bank was having its own difficulties with funding and needed to pull back on its lending book—you would not be able to refinance, and your house, which is your collateral, would be pulled.

13. See FCIC (2011), 286–87. Goldman later relented, but by then the damage was done.

14. When I was at Salomon in the 1990s, we faced a similar issue with Lehman in the events surrounding the failure of LTCM. Lehman was on the ropes, and we had to decide if we would take the low-risk course of declining to trade with them. If we had, it probably would have eroded confidence in Lehman and spelled the end of the firm, so we bit the bullet and continued to trade. And the stakes for us in that event were orders of magnitude greater than the novation of a $5 million derivative.

Chapter 14: Is It a Number or a Story? Model as Narrative

1. And thus there is no canonical agent-based model to use as a foundation for work in this area.

2. This might not be so foreign to Robert Lucas. He expresses the point of narratives in Lucas (2011), though in a different context: "Economists have an image of practicality and worldliness not shared by physicists and poets. Some economists have earned this image. Others—myself and many of my colleagues here at Chicago—have not. I'm not sure whether you will take this as a confession or boast, but we are basically story-tellers, creators of make-believe eco-

nomic systems. . . . We are storytellers, operating much of the time in the world of make believe. We do not find that the realm of the imagination and ideas is an alternative to, or a retreat from, practical reality. On the contrary, it is the only way we have found to think seriously about reality."

This gets to the point of how we test the models. Economists use econometric methods, but applied against make-believe, artificial worlds, and necessarily worlds that are very restrictive and unrealistic in that they are trapped, at a minimum, by the four limitations I have highlighted, and perhaps many more. So which is better, creating a world that allows for testing based on history that may not be relevant, or building a model that is restricted in using such tests?

3. Keynes (1936), 161.

4. Both quotations from Ford (2010), 49–51. Also see Bousquet (2009), and Hammond (2001).

5. Beinhocker (2013), 334.

6. See Lucas and Prescott (1971), and Muth (1961).

7. As an alternative, we have the context-sensitive contingent market hypothesis of Roman Frydman and Michael Goldberg (2011).

8. See Crawford, Costa-Gomes, and Nagore (2013), which presents limits to the number of iterations of this sort of gaming.

9. There is no possibility for a double-blind study or even a less than gold-standard controlled experiment—even if you were to do one, the effects of experience (one person gets bored, another gun-shy), not to mention reflexivity, will not allow it to be repeated.

10. Ulrich chose the essay rather than the more scientific concept of a hypothesis because (Musil 1996, 270) "it was approximately in the way that an essay, in the sequence of its paragraphs, takes a thing from many sides without comprehending it wholly—for a thing wholly comprehended instantly loses its bulk and melts down into a concept . . . that worked in a haphazard, paralyzing, disarming manner against logical systematization, against the one-track will," that is, adjacent to the strictures of the mathematical mind.

11. A detailed treatment of essayism is presented in Harrison (1992).

12. Posnock (2008, 68) refers in particular to this passage from Musil (1996, 269):

> His own nature's will to develop forbids him to believe in anything perfect; but everything that comes his way behaves as if it were perfect. He has a vague intuitive feeling that this order of things is not as solid as it pretends to be; nothing, no ego, no form, no principle, is safe, everything is in a process of invisible but never-ceasing transformation, there is more of the future in the unsolid than in the solid, and the present is nothing but a hypothesis that one has not yet finished with. What better can he do than hold aloof from the world, in that good sense exemplified by a scientist's attitude towards facts that are trying to tempt him into over-hastily believing in them? This is why he hesitates to become anything. A character, a profession, a definite mode of existence— for him these are notions through which the skeleton is already peering, the skeleton that is all that will be left of him in the end.

13. Rorty (1996), 8.

14. Ford (2010), 69.

15. If you are more attentive and get a jump on the ball at the beginning of its trajectory, change the third component of the gaze heuristic: adjust your running speed so that the image of the ball rises at a constant rate. That is, if you see the ball rising from the point at which it was hit with accelerating speed, run backward, because the ball will hit the ground behind you, whereas if the ball is rising with decreasing speed, run toward the ball instead.

16. Shaffer et al. (2004).

17. The problems of posing economics as a deductive science are treated extensively in Syll (2016). See, for example, 45–49, 60–69.

18. In mathematics, induction is a mode of proof and is thus a tool for getting to a deductive result. Induction is also used in an empirical sense, where the future is argued based on the past. Hume was a skeptic of this induction, and I am in the same camp: Why should the future look like the past? In a crisis it certainly does not. I am not using the term *induction* in either of these ways.

19. Dawkins (2006), 96.

20. Indeed, the deductive approach in economics goes back to Jevons. Jevons (1871, 24) reinforces the classical axiomatic approach by linking economics by analogy to mechanics: "A few of the simplest principles or axioms concerning the nature of the human mind must be taken as its first starting-point, just as the vast theories of mechanical science are founded upon a few simple laws of motion." This is discussed further in Schabas (1990), 84–89.

21. Borges (1973), 45.

22. As an effort to make fantasy become reality it is mirrored in Borges's "The Circular Ruins": An old man enters the ruins of an ancient temple that "contained a minimum of the visible world," his goal to create a son through dreams, to "dream him in minute entirety and insert him into reality," to dream him "entrail by entrail, feature by feature, in a thousand and one secret nights" and then to "insert him into reality." When the son finally awakes, the old man fears that his son will discover he is nothing more than "a mere simulacrum," and so it was "with relief, with humiliation, with terror he understood that he also was an illusion, that someone else was dreaming him." Earlier, I described the state of economics as being on the planet of Tlon, where reality pursues and is embraced by the dream. In "The Circular Ruins," the dream is made into a reality—but only the reality of the Dreamer. See commentary in Bell-Villada (1981), 92.

23. A variety of terms are used in philosophy for inferences of this kind. C. S. Peirce called these *abductive inferences* as opposed to inductive ones. Others have called them *explanatory inductions, theoretical inductions,* or *theoretical inferences.* More recently, many philosophers have used the term *inference to the best explanation* (Harman 1965; Lipton 2004).

Chapter 15: Conclusion

1. Lynch (2008) provides a history of the development of modern weather forecasting. John von Neumann, in addition to the roles I have already mentioned in developing game theory and conceptualizing replicating machines, and in addition to his foundational work in mathematics, physics, computer science, and economics, also was central in this effort.

2. This fits within an emerging interest among the socially minded in the financial community called impact investing, in which investments are made with an eye toward profits but also with an objective of social returns.

REFERENCES

Acemoglu, Daron, Asuman Ozdaglar, and Alireza Tahbaz-Salehi. 2015. "Systemic Risk and Stability in Financial Networks." *American Economic Review* 105, no. 2: 564–608. doi: 10.3386/w18727.

Ackerman, Frank. 2002. "Still Dead after All These Years: Interpreting the Failure of General Equilibrium Theory." *Journal of Economic Methodology* 9, no. 2: 119–39. doi: 10.1080/13501780210137083.

Adrian, Tobias, and Adam Ashcraft. 2012. *Shadow Banking: A Review of the Literature*. Staff Report No. 580. New York: Federal Reserve Bank of New York.

Adrian, Tobias, and Hyun Song Shin. 2013. *Procyclical Leverage and Value-at-Risk*. Staff Report No. 338. New York: Federal Bank of New York.

Aguiar, Andrea, Richard Bookstaber, Dror Kenett, and Tom Wipf. 2016. "A Map of Collateral Uses and Flows." *Journal of Financial Market Infrastructures* 5, no. 2: 1–28. doi: 10.21314/JFMI.2016.069.

Aguiar, Andrea, Richard Bookstaber, and Thomas Wipf. 2014. "A Map of Funding Durability and Risk." Office of Financial Research, OFR Working Paper 14-03.

Amihud, Yakov, and Haim Mendelson. 1988. "Liquidity and Asset Prices: Financial Management Implications." *Financial Management* 17, no. 1: 5–15. http://www.jstor.org/stable/3665910.

———. 1991. "Liquidity, Maturity, and the Yields on U.S. Treasury Securities." *Journal of Finance* 46, no. 4: 1411–25. doi: 10.1111/j.1540-6261.1991.tb04623.x.

Anderson, P. W., Kenneth J. Arrow, and David Pines, eds. 1988. *The Economy as an Evolving Complex System*. Redwood City, CA: Addison-Wesley.

Arthur, W. Brian. 1999. "Complexity and the Economy." *Science* 284, no. 5411: 107–9. doi: 10.1126/science.284.5411.107.

Bacher, Rainer, and Urs Näf. 2003. "Report on the Blackout in Italy on 28 September 2003." Swiss Federal Office of Energy.

Bargigli, Leonardo, Giovanni Di Iasio, Luigi Infante, Fabrizio Lillo, and Federico Pierobon. 2015. "The Multiplex Structure of Interbank Networks." *Quantitative Finance* 15, no. 4: 673–91. doi: 10.1080/14697688.2014.968356.

Becker, Gary S. 1976. *The Economic Approach to Human Behavior*. Chicago: University of Chicago Press.

Beinhocker, Eric D. 2006. *The Origins of Wealth: Evolution, Complexity, and the Radical Remaking of Economics*. Boston: Harvard Business School Press.

———. 2013. "Reflexivity, Complexity, and the Nature of Social Science." *Journal of Economic Methodology* 20, no. 4: 330–42.

Bell-Villada, Gene H. 1981. *Borges and His Fiction: A Guide to His Mind and Art*. Texas Pan American Series. Chapel Hill: University of North Carolina Press.

Bentham, Jeremy. 2007. *An Introduction to the Principles of Morals and Legislation*. Dover Philosophical Classics. Mineola, NY: Dover.

Berger, Allen N., and Christa H. S. Bouwman. 2009. "Bank Liquidation Creation." *Review of Financial Studies* 22, no. 9: 3779–3837. doi: 10.1093/rfs/hhn104.

Bloch, William Goldbloom. 2008. *The Unimaginable Mathematics of Borges' Library of Babel.* Oxford: Oxford University Press.

Boccaletti, Stefano, Ginestra Bianconi, Regino Criado, Charo I. Del Genio, Jesus Gómez-Gardeñes, Miguel Romance, Irene Sendiña-Nadal, Zhen Wang, and Massimiliano Zanin. 2014. "The Structure and Dynamics of Multilayer Networks." *Physics Reports* 544, no. 1: 1–122.

Bookstaber, Richard. 2007. *A Demon of Our Own Design: Markets, Hedge Funds, and the Perils of Financial Innovation.* Hoboken, NJ: J. Wiley.

Bookstaber, Richard, Jill Cetina, Greg Feldberg, Mark Flood, and Paul Glasserman. 2014. "Stress Tests to Promote Financial Stability: Assessing Progress and Looking to the Future." *Journal of Risk Management in Financial Institutions* 7, no. 1: 16–25.

Bookstaber, Richard, Paul Glasserman, Garud Iyengar, Yu Luo, Venkat Venkatasubramanian, and Zhizun Zhang. 2015. "Process Systems Engineering as a Modeling Paradigm for Analyzing Systemic Risk in Financial Networks." *Journal of Investing* 24, no. 2: 147–62.

Bookstaber, Richard, and Dror Y. Kenett. 2016. "Looking Deeper, Seeing More: A Multilayer Map of the Financial System." Office of Financial Research, OFR Brief 16-06.

Bookstaber, Richard, and Joseph Langsam. 1985. "On the Optimality of Coarse Behavior Rules." *Journal of Theoretical Biology* 116, no. 2: 161–93. doi: 10.1016/S0022-5193(85)80262-9.

Bookstaber, Richard, Mark Paddrik, and Brian Tivnan. Forthcoming. "An Agent-Based Model for Financial Vulnerability." *Journal of Economic Interaction and Coordination.*

Borges, Jorge Luis. 1969. *Ficciones.* New York: Grove Press.

———. 1973. *Borges on Writing.* New York: E. P. Dutton & Co.

———. 2004. *The Aleph and Other Stories.* Translated by Andrew Hurley. New York: Penguin.

Bouchaud, Jean-Philippe, J. Doyne Farmer, and Fabrizio Lillo. 2008. "How Markets Slowly Digest Changes in Supply and Demand." In *Handbook of Financial Markets: Dynamics and Evolution*, edited by Thorsten Hens and Klaus Reiner Schenk-Hoppé. Amsterdam: North-Holland. http://arxiv.org/pdf/0809.0822.pdf.

Bousquet, Antoine. 2009. *The Scientific Way of Warfare: Order and Chaos on the Battlefields of Modernity.* New York: Columbia University Press.

Brunnermeier, Markus K. 2009. "Deciphering the Liquidity and Credit Crunch 2007–2008." *Journal of Economic Perspectives* 23, no. 1: 77–100. https://www.princeton.edu/~markus/research/papers/liquidity_credit_crunch.pdf.

Brunnermeier, Markus, and Lasse Heje Pedersen. 2009. "Market Liquidity and Funding Liquidity." *Review of Financial Studies* 22, no. 6: 2201–38. doi: 10.1093/rfs/hhn098.

Buldyrev, Sergey, Roni Parshani, Gerald Paul, H. Eugene Stanley, and Shlomo Havlin. 2010. "Catastrophic Cascade of Failures in Interdependent Networks." *Nature* 464, no. 7291: 1025–28. doi:10.1038/nature08932.

Christian, Brian. 2011. "Mind vs. Machine." *The Atlantic*, March. http://www.theatlantic.com/magazine/archive/2011/03/mind-vs-machine/308386/.

Chowdhury, Debashish, Ludger Santen, and Andreas Schadschneider. 2000. "Statistical Physics of Vehicular Traffic and Some Related Systems." *Physics Report* 329, no. 4–6: 199–329. doi: 10.1016/S0370-1573(99)00117-9.

Clower, Robert. 1989. "The State of Economics: Hopeless but Not Serious." In *The Spread of Economic Ideas*, edited by David C. Colander and A. W. Coats. New York: Cambridge University Press.

Commodity Futures Trading Commission, and Securities and Exchange Commission. 2010.

"Findings Regarding the Market Events of May 6, 2010." Washington, DC: U.S. Commodity Futures Trading Commission, U.S. Securities and Exchange Commission.

Coram, Robert. 2002. *Boyd: The Fighter Pilot Who Changed the Art of War*. 1st ed. Boston: Little, Brown.

Crawford, Vincent P., Miguel A. Costa-Gomes, and Iriberri Nagore. 2013. "Structural Models of Nonequilibrium Strategic Thinking: Theory, Evidence, and Applications." *Journal of Economic Literature* 51, no. 1: 5–62. doi: 10.1257/jel.51.1.5.

D'Agostino, Gregorio, and Antonio Scala, eds. 2014. *Networks of Networks: The Last Frontier of Complexity*. Switzerland: Springer International.

Davis, Martin. 1958. *Computability and Unsolvability*. McGraw-Hill Series in Information Processing and Computers. New York: McGraw-Hill.

Dawkins, Richard. 2006. *The Selfish Gene: 30th Anniversary Edition with a New Introduction by the Author*. Oxford: Oxford University Press.

Dawson, John W. 1997. *Logical Dilemmas: The Life and Work of Kurt Gödel*. Wellesley, MA: A. K. Peters.

Dostoyevsky, Fyodor. 2015. *Notes from the Underground*. CreateSpace Independent Publishing Platform.

Duffie, Darrell. 2010. "Presidential Address: Asset Price Dynamics with Slow-Moving Capital." *Journal of Finance* 65, no. 4: 1237–67.

Ellsberg, Daniel. 1961. "Risk, Ambiguity, and the Savage Axioms." *Quarterly Journal of Economics* 75, no. 4: 643–69. doi: 10.2307/1884324.

Emerson, Ralph Waldo. 1983. *Essays and Lectures*. New York: Literary Classics of the United States.

Epstein, Larry G., Massimo Marinacci, and Kyoungwon Seo. 2007. "Coarse Contingencies and Ambiguity." *Theoretical Economics* 2, no. 4: 355–94. https://econtheory.org/ojs/index.php/te/article/viewFile/20070355/1486.

Epstein, Larry G., and Tan Wang. 1994. "Intertemporal Asset Pricing under Knightian Uncertainty." *Econometrica* 62, no. 2: 283–322. doi: 10.2307/2951614.

Evans, George W., and Seppo Honkapohja. 2005. "An Interview with Thomas J. Sargent." *Macroeconomic Dynamics* 9, no. 4: 561–83. doi: 10.1017/S1365100505050042.

Fama, Eugene F., and James D. MacBeth. 1973. "Risk, Return, and Equilibrium: Empirical Tests." *Journal of Political Economy* 81, no. 3: 607–36. http://www.jstor.org/stable/1831028.

Farmer, J. Doyne. 2002. "Market Force, Ecology and Evolution." *Industrial and Corporate Change* 11, no. 5: 895–953. doi: 10.1093/icc/11.5.895.

Farmer, J. Doyne, and John Geanakoplos. 2009. "The Virtues and Vices of Equilibrium and the Future of Financial Economics." *Complexity* 14, no. 3: 11–38. doi: 10.1002/cplx.20261.

Financial Crisis Inquiry Commission [FCIC]. 2011. *The Financial Crisis Inquiry Report: Final Report of the National Commission on the Causes of the Financial and Economic Crisis in the United States*. Washington, DC: Government Printing Office. https://www.gpo.gov/fdsys/pkg/GPO-FCIC/pdf/GPO-FCIC.pdf.

Fisher, Irving. 1892. "Mathematical Investigations in the Theory of Value and Prices." *Connecticut Academy of Arts and Sciences Transactions* 9: 1–124.

Ford, Daniel. 2010. *A Vision So Noble: John Boyd, the OODA Loop, and America's War on Terror*. Durham, NH: Warbird Books.

Fostel, Ana, and John Geanakoplos. 2008. "Leverage Cycles and the Anxious Economy." *American Economic Review* 98, no. 4: 1211–44. doi: 10.1257/aer.98.4.1211.

Friedman, Milton. 1953. *Essays in Positive Economics*. Chicago: University of Chicago Press.

Frydman, Roman, and Michael D. Goldberg. 2011. *Beyond Mechanical Markets: Asset Price Swings, Risk, and the Role of the State*. Princeton, NJ: Princeton University Press.

Gabrielsen, Alexandros, Massimiliano Marzo, and Paolo Zagaglia. 2011. "Measuring Market Liquidity: An Introductory Survey." Quaderni DSE Working Paper no. 802. doi: 10.2139 /ssrn.1976149.

Gardner, Martin. 1970. "Mathematical Games: The Fantastic Combinations of John Conway's New Solitaire Game 'Life.'" *Scientific American* 223: 120–23.

Gigerenzer, Gerd. 2008. *Rationality for Mortals: How People Cope with Uncertainty*. Evolution and Cognition. Oxford: Oxford University Press.

Gigerenzer, Gerd, and Henry Brighton. 2009. "Homo Heuristics: Why Biased Minds Make Better Inferences." *Topics in Cognitive Science* 1: 107–43. http://onlinelibrary.wiley.com/doi/10.1111 /j.1756-8765.2008.01006.x/pdf.

Gigerenzer, Gerd, and Wolfgang Gaissmaier. 2011. "Heuristic Decision Making." *Annual Review of Psychology* 62: 451–82. doi: 10.1146/annurev-psych-120709-145346.

Glasserman, Paul, and H. Peyton Young. 2015. "Contagion in Financial Networks." Office of Financial Research, OFR Working Paper no. 15-21. https://financialresearch.gov/working-papers/files/OFRwp-2015-21_Contagion-in-Financial-Networks.pdf.

Gorton, Gary. 2010. *Slapped by the Invisible Hand: The Panic of 2007*. Financial Management Association Survey and Synthesis Series. Oxford: Oxford University Press.

Gray, Robert M. 2009. *Probability, Random Processes, and Ergodic Properties*. 2nd ed. New York: Springer.

Haldane, Andrew G., and Robert M. May. 2011. "Systematic Risk in Banking Ecosystems." *Nature* 469: 351–55. doi: 10.1038/nature09659.

Hammond, Grant Tedrick. 2001. *The Mind of War: John Boyd and American Security*. Washington, DC: Smithsonian Institution Press.

Harman, Gilbert H. 1965. "The Inference to the Best Explanation." *Philosophical Review* 74, no. 1: 88–95.

Harrison, Thomas J. 1992. *Essayism: Conrad, Musil and Pirandello*. Baltimore: John Hopkins University Press.

Hasbrouck, Joel, and Duane J. Seppi. 2001. "Common Factors in Prices, Order Flows, and Liquidity." *Journal of Financial Economics* 59, no. 3: 383–411. doi: 10.1016/S0304-405X(00) 00091-X.

Helbing, Dirk, Illés Farkas, and Tamás Vicsek. 2000. "Simulating Dynamical Features of Escape Panic." *Nature* 407: 487–90. doi: 10.1038/35035023.

Helbing, Dirk, and Pratik Mukerji. 2012. "Crowd Disasters as Systemic Failures: Analysis of the Love Parade Disaster." *EPJ Data Science* 1: 7. doi: 10.1140/epjds7.

Hemelrijk, Charlotte K., and Hanno Hildenbrandt. 2012. "Schools of Fish and Flocks of Birds: Their Shape and Internal Structure by Self-Organization." *Interface Focus* 8, no. 21: 726–37. doi: 10.1098/rsfs.2012.0025.

Hobsbawm, Eric. 1999. *Industry and Empire: The Birth of the Industrial Revolution*. New York: New Press.

Hollier, Denis. 1989. *Against Architecture: The Writings of Georges Bataille*. Translated by Betsy Wing. Cambridge, MA: MIT Press.

Humphrys, Mark. 2008. "How My Program Passed the Turing Test." In *Parsing the Turing Test: Philosophical and Methodological Issues in the Quest for the Thinking Computer*, edited by Robert Epstein, Gary Roberts, and Grace Beber. New York: Springer.

Hutchison, Terence W. 1972. "The 'Marginal Revolution' Decline and Fall of English Political Economy." *History of Political Economy* 4, no. 2: 442–68. doi: 0.1215/00182702-4-2-442.

International Monetary Fund. 2007. *World Economic Outlook: Globalization and Inequality*. World Economic and Financial Surveys. Washington, DC: International Monetary Fund.

Jevons, William Stanley. 1871. *The Theory of Political Economy*. New York: Macmillan.

————. 1874. *The Principles of Science: A Treatise on Logic and Scientific Method*. London: Macmillan.

————. 1879. "Preface to the Second Edition." In *The Theory of Political Economy*. London: Macmillan.

————. 1918. *Elementary Lessons in Logic: Deductive and Inductive with Copious Questions and Examples, and a Vocabulary of Logical Terms*. New York: Macmillan.

Jevons, William Stanley, and H. S. Foxwell. 1884. *Investigations in Currency and Finance*. London: Macmillan.

Kahneman, Daniel. 2011. *Thinking, Fast and Slow*. New York: Farrar, Straus and Giroux.

Kay, John. 2012. "The Map Is Not the Territory: Models, Scientists, and the State of Macroeconomics." *Critical Review* 24, no. 1: 87–99. http://dx.doi.org/10.1080/08913811.2012.684476.

Keynes, John Maynard. 1936. *The General Theory of Employment, Interest, and Money*. London: Harcourt Brace Jovanovich.

————. 1937. "The General Theory of Employment." *Quarterly Journal of Economics* 51, no. 2: 209–23.

————. 1938. Letter to Harrod. 4 July. Retrieved from http://economia.unipv.it/harrod/edition/editionstuff/rfh.346.htm.

————. 1973. *The Collected Writings of John Maynard Keynes*. Vol. 8, *A Treatise on Probability*. London: Macmillan.

Khandani, Amir E., and Andrew W. Lo. 2011. "What Happened to the Quants in August 2007? Evidence from Factors and Transactions Data." *Journal of Financial Markets* 14, no. 1: 1–46. doi: 10.1016/j.finmar.2010.07.005.

Kirilenko, Andrei A., Albert S. Kyle, Mehrdad Samadi, and Tugkan Tuzun. Forthcoming. "The Flash Crash: The Impact of High Frequency Trading on an Electronic Market." *Social Science Research Network*. doi: 10.2139/ssrn.1686004.

Kirman, Alan. 1989. "The Intrinsic Limits of Modern Economic Theory: The Emperor Has No Clothes." *Economic Journal* 99, no. 395: 126–39. doi: 10.2307/2234075.

————. 1992. "Whom or What Does the Representative Individual Represent?" *Journal of Economic Perspectives* 6, no. 2: 117–36.

Knight, Frank H. 1921. *Risk, Uncertainty, and Profit*. Boston: Houghton Mifflin.

Krugman, Paul. 2009. "How Did Economists Get It So Wrong?" *New York Times*, September 6. http://www.nytimes.com/2009/09/06/magazine/06Economic-t.html.

Kuhn, Thomas S. 1962. *The Structure of Scientific Revolutions*. Chicago: University of Chicago Press.

Kundera, Milan. 1984. *The Unbearable Lightness of Being*. Translated by Michael Henry Heim. New York: Harper & Row.

————. 1988. "Key Words, Problem Words, Words I Love." *New York Times*, March 6.

————. 2003. *The Art of the Novel*. Translated by Linda Asher. First Perennial Classics. New York: Perennial.

Kyle, Albert S. 1985. "Continuous Auctions and Insider Trading." *Econometrica* 53, no. 6: 1315–35. http://www.jstor.org/stable/1913210.

Kyle, Albert S., and Anna A. Obizhaeva. 2011a. "Market Microstructure Invariants: Empirical Evidence from Portfolio Transitions." *Social Science Research Network*, December 12. doi: 10.2139/ssrn.1978943.

————. 2011b. "Market Microstructure Invariants: Theory and Implications of Calibration." *Social Science Research Network*, December 12. doi: 10.2139/ssrn.1978932.

Kyle, Albert S., and Wei Xiong. 2001. "Contagion as a Wealth Effect." *Journal of Finance* 56, no. 4: 1401–40. doi: 10.1111/0022-1082.00373.

Lewis, Michael. 2010. *The Big Short: Inside the Doomsday Machine*. New York: W. W. Norton.

Lloyd, Seth. 2007. *Programming the Universe: A Quantum Computer Scientist Takes on the Cosmos.* New York: Vintage Books.

Lipton, Peter. 2004. *Inference to the Best Explanation.* 2nd ed. London: Routledge.

Lo, Andrew W. 2012. "Reading about the Financial Crisis: A Twenty-one-Book Review." *Journal of Economic Literature* 50, no. 1: 151–78. doi: 10.1257/jel.50.1.151.

Lorenz, Edward N. 1963. "Deterministic Nonperiodic Flow." *Journal of the Atmospheric Sciences* 20, no. 2: 130–41. doi: 10.1175/1520-0469(1963)020<0130:DNF>2.0.CO;2.

Lowenstein, Roger. 2000. *When Genius Failed: The Rise and Fall of Long-Term Capital Management.* New York: Random House.

Lucas, Robert, Jr. 1977. "Understanding Business Cycles." *Carnegie-Rochester Conference Series on Public Policy* 5: 7–29. doi: 10.1016/0167-2231(77)90002-1.

———. 1981. *Studies in Business-Cycle Theory.* Cambridge, MA: MIT Press.

———. 2009. "In Defense of the Dismal Science." *The Economist,* August 6. http://www.econo mist.com/node/14165405.

———. 2011. "What Economists Do." *Journal of Applied Economics* 14, no. 1: 1–4.

Lucas, Robert, Jr., and Edward C. Prescott. 1971. "Investment under Uncertainty." *Econometrica* 39, no. 5: 659–81. doi: 10.2307/1909571.

Luria, A. R. 1968. *The Mind of a Mnemonist: A Little Book about a Vast Memory.* Trans. Lynn Solotaroff. New York: Basic Books.

Lynch, Peter. 2008. "The Origins of Computer Weather Prediction and Climate Modeling." *Journal of Computational Physics* 227: 3431–44. doi: 10.1016/j.jcp.2007.02.034.

Maerivoet, Sven, and Bart De Moor. 2005. "Cellular Automata Models of Road Traffic." *Physics Report* 419, no. 1: 1–64. doi: 10.1016/j.physrep.2005.08.005.

Majdandzic, Antonio, Boris Podobnik, Sergey V. Buldyrev, Dror Y. Kenett, Shlomo Havlin, and H. Eugene Stanley. 2014. "Spontaneous Recovery in Dynamical Networks." *Nature Physics* 10, no. 1: 34–38. doi: 10.1038/nphys2819.

Martel, Robert. 1996. "Heterogeneity, Aggregation, and a Meaningful Macroeconomics." In *Beyond Microfoundations: Post-Walrasian Macroeconomics,* edited by David Colander. New York: Cambridge University Press.

Merton, Robert K. 1948. "The Self-Fulfilling Prophecy." *Antioch Review* 8, no. 2: 193–210. doi: 10.2307/4609267.

Mill, John Stuart. 2004. *Principles of Political Economy.* Great Minds Series. Amherst, NY: Prometheus Books.

Miller, John H., and Scott E. Page. 2007. *Complex Adaptive Systems: An Introduction to Computational Models of Social Life.* Princeton Studies in Complexity. Princeton, NJ: Princeton University Press.

Morris, Stephen, and Hyun Song Shin. 2004. "Liquidity Black Holes." *Review of Finance* 8, no. 1: 1–18. doi: 10.1023/B:EUFI.0000022155.98681.25.

Mosselmans, Bert. 2013. *William Stanley Jevons and the Cutting Edge of Economics.* New York: Routledge.

Musil, Robert. 1996. *The Man without Qualities,* vol. 2, *Into the Millennium.* Translated by Sophie Wilkins. New York: Vintage Press.

Muth, John F. 1961. "Rational Expectations and the Theory of Price Movements." *Econometrica* 29, no. 3: 315–35. doi: 10.2307/1909635.

Nietzsche, Friedrich. 2006. *The Gay Science.* Translated by Thomas Common. Dover Philosophical Classics. Mineola, NY: Dover Publications.

Office of Financial Research. 2012. *Annual Report.* Washington, DC: Office of Financial Research. https://www.treasury.gov/initiatives/wsr/ofr/Documents/OFR_Annual_Report_071912 _Final.pdf.

Page, Scott E. 2011. *Diversity and Complexity*. Primers in Complex Systems. Princeton, NJ: Princeton University Press.

Peters, Ole, and Alexander Adamou. 2015. "The Evolutionary Advantage of Cooperation." *Nonlinear Sciences: Adaptation and Self-Organizing Systems* arXiv, no. 1506.03414.

Polanyi, Michael. 1974. *Personal Knowledge: Towards a Post-Critical Philosophy*. Chicago: University of Chicago Press.

Poovey, Mary. 2008. *Genres of the Credit Economy: Mediating Value in Eighteenth- and Nineteenth-Century Britain*. Chicago: University of Chicago Press.

Popper, Karl R. 1957. *The Poverty of Historicism*. New York: Harper Torchbooks.

Posnock, Ross. 2008. *Philip Roth's Rude Truth: The Art of Immaturity*. Princeton, NJ: Princeton University Press.

Rizvi, S. Abu Turab. 1994. "The Microfoundations Project in General Equilibrium Theory." *Cambridge Journal of Economics* 18, no. 4: 357–77.

Rolnick, Art. 2010. "Interview with Thomas Sargent." *The Region* [published by the Federal Reserve Bank of Minneapolis], September, 26–39. https://www.minneapolisfed.org/~/media/files/pubs/region/10-09/sargent.pdf.

Rorty, Richard. 1996. "Something to Steer By." *London Review of Books* 18, no. 12: 7–8.

Rucker, Rudy. 2005. *Infinity and the Mind: The Science and Philosophy of the Infinite*. Princeton Science Library. Princeton, NJ: Princeton University Press.

Russell, Bertrand. 1995. *My Philosophical Development*. London: Routledge.

———. 2000. *The Autobiography of Bertrand Russell*. 2nd ed. New York: Routledge.

Saari, Donald G. 1995. "Mathematical Complexity of Simple Economics." *Notices of the American Mathematical Society* 42: 222–30.

———. 1996. "The Ease of Generating Chaotic Behavior in Economics." *Chaos, Solitons and Fractals* 7, no. 12: 2267–78. doi: 10.1016/S0960-0779(96)00085-9.

Samuelson, Paul Anthony. 1969. "Classical and Neoclassical Theory." In *Monetary Theory*, edited by Robert W. Clower. London: Penguin Books.

Sargent, Thomas J. 1993. *Bounded Rationality in Macroeconomics*. New York: Oxford University Press.

Scarf, Herbert. 1960. "Some Examples of the Global Instability of the Competitive Equilibrium." *International Economic Review* 1, no. 3: 157–72. doi: 10.2307/2556215.

Schabas, Margaret. 1990. *A World Ruled by Number: William Stanley Jevons and the Rise of Mathematical Economics*. Princeton Legacy Library. Princeton, NJ: Princeton University Press.

Schivelbusch, Wolfgang. 2014. *The Railway Journey: The Industrialization of Time and Space in the Nineteenth Century*. Berkeley: University of California Press.

Schooler, Lael J., and Ralph Hertwig. 2005. "How Forgetting Aids Heuristic Inference." *Psychological Review* 112, no. 3: 610–28. doi: 10.1037/0033-295X.112.3.610.

Schumpeter, Joseph A. 1954. *History of Economic Analysis*. New York: Oxford University Press.

Seligman, M.E.P. 1972. "Learned Helplessness." *Annual Review of Medicine* 23, no. 1: 407–12. doi: 10.1146/annurev.me.23.020172.002203.

Shackle, G.L.S. 1972. *Epistemics and Economics: A Critique of Economic Doctrines*. Cambridge: Cambridge University Press.

Shaffer, Dennis M. Scott M. Krauchunas, Marianna Eddy, and Michael K. McBeath. 2004. "How Dogs Navigate to Catch Frisbees." *Psychological Science* 15: 437–41. doi:10.1111/j.0956-7976.2004.00698.

Shleifer, Andrei, and Robert Vishny. 2011. "Fire Sales in Finance and Macroeconomics." *Journal of Economic Perspectives* 25, no. 1: 29–48. doi: 10.1257/089533011798837710.

Simon, Herbert. 1947. *Administrative Behavior: A Study of Decision-Making Processes in Administrative Organizations*. New York: Macmillan.

Singer, Tania, and Matthias Bolz, eds. 2013. *Compassion: Bridging Practice and Science.* Munich, Germany: Max Planck Society. http://www.compassion-training.org/en/online/index.htm l?iframe=true&width=100%&height=100%#22.

Smith, Rupert. 2008. *The Utility of Force: The Art of War in the Modern.* New York: Vintage.

Solow, Robert. 2010. "Building Science for a Real World." Testimony presented at a hearing before the Subcommittee on Investigations and Oversight, Committee on Science and Technology, U.S. House of Representatives, July 20. https://www.gpo.gov/fdsys/pkg/CHRG -111hhrg57604/pdf/CHRG-111hhrg57604.pdf.

Soros, George. 1987. *The Alchemy of Finance: Reading the Mind of the Market.* Hoboken, NJ: Wiley & Sons.

———. 2010. *The Soros Lectures: At the Central European University.* New York: BBS / Public Affairs.

———. 2013. "Fallibility, Reflexivity, and the Human Uncertainty Principle." *Journal of Economic Methodology* 20, no. 4: 309–29. doi: 10.1080/1350178X.2013.859415.

Summer, Martin. 2013. "Financial Contagion and Network Analysis." *Annual Review of Financial Economics* 5: 277–97. doi: 10.1146/annurev-financial-110112-120948.

Sun Tzu. 2009. *The Art of War.* Translated by and with commentary by Lionel Giles, Barton Williams, and Sian Kim. Classic Collector's Edition. El Paso, TX: Special Edition Books.

Šuvakov, Milovan, and Veljko Dmitrašinović. 2013. "Three Classes of Newtonian Three-Body Planar Periodic Orbits." *Physical Review Letters* 110: 114301. doi: 10.1103/PhysRevLett .110.114301.

Syll, Lars Pålsson. 2016.Error! Hyperlink reference not valid. *On the Use and Misuse of Theories and Models in Mainstream Economics.* World Economics Association Book Series, vol. 4. London: College Publications.

Tames, Richard L., ed. 1971. *Documents of the Industrial Revolution, 1750–1850.* London: Hutchinson Educational.

Tirole, Jean. 2011. "Illiquidity and All Its Friends." *Journal of Economic Literature* 49, no. 2: 287–325. https://www.imf.org/external/np/seminars/eng/2013/macro2/pdf/tirole2.pdf.

Tversky, Amos, and Daniel Kahneman. 1974. "Judgment under Uncertainty: Heuristics and Biases." *Science* 185, no. 4157: 1124–31.

———. 1983. "Extensional versus Intuitive Reasoning: The Conjunction Fallacy in Probability Judgment." *Psychological Review* 90, no. 4: 293–315. doi: 10.1037/0033-295X.90.4.293.

U.S. Senate, Committee on Homeland Security and Governmental Affairs, Permanent Subcommittee on Investigations. 2011. *Wall Street and the Financial Crisis: Anatomy of a Financial Collapse.* Washington, DC: Government Printing Office. http://www.hsgac.senate.gov// imo/media/doc/Financial_Crisis/FinancialCrisisReport.pdf.

Vayanos, Dimitri. 2004. "Flight to Quality, Flight to Liquidity, and the Pricing of Risk." NBER Working Paper, no. 10327. doi: 10.3386/w10327.

Wallace, Anise. 1980. "Is Beta Dead?" *Institutional Investor,* July, 23–30.

Walras, Léon. 1984. *Elements of Pure Economics.* Translated by William Jaffé. Philadelphia: Orion.

Wang, Bing-Hong, Yvonne-Roamy Kwong, and Pak-Ming Hui. 1998. "Statistical Mechanical Approach to Fukui-Ishibashi Traffic Flow Models." *Physical Review E* 57, no. 3: 2568–73. http:// dx.doi.org/10.1103/PhysRevE.57.2568.

Watson, Matthew. 2014. *Uneconomic Economics and the Crisis of the Model World.* Houndmills, Basingstoke: Palgrave Macmillan.

Wells, A. M. 1849. Review of *European Life and Manners; in Familiar Letters to Friends* by Henry Colman. *The American Review: A Whig Journal of Politics* NS 4/10, no. 20 (August): 159–75.

Wittgenstein, Ludwig. 1984. *Culture and Value.* Translated by Peter Winch. Chicago: University of Chicago Press.

Wolfram, Stephen. 2002. *A New Kind of Science.* Champaign, IL: Wolfram Media.

Zheng, Hong, Young-Jun Son, Yi-Chang Chiu, Larry Head, Yiheng Feng, Hui Xi, Sojung Kim, and Mark Hickman. 2013. "A Primer for Agent-Based Simulation and Modeling in Transportation Applications." Federal Highway Administration, Report No. FHWA-13-054. https://www.fhwa.dot.gov/advancedresearch/pubs/13054/13054.pdf.

Zhou, Dong, Amir Bashan, Reuven Cohen, Yehiel Berezin, Nadav Shnerb, and Shlomo Havlin. 2014. "Simultaneous First- and Second-Order Percolation Transitions in Interdependent Networks." *Physical Review E* 90, no. 1: 012803. doi: 10.1103/PhysRevE.90.012803.

INDEX

A NOTE ON THE TYPE

This book has been composed in Adobe Text and Gotham. Adobe Text, designed by Robert Slimbach for Adobe, bridges the gap between fifteenth- and sixteenth-century calligraphic and eighteenth-century Modern styles. Gotham, inspired by New York street signs, was designed by Tobias Frere-Jones for Hoefler & Co.